chicken and charcoal

Yakitori, Yardbird, Hong Kong   Matt Abergel

Φ

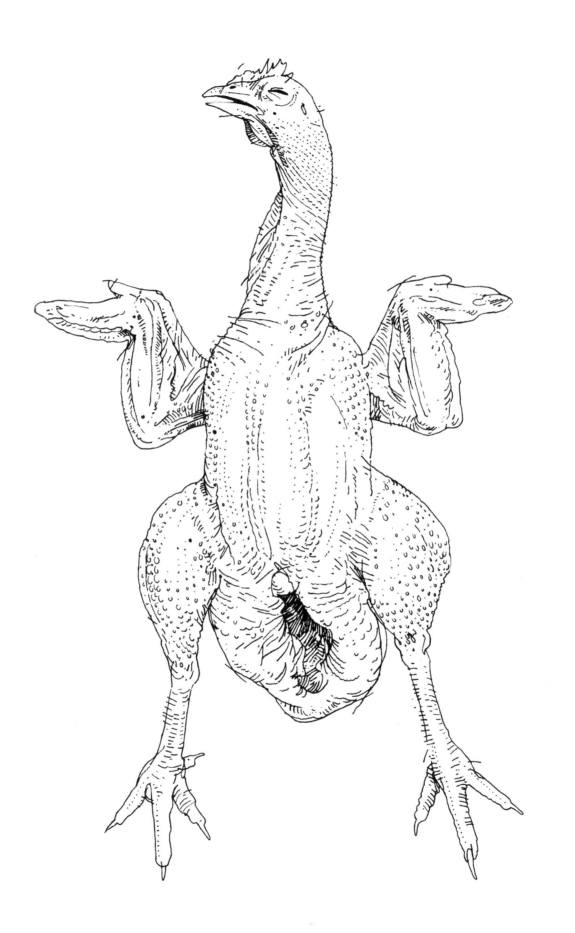

what came first

I've always loved chicken. Roasted Cornish hens by my Bubby (Yiddish for grandmother), braised by my Safta (Hebrew for grandmother), fried at the St Louis Hotel, rotisseried at Swiss Chalet, in nugget form by you-know-who, but most of all, I love chicken when it's grilled over charcoal. Chicken is a food that I connected with at a very early age. Each year, my brother and I would spend some of the summer months visiting our dad in Israel. On Saturday afternoons we would always barbecue. The cut-in-half oil barrel, with welded rusty legs and thick wire grate, would be filled with dried branches, pine needles, and acorns ready to light the solid wood charcoal. It was a job I loved to do, probably because it allowed me to play with fire and figure out the best way to get the charcoal perfectly hot. From there, it really depended on which of my six aunts were coming over for lunch; each of them had their own special kabob recipe, personal connection to a butcher, and incredible array of sides, salads, sauces, and dips. Chicken wings—seasoned with paprika, salt, and pepper—and chicken hearts—skewered whole with small pieces of lamb fat in-between— were the constant items. The wings got so crispy that even the bones were edible, and the hearts were so meaty and juicy. These were the highlight of my day. It really made me think about all the parts of this incredible bird, and how much I enjoyed eating them.

Fast-forward to the age of seventeen. During the later years of high school, I was working two part-time jobs to earn enough money to travel: one in a local kitchen, and the other in a skateboard shop called The Source (where I would later meet the mother of my children and business partner, Lindsay). And immediately after high school, I traveled to Korea, Japan, and Malaysia. The most memorable part of the trip was my time spent in Japan. Friends introduced me to some great local guides in Tokyo and, in true Japanese fashion, their hospitality was outstanding. I was offered a place to stay in Kichijōji, right on the edge of Inokashira Park, where there was a small stand with a smoky grill around which people gathered, eating sticks of yakitori. I ate there every day I was in Tokyo, sampling just a few skewers of each variety before moving on to the next. It was here that I first tasted the neck, tail, and soft bone of a chicken.

Time went on. I continued to cook. By the age of nineteen, I was living in Vancouver. I was working at a little fish shack and an art gallery, but any chance I had, I found myself eating Japanese food. It was then that I realized that I should be cooking what I love to eat the most. So I applied to an izakaya I frequented. Shiru Bay was an open kitchen with a rotating cast. Chefs came from one of the ten izakayas the restaurant owned in Tokyo. Each chef had their own set of skills and passions. Japanese chefs at this level are eager to teach. The izakaya culture isn't as constrained by tradition as the kaiseki or sushi worlds. Despite me being the only non-Japanese chef in the kitchen, they showed me the ropes.

The work ethic of these chefs was incredible, working twelve-hour shifts, then drinking for six hours, and sleeping for the remainder. But the chefs always came in fully charged for service, ready to give everything they could. They believed in the restaurant, they believed in each other, and they respected everyone. For me, this provided the template of how I strive to run my kitchens. I'm not saying that I don't lose my temper from time to time, but at the end of the day, there is only one common goal and we're all willing and able to do everything we can to achieve it. No titles, no barriers, just the tools you need to get the job done as best you can, and with the intention of always improving. I left Shiru Bay too soon. A couple of regular customers offered me the chef position at a new fusion restaurant they were opening. I was being paid in cash, given a car, supplied with endless weed, and had full creative control: this was an instance of too good to be true, way too soon.

Looking back, I think we actually did an okay job with the restaurant. However, its sole purpose proved not to be a functional business model. Lindsay came to Vancouver to work with me at the restaurant, taking a break from the New York summer heat. It was then that we fell in love and I decided to leave Vancouver and make the move to NYC. Once in New York, I was miserable. I couldn't find a job I really wanted. Besides, as a Canadian, I wasn't really able to work. After a few failed attempts at finding my place, Lindsay pushed me to apply to Masa. I said to myself that there is no way in hell this will happen, they will never hire me. It turns out I was wrong. I went to Masa for a trial and was called back just a few days later. This was the beginning of a whole new chapter for me.

Masayoshi Takayama is, and will always be, the most influential person to the way that I not only cook and see food, but the ways in which all of these things intertwine. Masa was very generous with our family meals. We made breakfast, lunch, and dinner for all the staff, including Masa. It was of the utmost importance that every meal was delicious, balanced, and enough. On Saturday nights we would often have a fourth meal together, something more luxurious or involved, often enjoyed with whisky or beer, sitting together until the middle of the night. These meals were almost always dictated by Taisho, which is the name we gave Masa in the kitchen. Taisho translates as "general", "admiral", or "boss". He frequently wanted to eat yakitori, so we would order freshly slaughtered birds from Carlo at La Pera Brothers in Brooklyn, then butcher and skewer them the best way we knew how. Each time we would improve our technique, trying to emulate what

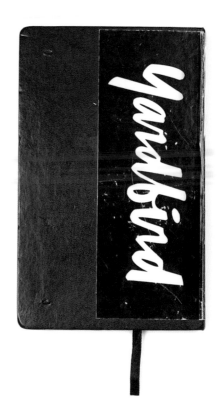

SHIN-D COOKED WITH ROSEMARY
THYME/LEMON SKIN
INFUSED SALT

FINISHED WITH LEMON ZEST
BLACK PEPPER.

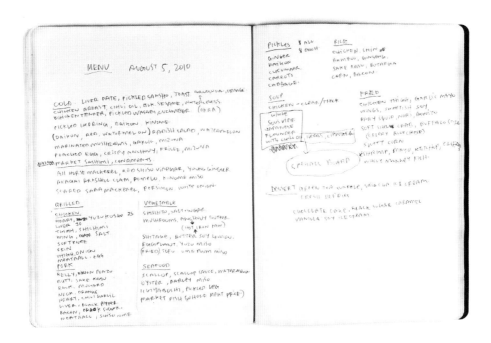

I would so often eat with Lindsay on Sundays. We would spend most of our Sunday dinners at Yakitori Totto. We talked about how amazing it would be to have this kind of food and drink with a more informed, engaged, western-style service. These ideas were the beginning of what would become Yardbird.

After some time, Lindsay became pregnant and we began to realize our time in NYC was coming to an end. During my time in the city, I've had the pleasure of cooking for, and becoming friends with, one of the most frequent customers of Masa, Savva Pavlov. When he found out I was leaving, he asked whether I wanted to cook for him a few times a week at his apartment on Long Island. I knew what Savva liked to eat, so I would go on missions to find the best ingredients I could buy for his lunch and dinner. Little did I know that this would solidify my relationship with one of the most generous and understanding investors and partners anyone would be lucky enough to have. Shortly after that, I got a job at a newly opened yakitori restaurant, Tori Shin. It was there where I began to fully understand how specialized yakitori is, and that I wanted to focus on it.

Lindsay and I had our first child, Lili Sunday, in NYC. Just six weeks later we began our travels to show off our newborn. We also realized that it was time for me to get a job. Over the years, I had been offered jobs in various places. We ended up picking Hong Kong as our destination. This was the best decision we ever made. After two years doing the job I came to do, we were ready for our own place. Our business plan evolved. I spent many nights sketching ideas, writing menus, and eating chicken. In the last few months at my previous job, I ordered, cooked, and tasted many different types of chicken from all over the world, unaware of the incredible triple yellow birds right in my proverbial backyard. Standing outside the half-built Yardbird, I ran into a good friend and chef, Vinny Lauria. He gave me the contact of Ivan Wong at Hop Wo Poultry. The rest is history.

These birds are hands-down the most delicious chicken I have ever tasted and had the pleasure to cook. I knew that if their chicken was going to be my primary ingredient, my relationship with the great people at Hop Wo had to be strong. When we opened, we were ordering ten birds every day. That escalated to fifteen. Then to thirty. Now, in the same 1,400 square foot restaurant, we average fifty birds every day. We are Hop Wo's biggest customer. I proudly introduce them to other chefs who I feel will not only respect their product but also treat the producers in the way they deserve.

When we opened Yardbird, our intention was to be a well-rounded neighborhood yakitori restaurant. We wanted to grow slowly and maintain our ideals as best we could. Growth happened quickly; much of those first years are a blur. While Lindsay and I separated, our restaurant was one continuous house party—drinking for days on end—yet somehow always getting things done the way they should be. This was entirely due to the incredible humans we worked with, to their strengths and weaknesses, and their dedication to the success of our little restaurant. It's been almost seven years, but it never ceases to amaze me all the different types of people who are brought together by smoky chicken on a stick, free-flowing booze, and music that's often played too loud. Yardbird is our dream restaurant; a place where I can cook the food I love, create the environment I envisioned, and be surrounded by both my family and best friends in the world.

service

When you go to Yardbird and meet the strangers sitting next to you at the bar or having a drink outside while waiting for a table, they often tell you how good the place is. They feel a sense of ownership; they introduce you to the servers they know by name and act like it's theirs as much as anyone else's. They feel like a part of it. In that respect, Yardbird is unlike any other restaurant you might have visited. And you have to wonder how this feeling was cultivated. How does everyone in the room, no matter who they are, feel like they're at a friend's home or house party? We pick up the story early: with Matt and Lindsay growing up in different parts of Canada before working at Masa and Nobu Fifty Seven in New York, respectively, then moving to Hong Kong together and opening Yardbird in 2011.

Matt Abergel, co-founder, co-owner, head chef: My grandparents had a big, unfinished basement. My grandfather is a carpenter, so he built us these amazing boxes [for skateboarding] and the house ended up being this hangout, because it would snow six months out of the year. My grandmother called it "the UN" because we were all first-generation Canadians. We'd skate, and my grandmother would cook us food, and we'd hang out, and it was a very family-oriented thing. I think that's where this whole philosophy started: of not just working together. You don't just work together—it becomes more than that.

It's a community. And it's the same thing with our customers now: you see them all the time and you're always there to provide, but it's something that you're very proud and privileged to do. It's not like you're working because you have to work, or like you're working in a shitty place where you hate your job. It's something that you're passionate about, that you're knowledgeable about, and you're sharing that. You know: "See you next week!"

Lindsay Jang, co-founder, co-owner, implementer of the front-of-house service style: I'd been working at my parents' restaurant since I was about eleven, and Starbucks opened up in Sherwood Park, where I grew up outside of Edmonton. I was fifteen or sixteen and thought, "I want to learn how to be a barista." I was definitely cocky: "Of course I'm going to get this job—I've been working in a restaurant." And I didn't get hired. I remember asking, "Do you mind if I just ask for some feedback, so I could improve my interview skills?" I was thinking, "Who would not want me on their team?!" And they told me, "You have too much experience. We want to train people from our point of view."

Matt: I went skating with Daewon Song once, and he's the nicest guy ever—also the best skateboarder I've ever seen. You start to realize these guys are just cool. They're not dicks; they're living the dream, and they realize it. And they have problems. Everyone's got problems. I don't shy away from people with problems. I don't shy away from that because those are the people who have the most to give. They're the ones who will risk everything—who will really wear their heart on their sleeve, and cry, and yell, and scream, and shout. They're going to be the best ones. They're the ones who are going to ride or die. When we started Yardbird, we advertized "No experience necessary." It's hard to unlearn things.

Lindsay: This was the best idea, because I've been in hospitality my entire life, or at least around it, and Matt has also been working in kitchens since he was about fifteen. When we opened Yardbird, we just made it exactly what we wanted it to be. We never wanted to work on a Sunday and we never wanted to work a lunch shift, so that's why we don't open on Sunday and we don't open for lunch.

Matt: The place I worked at before we moved to Hong Kong was $500 per person [for a meal]. It was the last place any of my friends could ever go. And I always wanted a restaurant where all my friends could visit.

Lindsay: People would say, "It will never work. You need to open for lunch. Blah, blah, blah." And we'd say, "Yeah, well, we're not going to." Greed and money have never been our main motivators.

Cody Allen, founder of Shanghai's Le Baron nightclub, close friend of Matt and Lindsay: At that early time, it was investors, and then it was some customers, and then it was whoever—critics and outside voices. Constantly there were, and still are, people who just don't get it. And I think Matt and I share a way of doing things that is like, "Oh, man, if these people don't get it, we're definitely doing it the right way. We're definitely in the right zone here."

Matt: I owned yardbirdrestaurant.com for five years before we opened. I knew the name, I knew the menu, I knew the music I was going to play. I draw everything; all my ideas come out on paper. In my room, there are about fifty old Moleskines sitting there—I have ones from 2003, 2004, 2005—all these menus that were already coming together. So the idea was whole; the idea was complete.

Cody: I don't think they've got many things wrong in terms of how to set up a business, how to treat your customer, how to treat your employee, the pride in their product, their singularity of vision. I mean, how much has the menu at Yardbird changed in six years? Very, very, very little. Matt has added some specials, but basically it's the same. The consistency of that offering, and a drilling of systems and consistency into people who also have great personalities and can bring both those things to the customer experience at the same time—it's such a good recipe for success, and it's so hard to do. I've been trying to do it myself for five years and I still can't get it right. They got it right on the first try.

Kenneth Chan, Yardbird head of operations: Every aspect of our service and our food is meant to be without pretense. I guess it's a weird metaphor, but it's "easily digestible." Nothing's stressful. The customer doesn't have to worry about, "Oh, am I dressed properly?" You can come in flip-flops and a tank top and you're fine; you can come in with some crazy hat on, looking like you just walked off a

runway, and that's fine. You can be whoever you want, and you can look at the menu and it's all pretty simple. We've designed it so we have a lot of interaction with people, and it allows us to give just enough information so you can make a good decision about what to eat that night. Everything's like that. If you look at the room, it's not decorated with any type of flair. Even our uniform is just jeans, T-shirt, and apron. And there's not too much going on at the table, just what you need. Our service is the same way: we want to be around, but we don't want to be in the way.

Lindsay: Nobu Fifty Seven is, I think, the only three-star restaurant without tablecloths. Most starred restaurants have white-tablecloth service, and I just loved the idea that it was somewhat casual and yet very engaged. You're really a part of the diner experience. And so Yardbird, for us, was taking that exact same model of giving elite service, but in an environment that didn't feel stuffy, because nobody really likes to eat that way. I don't know anyone who likes someone wiping their face after they've eaten.

Kenneth: You know how you get those servers where it's like, "Shit, if I wanted to eat dinner with you, I would have invited you to pull up a chair," right? But it's also not as if I'm a story in the background. You find that nice, comfortable way of being, and then you figure out what each guest wants, and then you do that. You figure out, "Okay, if they really want to engage, then I will engage with them; if they seem like they want to have their own private time, then I'll do that." And everything else is pretty simple. The food gets served, we bring it out at the right pace, and you don't have to think about anything. You don't have to sift through a menu that's five to twenty pages long.

Lindsay: I always equate good service with a ballet performance. We anticipate needs before they ask, and it's unobtrusive.

Tara Babins, Yardbird communications manager and "door bitch": I don't have a very clear understanding of how other restaurants work around the world, or in Hong Kong. All I know is this restaurant. But what they say is that, when Yardbird came to Hong Kong, it was definitely a different type of service in comparison to the majority of restaurants here—whether that was the no reservations, the no service charge, the staff vibe, the music, the loudness, the standing and eating. There's a list of things that were different, which ended up working. Service-wise, I know we're extremely determined, our crew is great and passionate, and, as a patron at other restaurants, I can see that's not always the case. You know, the team can look sad or miserable, or totally uninterested.

Cody: There was also no optional tipping in Hong Kong at the time. Matt and Lindsay say it was them and a couple of other restaurants at the same time [that introduced optional tipping]. That might be true, but I, and no one else, know what those two other restaurants are. So let's give Yardbird full credit for introducing an entire new structure into the economy of service in Hong Kong.

Lindsay: We were the second restaurant in Hong Kong to not impose a service charge. Service culture here is very transactional and quick and not fun, unless you go to some super-fancy restaurant. Most restaurants take a service charge, and that ten percent goes to the

as the "cool, hip" restaurant. But I don't think that was ever the goal. It was nice, but being professional, being good at what you do, being welcoming, being hospitable, and paying attention to those details have always been more important, because those are the things that keep people coming back. Those are the things that outlast what's cool.

Cody: In the cities of Hong Kong, Shanghai, Beijing, Taipei, Singapore, there's a handful of people doing things, who really care about it—who have great service, great food, cool music, good design, cool community, great space. They've got the whole holistic hospitality experience figured out. But it's really slim, and at the time when Yardbird opened, no one had cracked that code altogether. What Matt and Lindsay brought was a completely different option: here's this other segment of people who are more artistically inclined, who are a little bit more street-oriented, a little bit more art-oriented. I think that that was them showing to young Hong Kongers, "Hey, here's another scene you can be a part of."

Kenneth: We know who we are, and I think that helps us to have an identity of our own. The restaurant is not meant for everyone; if you can't handle standing around the bar, or waiting a little bit and having a drink, or even walking around and coming back, then maybe it's not the right restaurant for you, and we're fully okay with that. If you want to come in, we'll do our best to accommodate you, to meet your needs, to cater to what you're looking for. But there's a certain level at which we can't be that flexible, or bend that way—you just can't do it sometimes. And that's totally fine, so long as we've given it our best shot to get them what they want.

Cody: That lack of fear really does come across to the customer and to potential employees. People love to be on a train driven by a madman with a singular vision—like, "This is what we're doing. We're going to do it every day. We're going to do it because we're the best, and this is the best idea. Let's go." That's the attitude at Yardbird every day, and I think that's why they have such great staff retention and why they have such great community retention there.

Matt: The way we welcome most people, is as if they're a part of the family, then they're a part of the family. Immediately. It doesn't matter where you're from, who you are, what you've done. Who gives a fuck? It's not about that. This is a family. And it's an open family, and it's a diverse family, and it's a fucking weird, dysfunctional family.

Lindsay: I learned from a very young age the positive effect you can have by being hospitable and hosting, feeding people, and making sure people have a good time. Training our staff in a country where service is not something that you aspire to work in, there's just been so much gratification in that.

house, and not to the waiter. So we decided, "We don't care—we want you guys to earn your tips." We could have taken an extra ten percent off every bill, but we didn't want to. I don't think Matt and I have taken a raise in over three years. Our goal is to make sure that we're growing our team.

Cody: They didn't take reservations, and they played music loud, and they didn't do any substitutions. If you were a real asshole to the employees, Matt would just come up and say, "Hey, you don't owe us any money, it's all good, but please, can you leave?" There were just things happening there you never saw people do in other parts of Hong Kong. It's mind-numbing to think that didn't exist here before, but it really is just a place where you walk in and there's something that feels cool about it. The waiters are cool, and the music is cool, and it looks cool. And people complained: "Oh, there's no reservations, and there's a long line, and there's nothing on the wall. It's just a boring space"—all this stuff. Now you have this complete industry of a whole thriving sector of restaurants here that are somehow like that.

Kenneth: I hate cool restaurants. I don't mind if you think something's cool. And I don't mind if you're cool or anything like that, but I think if your desire is to be a cool restaurant, you're looking to make it a very short run, because cool is a very fleeting idea. What's cool and hip changes—that's the definition of those words, right? It's something that will evolve and change, and I don't think that that's a way to create community and build longevity. If it's a by-product of being good at what you're doing and your natural state of being, then that's wonderful. That's amazing. Especially in the beginning, it was seen

Lindsay Jang

Lindsay Jang has a lot going on. There are the restaurants she founded with Matt Abergel: Yardbird and RŌNIN. There's Sunday's Grocery, a globally curated digital store and blog for everything Yardbird and RŌNIN, particularly the various collaboration products they've made—such as their Sunday's Whisky, two brands of Sunday's Sake, Sunday's Coffee Shochu, or their new RŌNIN x Carhartt WIP apparel. There's the agency, Hecho, born of Lindsay and Co. doing all their own marketing and creative, and which now handles digital communication and branding work for a bunch of other brands. She's the CEO of MISSBISH, the rising editorial platform she co-founded that focuses on strong, female-driven content, which has scheduled the release of its first apparel line. Out on the horizon too, there's the first overseas endeavor, a Yardbird-inspired concept, opening in Los Angeles in 2019.

Lindsay's got all these plates spinning—really impressive plates—but there's no frantic rushing, no shakiness, no risk of smashed crockery. She is a mother of two, often teaches yoga, and manages to get a fair chunk of valuable travel time. Pile all these roles, responsibilities, and pursuits into one working week, and it's hard to comprehend how they can all fit and balance without toppling one another over.

"People are always asking, 'How? How do you do all these things? How do you teach yoga, and then you travel, and then you do MISSBISH, and blah, blah, blah.' But I actually think—and there's an article somewhere you can Google that shows—that women are more productive after they have children. I think it's 'cause you learn you have so much shit to do, and you just become faster at it.

"When we moved here, I didn't think I had that entrepreneurial bug. I didn't really understand the legal side of it all. But then, once Yardbird opened, I realized, 'Oh, this is easy.' Well, not easy, but the barrier to entry to owning your own thing—it's attainable. Matt and I had talked about opening a place like Yardbird for years—since way back in 2003, when I visited Matt in Vancouver for a summer and got some work at the same restaurant where he cooked. We started writing menus. He said, 'I can do back of house and you can do front of house.' A perfect partnership, because I liked his food and he obviously believed in my service. After moving to Hong Kong, while Matt was working as the executive chef at a large, corporate restaurant, I dove into the business plan for Yardbird. What I got from Nobu Fifty Seven was the best you could possibly get—I wanted to apply top-of-the-line service without white-tablecloth formality."

Originally, Lindsay was going to have a more hands-off role when the doors opened. "I'd worked in hospitality for years, and grew up in a typical, small-town Chinese–Canadian restaurant just outside of Edmonton, then worked service jobs through my twenties in Vancouver and New York. I was done with it. I told Matt I didn't want to work in the restaurant. I would help him open it, and I would do the training, but I wasn't interested in hospitality anymore. My whole life had shifted: I was teaching yoga. I was raising our daughter. I didn't want to work those restaurant hours anymore. And then we opened… and I got back into the space, and I was training the staff, and I recognized that it was actually my second nature. That is what I'm good at, so I fell right back in love with hospitality.

"I worked at Yardbird every single day for a year and half. The host or maître d' role—we call it the 'door bitch'—was possibly the most important in the early days. Not from a laborious perspective, but from a controlling-the-crowd perspective, managing expectations, that was the hardest job in the restaurant. I was the one standing at the door, telling people they would have to wait one or two hours to sit down, then convincing them to stay and have a drink. Hong Kong wasn't yet used to that kind of service. It took me time to sort of define and articulate that position.

"My philosophy was always to train people to train other people—to strip yourself of ego, of any fear of being replaced or undervalued, so you can grow. And that's how Yardbird, RŌNIN, Sunday's Grocery, MISSBISH, and all the projects and businesses to come as well, continue to grow, to work, to quietly succeed. Yardbird over the last almost-seven years has just been such an incredible source of true connection. And I think it's helped me really figure out what I'm passionate about and good at. Hospitality, obviously, runs in my blood because of my family restaurant and always working in restaurants and bars. But I think I've always had that natural entrepreneurial spirit, because that's what my parents were like: you keep it in the family, and you work your ass off."

sean dix

Furniture designer, interior architect, and functioning chair addict; it was chairs that led Sean to designing the interior of Yardbird; Matt Abergel had been on the hunt for some, and came across one of Sean's online. "Somebody in the office got a call from 'some guy, says he's a chef, saw a chair of mine somewhere and wants to buy some,'" Sean says. Only after he called Matt back did they realize that they were both in Hong Kong—they hit it off immediately.

The collaboration with Matt would go from him wanting to order some Sean Dix-designed chairs that already existed, to Sean creating a custom "Yardbird chair"—now one of his best-selling, well-known creations—and eventually becoming the architect of the entire restaurant interior. The working relationship between Sean and Matt has flourished, underpinned by a shared appreciation for function, simplicity, and, as Sean says, "A kind of philosophy that both of us have about stripping things away. I think that, working with Matt, we spend more time taking the design out than we do adding it in."

When Sean designs a chair (be it the Yardbird chair or any other) and the interior of a restaurant (Yardbird or any other), he's making them fit together. "I try to control every single detail [on a project] and I only specify something when I have to," Sean explains. "In other words,

I don't buy doorknobs, I design them, and we use those doorknobs. Now that I do these interior projects, I have a better idea of how that design operates in the context of other things—because a lot of furniture designers, they just design furniture. They don't think too much about how that's going to fit into the crap that people already have. What's the old thing from report cards? 'Plays well with others.' I like stuff that plays well with others."

"I've described it before as being something like a carburetor," says Sean. "You know you need it, and you know it's really good, but do you really want to sit around talking about it? It's better if it's kind of in the background. That's what design should be." And that philosophy for design is also something Sean attributes to the greater success of Yardbird. "You know, aside from all the obvious things—like the talent of Matt and their team and the enthusiasm they bring to it, and the great food and all that—one of the reasons is that, in this kind of philosophical sense, it's not trying too hard. Nothing is trying too hard. Everything is kind of, 'Fucking take it easy.'"

Sean Dix: I've told him over and over again, if he ever wants to quit his night job, he's got a day job here. He's got a crazy good eye. I remember that the first time we met, he paid me what, for me, was an awesome compliment: he said, "I already put a deposit down on fifty vintage Friso Kramer chairs, but I saw yours and I liked them better." First of all, I was amazed, because Friso Kramer is a pretty obscure 1950s, 1960s Dutch-School furniture designer. So to tell me he'd rejected Friso Kramer for me was like the biggest compliment ever. Kramer, an under-appreciated Dutchman, created dozens of great designs that sit quietly and do precisely what they need to do. It turns out that Matt is another spiritual son of Kramer—everything he's done in Yardbird follows that same unpretentious logic.

The Yardbird chair (see pages 26–27) is inspired by my favorite typology of furniture—anonymously designed furniture for factory workers, hospitals, police stations, elementary schools; institutional furniture with understated character, designed thoughtfully by somebody with direct personal knowledge of materials and means of construction, and a deep suspicion of applied decoration.

It's an approach to design (or just about anything, really) that is largely forgotten, built on a deep knowledge and respect for materials—what they can do, what they can't, and how they age. That's the kind of design I love, the kind of design that informed my work for Yardbird.

I imagine the original designer of these archetypes as a grumpy older guy in dirty jeans and scuffed workboots, squinting over a problematic component on his old factory workbench with some calipers and a sledgehammer, a Gauloises dangling from his lips. He's got a lifetime of grease worked into the joints and under the chipped nails of his blunt fingers. He's got great smile wrinkles around his eyes, hundreds of stained old cardboard templates hanging above, and a lifetime of rough 1:1 grease-penciled drawings stacked in a drawer by his side.

Like me, I guess, except that the grease on my fingers is schmaltz from Yardbird's chicken skewers.

Sean Dix, Yardbird chair, 2011

evan hecox

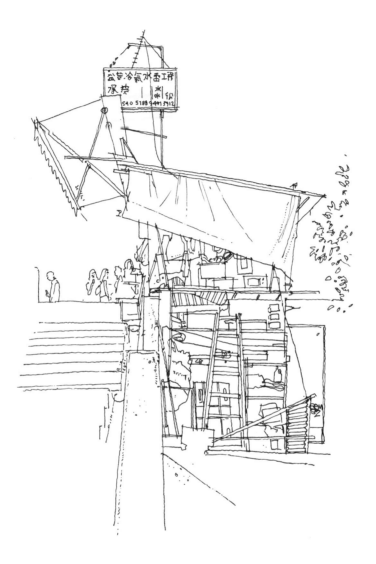

Long before he agreed to design the Yardbird logo, to create incredible art for both the restaurant and this book, and became a friend, Evan Hecox was the legendary artist responsible for the graphics of Chocolate, my favorite skateboard company growing up. The artwork Evan created for each new series of boards was the reason I began to understand the connections between fine art and commercial art, and the importance of a consistent identity for a brand. In some way, skateboarding taught me the most valuable lessons, both in life and in business. Chocolate's brand identity, driven by Evan, was most influential in the development of Yardbird as a brand.

When I began to work on the Yardbird brand, I decided to go out on a limb and try contacting Evan through my friend Eugene Whang. Sometimes all you need to do is ask. To my surprise, Evan responded almost immediately. In only a couple of days, he'd sent possible Yardbird logos to me. With very little adjustment, we had exactly what I'd always dreamt of. Having Evan create the logo for Yardbird merged my young life as a skateboarder with my current life as a chef and restaurant owner. I truly want to thank Evan for being so generous with his talents over the past seven years. It's very hard to imagine our Yardbird brand without Evan as a part of it.

Evan Hecox, Key Shop, 2018, gouache and acrylic on paper

Evan Hecox, Morning Sun, 2018, gouache and acrylic on paper

Evan Hecox, Shoe Repair, 2018, gouache and acrylic on paper

Evan Hecox, Street Market, 2018, gouache and acrylic on paper

you've just got to ask for it

Yardbird has created and worked on an extraordinary number of events, products, and general cool shit for any brand or type of enterprise, let alone a chicken restaurant in Sheung Wan, Hong Kong. From a pair of custom Vans, to a candle that smells like whisky, to a range of actual whiskies and sakes, to a chair that you sit on—the Yardbird chair that you can purchase, bring home, then sit on in your own kitchen—when teaming up with someone, it seems there are no limits to what Yardbird could go ahead and create tomorrow.

The first and most notable collaboration has to be from before the Yardbird doors even opened: the logo and lettering—or wordmark—of Yardbird itself. The words stuck on the restaurant window, the menus, even the t-shirts worn by the staff, were all created by iconic skate artist Evan Hecox.

The roots of this collaboration—and in some ways, every Yardbird collaboration—were planted decades before those words were painted onto the restaurant window. They hark back to growing up through skate and street culture, to working at The Source (the skate store in Calgary that both Matt and Lindsay did serious time in). Selling skateboards, Matt would see firsthand a new deck released twice a month, each with its own iconic design and artwork. That era—the mid-to late nineties—was a true golden period for skate culture, led by the companies Chocolate and Girl Skateboards. Many of the artists who worked on these skateboards went on to become some of the world's best and most renowned contemporary skate artists. Nearly twenty years later, when it came to making a brand of his own, there was an obvious dream choice as to who Matt would like to design the Yardbird logo.

"It was amazing because it took literally two rounds," tells Matt. "I sent Evan a picture of a chicken, asked him to draw it, and told him the restaurant name. He sent me two versions of the Yardbird name. One was lower case with very thin writing, and the other was what we have. That was it. The first chicken Evan sent was too detailed. I asked him to make it less detailed, so that it would work when we print it both large and small, but that was it."

If it hadn't lit already, the light bulb then went on for Matt and Lindsay, illuminating the idea that working with their heroes and inspirations, their favorite culture shifters, was not just a possibility, but relatively easy to achieve.

"When it happened it was insane. That's when I kind of realized, too, that if you want something in life, you've just got to ask for it. You've just got to put yourself out there," says Matt. "And also that these people, who I looked up to for so long in my life, are super-accessible human beings. These are the salt-of-the-earth kind of people who, if you just reach out to them, everyone's down."

Again, that collaborative creative ethos comes back to their roots in skateboarding; a youth spent entrenched in a community hanging around a skate store, like The Source. A cool community, no matter where it's at, is into working on cool projects. "Everyone's down," including a lot of interesting people making a lot of things together with Yardbird, like famed artist Cody Hudson creating artwork for the original Yardbird Nigori Sake bottle, which also became a run of t-shirts.

Vans x Yardbird

Yardbird collaborated with Vans, the original skateboarding footwear company, on two signature pieces of footwear. The collaboration launched with Sk8-Hi Notchback Pro and Authentic Pro, both inspired by Yardbird's favorite traditional Japanese "Tenugui" pattern. Both Yardbird and Vans share the same values in creating environments with a sense of community and creativity rooted in skateboarding culture.

Yardbird Junmai Sake

Yardbird partnered with acclaimed artist and designer, Evan Hecox, on the Yardbird wordmark and chicken logo. Hecox is widely known for his graphics for Chocolate Skateboards and his work often portrays the essence of urban environments. Hecox is based in Colorado but has exhibited worldwide, including in Los Angeles, London, and Tokyo.

Yardbird Nigori Sake

Yardbird worked with artist Cody Hudson to create one-of-a-kind artwork for the original Yardbird Nigori Sake bottle. This artwork was subsequently used for a limited edition T-shirt. Hudson began as a graphic designer but has since experimented with nearly every medium. His work has been featured in galleries around the world and he is also the founder of Struggle Inc., a Chicago-based commercial art house.

INTERNATIONAL CHICKEN TRIBE

YARDBIRD
SHEUNG WAN
IT AINT WHERE YA FROM, ITZ WHERE YA AT!!
HONG KONGERZ

Stüssy x Yardbird

Yardbird worked with famed streetwear brand, Stüssy, to create a collaborative t-shirt and beer koozie for
their first 'Fried Chicken Feast' in March 2013.

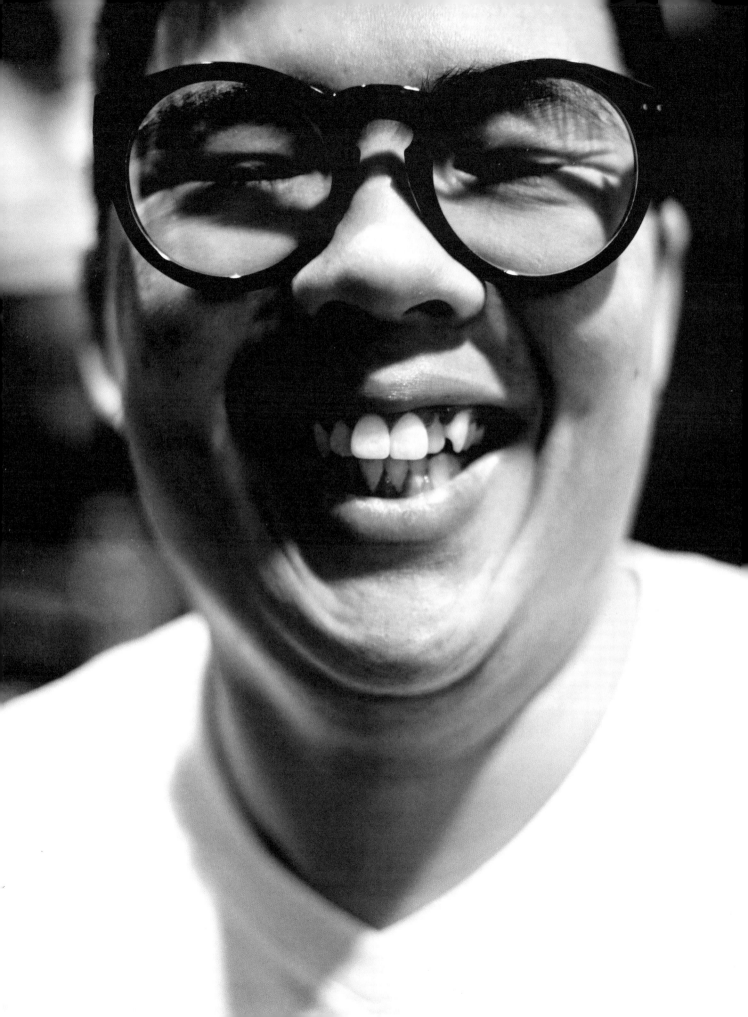

the Chicken

While sourcing the best chicken we could find for Yardbird, I was lucky to be put in touch with Wong Sir and his son Ivan at Hop Wo Poultry. Since tasting these freshly killed, triple yellow chickens, we have never turned back. For me, these birds embody the true taste of chicken, and help us exist within the culinary fabric of Hong Kong.

Every day, except Sundays, between forty-five and fifty locally reared, triple yellow chickens are slaughtered three blocks away at the Sheung Wan Market. The birds' throats are slit, then they are bled, feathered, eviscerated, and packed into individual bags before being delivered to our kitchen. Less than two hours pass between the chickens being alive and us butchering them. I know this is a luxury that I enjoy through living in Hong Kong and being introduced to Wong Sir and his son Ivan at Hop Wo Poultry. That said, if you live in a city with a sizeable Chinese, Muslim, or Hispanic population, the chances are high that you will have access to a live poultry market.

Over and above organic, free-range, hormone-free, heirloom-breed, and any of the many other labels that are put on poultry these days, I value freshness the most. In Hong Kong, freshness often has a different meaning than in the rest of the world, where supermarket "fresh" chicken has most likely been dead in a package for days before it reaches the shelves. Even then, we have no idea what happened to the birds on the journey from wherever they came from to where they were slaughtered. In my opinion, picking a live bird, seeing the condition it's in while it's still clucking, seeing the conditions it's about to be killed in, and meeting the person responsible for that creature's welfare, is the best way to control the quality of the poultry that you eat.

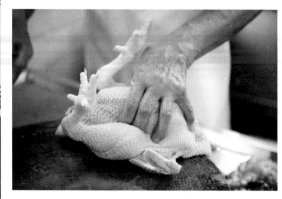

The taste known as "umami" has been scientifically boiled down to the presence of glutamic acid in food. Our chicken—sprayed liberally with sake, seasoned generously with seaweed salt, then cooked over binchotan charcoal—is most definitely full of it. But Masa explained umami differently. Masa felt umami was the essence of any ingredient and that with the experience of selection, and skill in preparation and cooking, we could bring out the umami in each ingredient. It is with this philosophy that we approach the chicken at Yardbird. We separate the chicken into as many parts as we can envisage, then we cook each part to best bring out its unique umami quality. The essence of the liver is best retained when cooked to a medium rare, and you're still able to appreciate the iron and texture of this most delicate part of the bird before it becomes acrid and chalky from overcooking. Where the chicken's skin is thick and layered with fat, such as the oyster, we grill it slowly to crisp the skin and fully cook the meat. With each day that goes by, we understand more about the chickens we cook and serve. We fine-tune how we cut, skewer, and grill our birds. Even after all this time, we continue to find parts that can be treated in new ways. The more you experiment with cooking these amazing birds, the more you will find the same.

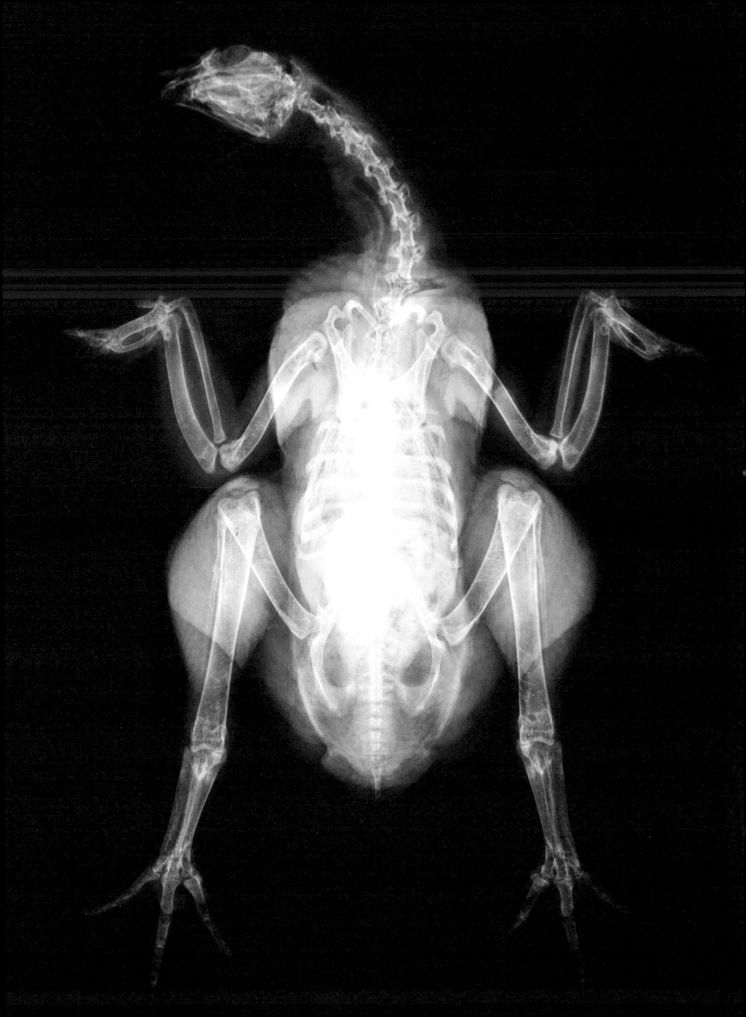

butchering

Our days at Yardbird always start the same: freshly killed local chickens are delivered whole, and immediately, the chefs get started on the butchering process. The process is broken down into three main stages, the main breakdown where the legs, breasts, and wings are removed, then the secondary parts such as the neck, rib, and tail, and lastly each leg and wing is broken down into all its parts, ready to be used in more than twenty five different items on our menu. Chicken is the most available meat on the planet, and this next section will give you some insight how to apply traditional Japanese butchering techniques so as to not waste anything.

Tsubaya
Kappabashi, Tokyo

Moritaka Ishime
Kumamoto, Kyushu

Sugimoto
Tsukiji, Tokyo

First, you will need a sharp knife. One of the main points to understand when butchering chicken is that 60 percent will be done with this, and 40 percent with your hands, pulling, pushing, and manipulating the bird to separate the parts. The type of knife used in Japanese poultry butchery is called honesuki, which translates as "bone knife." It has a thin, sharply angled tip allowing you to get between joints, a broad bevel which allows for ease of sharpening, and a thicker heel, which gives it strength when cracking through bone. Next, a large cutting board needs to be firmly placed on a clean surface. Use a damp towel or non-slip mat to help secure the board. Third, access to refrigeration, because it's important to keep the parts cold as you go, reserving them for the skewering later on.

01. Start by hyperextending the right leg. To remove the foot, cut through the joint just below the bone. Repeat with the other foot.

02. With the breast up, cut through the loose skin between the left leg and rib cage, taking care not to cut through any muscles. Repeat on the right side.

03. Once the skin has been slit open, cut at a 45 degree angle along the flat bone closest to the tail, where the leg is attached to the body. Repeat on the other side.

04. Once the skin and meat are separated on both sides, grab both legs and hyperextend the legs out of their joints.

05. Ensure that both legs are bent back completely.

06. Turn the bird onto its left side and start to cut away at the skin on the upper part of the right leg. Locate the joint of the upper thigh where the oyster is attached.

07. Using the tip of the knife, carefully cut at the outer edge of the oyster. Gently place your thumb against the bone, applying pressure while pulling and cutting along the joint at the same time. Once through, only the skin will be left to cut.

08. Continue pulling and cutting the skin until the right leg is completely detached. Reserve the leg to butcher later.

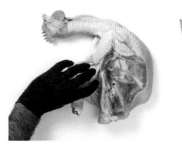

09. Hold the remaining left leg, turn the chicken over onto its other side.

10. Place the bird right-side down on the cutting board, ready to work on the left leg.

11. Starting at the bottom of the leg this time, cut downwards, following the main carcass continuing towards hip joint.

12. Remove the oyster in the same way as the previous oyster, partially using the tip of the knife and by pulling with your thumb.

13. Continue pulling and cutting the skin until the left leg is completely detached. Reserve the leg to butcher later.

14. Holding the left wing, manouevre the chicken onto its breast.

15. With some pressure, pull the left wing away from the body while cutting through the upper shoulder down towards the back. Cut through the tendon that sits at the top of the drumstick attaching the wing to the breast.

16. Continue cutting downwards and towards the back of the breast, tracing the outer edge of the breast along the ribs. Again, use your non-cutting hand to pull with some force.

17. Run your finger between the fillet and breast.

18. Once the outer breast is separated, the whole breast should separate easily from the fillet.

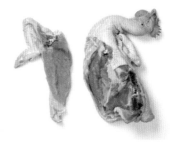

19. Cut along the breast bone and through the skin to completely remove the breast and wing.

20. Cut through the upper part of the breast, removing the wing while retaining some breast meat on the drumstick.

21. Reserve the wing to butcher later. Reserve the breast to skewer.

22. Cut through the small tendon at the top of the fillet.

23. Continue to cut along the outer edge of the fillet, from the top to the bottom.

24. Gently pull the fillet off the bone, from the tendon down towards the breast bone, using the tip of the knife to remove any remaining meat. This action should be about 80 percent pulling and 20 percent knifework.

25. Reserve the fillet for the skewer.

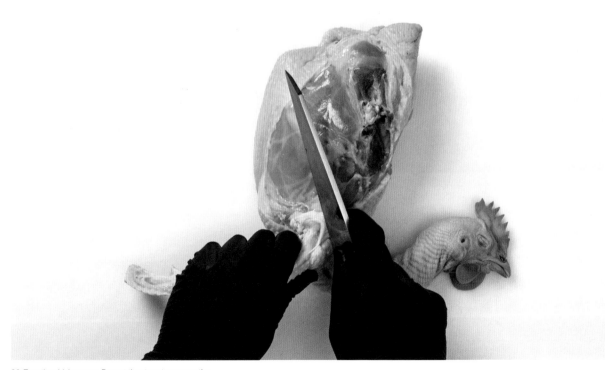

26. Turn the chicken over. Repeat the steps to remove the remaining breast, wing, and fillet, but in the reverse direction.

27. With some pressure, pull the left wing away from the body while cutting through the upper shoulder down towards the back. Cut through the tendon that sits at the top of the drumstick, attaching the wing to the breast.

28. Continue cutting downwards and towards the back of the breast, tracing the outer edge of the breast along the ribs. Again, use your non-cutting hand to pull with some force.

29. Run your finger between the fillet and breast, then completely remove the breast by cutting along the breast bone and through the skin.

30. Cut just below the joint of the wing keeping a small amount of the breast meat attached. Reserve the wing to butcher later. Reserve the breast to skewer.

31. Cut along the outside of the fillet, this time starting from the bottom.

32. Remove the fillet completely by cutting through the tendon at the top. Reserve the fillet to skewer.

33. Cut along the bottom of the hip and the inner section of the ribs to remove the triangular muscle called the rib.

34. Reserve the rib for skewering.

35. Turn the chicken over and repeat Step 32 to remove the other rib. Reserve the rib for the skewer.

36. Cut the soft breast bone at the point where there is a visible color difference. Reserve the soft bone for the meatball skewer.

37. Pull the neck skin over the head of the bird, until the base of the skull is exposed.

38. Cut through the neck, removing the head and neck skin.

39. Separate the neck skin from the head.

40. Separate the thyroid gland from the inside of the neck skin, by turning the skin inside out and carefully cutting it away.

41. Reserve the thyroid for thyroid skewer. Reserve the neck skin for rendered chicken fat. Reserve the thyroid for the skewer.

42. Remove the meat along the upper back, called the shoulder, cutting along the "wishbone" just below the neck.

43. Repeat on other side and reserve for the meatball skewer.

44. Using the heavy base of the knife blade, cut through the rib cage, separating the upper and lower parts of the carcass.

45. Reserve the upper part of the carcass for making the stock.

46. With the rib cage facing down, and securely pressed against the cutting board, start cutting at a 45 degree angle into the base of the neck.

47. Adjust the knife until it's more or less parallel to the neck. Use long strokes to remove the meat. The knife blade should barely scrape the vertebrae. A very sharp knife really helps to achieve the best results.

48. Pinch the meat firmly and pull away from the direction you are cutting, keeping the meat tight.

49. Flip the carcass over. Repeat on the underside of the neck. There is significantly less meat on this bottom side.

50. Reserve the meat for the neck skewer.

51. Cut along the back fat towards the tail.

52. Cut straight down to remove the tail. Reserve for the tail skewer.

53. Trim any excess skin from the tail and reserve for rendering. Reserve the carcass for making stock and tare sauce.

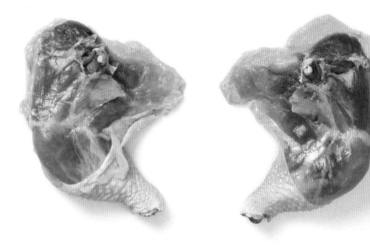

54. Start the leg breakdown by placing them skin-side down on the cutting board.

55. With your non-cutting hand, put pressure on both sides of the thigh bone. Get the tip of your knife firmly against the inside of the bone.

56. Cut all the way down on the side of the leg bone. Maintain the pressure on the muscle as you do so.

57. If done correctly it should expose the bone all the way down, on one side.

58. Get the tip of your knife under the bone and start to remove the bone from the meat at both ends of the joint.

59. Cut along the inner side of the middle joint, being careful to keep the soft knee joint attached to the meat side. Hyperextend the shorter bone and cut down until the knee joint separates.

60. Cut through the part of the soft bone closest to the longer leg bone and remove.

61. Separate the lower leg and upper leg, cutting just below the knee joint.

62. Reserve for the Achilles skewer and fried chicken.

63. There is a small muscle opposite the oyster that would have sat just above the bone—we call this the inner thigh. Pinch this muscle and cut just underneath, it should come off easily.

64. Reserve for the inner thigh skewer.

65. Cut the oyster off the rest of the leg with the skin and the smooth triangular piece.

66. Reserve for the oyster skewer.

67. Cut the soft knee joint with approximately ½ inch (1 cm) of meat surrounding it on all sides. Remove the skin and reserve for the knee skewer.

68. Remove the skin from the remaining thigh. Separate the thigh into 3 pieces.

69. Reserve all 3 for the thigh skewer and the 2 smaller pieces for the ume thigh skewer. Reserve the skin for the chicken and egg rice.

70. Next, begin the wing breakdown.

71. While pinching the loose skin between the mid wing and drumstick, cut along the drumstick down towards the joint.

72. Remove the triangular piece of skin from the mid wing.

73. Reserve for the skin skewer.

74. Cut a straight line just below the smaller of the two mid wing bones.

75. Run the tip of the knife blade at a 45 degree angle against the second and larger of the two mid wing bones, fully exposing it and butterflying the wing open.

76. Trim the small piece of meat left at the end of the wing.

77. Reserve the wing for the wing skewer. Reserve the small piece of meat for the neck skewer.

78. Pinch the thicker, meaty side of the wing tip and cut down as close to the bone as possible.

79. Reserve for the wing tip skewer.

80. Starting at the top of the drumstick, cut down as close to the bone as possible. Repeat on all sides until all the meat has been separated from the bone.

81. Reserve the meat for the meatball skewer. Reserve the bone for making stock.

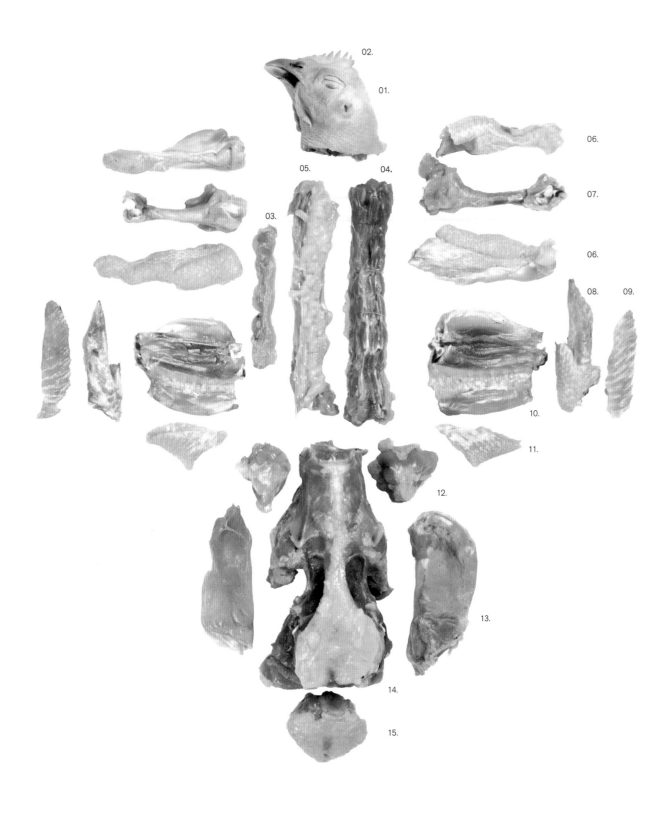

01. Head
02. Cockscomb
03.Thyroid
04. Neck bone

05. Neck meat
06. Drumstick meat
07. Drumstick bone
08. Wing tip

09. Wing tip skin
10. Wing
11. Wing skin
12. Shoulder meat

13. Rib meat
14. Lower carcass
15. Tail

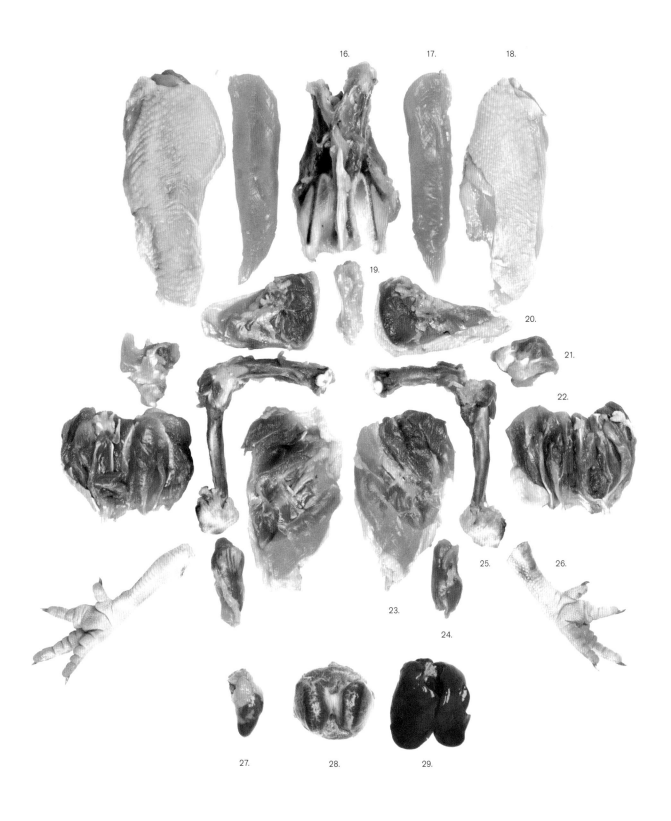

16. Upper carcass
17. Fillet
18. Breast
19. Soft breast bone

20. Oyster
21. Soft knee bone
22. Achilles (Lower leg)
23. Thigh

24. Inner thigh
25. Leg bone
26. Foot

27. Heart
28. Gizzard
29. Liver

skewering

Like all good things in life, skewering takes time and patience. From the fifty chickens we butcher every day, we get close to five hundred skewers. Each piece of chicken is carefully threaded on to our square bamboo skewers, ready to be grilled a few hours later. The time taken over these stages, ensuring each skewer is balanced and consistent, makes the time spent over the grill that much more enjoyable.

After the chicken, skewering is the most critical part of yakitori. A well-balanced skewer allows the chef to cook a single cut of meat with far more accuracy and control than in almost any other type of cooking. It's important to take your time with each skewer. Focus on centering each piece of chicken on the skewer, balancing the size of the meat from the largest at the top to smallest at the bottom, piercing it as little as possible to maintain the integrity of each piece, and keeping the pieces tight on the skewer so when the time comes to grill, the meat doesn't move.

At Yardbird we use square bamboo skewers, known as kaku kushi in Japanese. We prefer square skewers to round for their ability to hold the meat firmly, as well as their stability on the grill, balanced between the iron bars.

When you start the skewering process, it's very important to have your workstation set up in the most organized and efficient way: always try to minimize the amount of movement needed to complete each job. This is mostly common sense, and you will discover what works best for you, but here are a few rules to start with:

01. Use a large, clean cutting board, held in place by sitting it on either a non-slip mat, a damp kitchen towel or, in a pinch, some damp paper towels. This prevents the cutting board from moving, allowing you to bring it as close to the edge of your work surface as possible, minimizing the risk of slipping and stabbing yourself with a skewer (which especially hurts when it jabs under the thumbnail.)

02. Keep the chicken pieces as cold as possible, before, during, and after the skewering process. Again, this seems like common sense from a hygiene perspective, but it also helps to keep the muscles in the meat tight and stops the fat from melting, which makes the skewering process much easier.

03. If you are right handed, keep the skewers in a cup on the right side of the cutting board, the chicken pieces ready to be skewered organized neatly on the left side, and a tray or box at the top right for the finished product. If you are a lefty, switch it up. We layer the skewers with a Japanese paper towel specially designed to prevent meat from oxidizing, but regular paper towel will work as well.

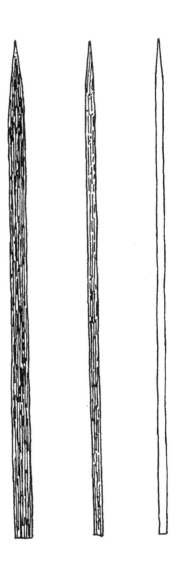

Breast   Green Miso Breast   Fillet   Thigh, Tokyo Onion   Thigh, Ume Shiso   Inner Thigh

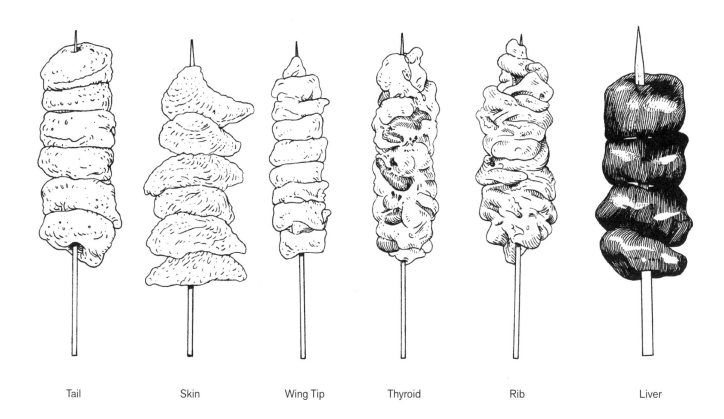

Tail   Skin   Wing Tip   Thyroid   Rib   Liver

Oyster   Achilles   Soft Knee Bone   Neck   Wing

Heart   Ventricle   Gizzard   Meatball   Duck Meatball

Breast
Mune

When it comes to chicken, the general consensus in Asia is that the breast is the most boring part, and I have to agree. Luckily, the birds we use have relatively small breasts, and this skewer utilizes almost the whole breast, save for trim. Most readily available breeds have much larger breasts, which means you will probably be able to get two or three skewers out of one.

Chickens needed:

Ingredients:	Amounts:
Breast	1 piece (45 g)

01. Trim the thick end of the breast.

02. Trim any excess fat from the outside of the breast.

03. Cut the the thin end of the breast into a 2-inch (5-cm) wide piece.

04. Cut the remaining piece lengthwise.

05. Then cut the resulting lengths in half.

06. Trim both ends of the breast so that you end up with 5 rectangular pieces that are quite even in size.

Green Miso Breast

Mune Miso

The inspiration for the Green Miso Breast came from the tried and true recipe of grilled pesto chicken. Rather than parmesan we use miso. The longer you marinade the chicken, the deeper the flavor will be, but since we are butchering and using the same chicken on the day, ours is only marinated for about an hour.

Chickens needed:

Ingredients:	Amounts:
Breast	1 piece (45 g)
Green Miso Pesto (page 188)	To cover

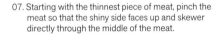

07. Starting with the thinnest piece of meat, pinch the meat so that the shiny side faces up and skewer directly through the middle of the meat.

08. Repeat step 7, being sure that the shiny side is facing up and that you are skewering directly through the middle of the meat.

09. Trim both sides of the skewer.

10. Keep ¼ inch (5 mm) of the skewer tip exposed.

Fillet

Sasami

In Japan, the fillet is most often served rare, just lightly grilled on the outside. This is because there is no fat and no real connective tissue except for the one easily removed tendon. Unfortunately eating rare or raw chicken is not something my customers tend to appreciate, so we decided to marinate the fillet in a slightly sweet yuzu miso so that we could get some caramelization on the chicken before it is fully cooked and dry.

Chickens needed:

Ingredients:	Amounts:
Fillet	2 pieces (45 g)
Yuzu Miso Marinade (see page 188)	To cover

01. Carefully remove the small tendon from the underside of the fillet by running the tip of the knife blade just under the visible part of the fillet.

02. Place the fillet on the cutting board. Pinching the end, run the knife along the tendon in a downward motion until removed. Repeat on the second fillet. Marinate for 1–2 hours (optional.)

03. Starting at the wider end, cut each fillet into three pieces to make a total of six pieces. Move one of the larger end pieces to the side of the smaller pieces.

04. Starting with the smaller pieces at the bottom of the skewer, pinch the meat so the rounded, smooth side faces up. Insert the skewer directly through the middle of the meat.

05. Continue skewering the rest of the fillet pieces, working up in size, keeping the smooth side of the meat facing up.

06. Trim any uneven parts along the length of the skewer. Keep ¼ inch (5 mm) of the skewer tip exposed.

Thigh, Tokyo Onion
Negima

This is probably the most iconic of all yakitori, available in every yakitori shop, not to mention most convenience stores and grocery stores in Japan. We use two different parts of the thigh, the two pieces above the onion take slightly longer to cook than the pieces below, this is because the heat at the middle of the grill is higher than the heat at the bottom. If you can't find Tokyo onion, you can use the base of the fattest spring onion you can find.

Chickens needed:

Ingredients:	Amounts:
Thigh	4 pieces (45–55 g)
Tokyo onion, washed and cut into 1 ¾-inch (4-cm) wide piece	1 piece (10 g)

01. Starting with the two smaller thigh pieces (see thigh butchering, page 56), pinch the meat so the rounded, smooth side faces up. Insert the skewer through the middle, keeping it tight on the skewer.

02. Repeat for the second piece. Then take the piece of Tokyo onion and insert the skewer directly through the middle.

03. Take the two larger thigh pieces. Again pinch the meat so the rounded, smooth side faces up. Insert the skewer directly through the middle of the meat.

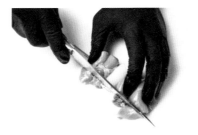

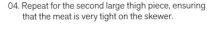

04. Repeat for the second large thigh piece, ensuring that the meat is very tight on the skewer.

05. Trim thigh along the length of the skewer on both sides. Reserve trimmings for Katsu Mix, page 174.

06. Make sure the skewer is balanced. Keep ¼ inch (5 mm) of the skewer tip exposed.

Ume Shiso Thigh

Shiso Maki Momo

Umeboshi and shiso are a classic combination in Japanese cooking, and are often found wrapped around or rolled into skewers in many yakitori shops around Japan. Shiso is an incredibly sturdy leaf and manages to hold up quite well in the grilling process. Here we use only the lower thinner part of the thigh, to allow the whole skewer to cook faster as not to burn the shiso.

Chickens needed:

Ingredients:	Amounts:
Thigh	4 pieces (45 g)
Shiso leaves	2

01. Prepare four pieces from the smaller part of the thigh (see thigh skewer, page 56). Remove the central spine from two shiso leaves.

02. Place the shiso leaves, shiny sides down, onto the smooth sides of the thigh. Make sure the straight cut edges of the shiso leaves face the same direction.

03. Pinch the meat wrapped in the shiso. Insert the skewer through the meat ⅛ inch (3 mm) from the bottom. Make sure the shiso is covering the meat.

04. Repeat for the other three pieces.

05. Be gentle when skewering being sure not to tear the shiso.

06. Ensure the skewer is balanced. Keep ¼ inch (5 mm) of the skewer tip exposed.

Inner Thigh
Rosu

The inner thigh is the darkest meat on the whole bird. It has a really unique combination of dark meat, fat, and tendon that gives it an incredible texture. It's probably a part of the leg that you've never really noticed, but when isolated and cooked properly it's really special.

Chickens needed:

Ingredients: Amounts:
Inner thigh .... 5 pieces (45 g)

01. With the inner thigh pieces smooth side up, pinch the meat until it is tight. Insert the skewer at a 45 degree angle, weaving upwards through the middle of the meat and out the other side.

02. Repeat for the next four pieces.

03. Make sure the skewer is inserted absolutely down the center, and that the skewer is not exposed on either side.

04. Make sure that the markings on the meat are all running in the same direction.

05. Adjust the meat on the skewer so that all the pieces are tightly pressed against each other.

06. Ensure the skewer is balanced. Keep ¼ inch (5 mm) of the skewer tip exposed.

Oyster
Sori re-su

The oyster, or as the Japanese call it the "sori re-su," is
the Japanese translation of the French name, sot l'y lasse,
meaning "only a fool leaves this behind." It is the muscle
that sits in the hip joint at the top of the thigh. This is
the hardest working part of a chicken, which gives it an
incredible texture and flavor.

Chickens needed:

Ingredients:	Amounts:
Oyster	2 pieces (50–55 g)

01. Using your thumb, press down on the top of the
round oyster muscle, while pulling the triangular
piece of skin until it is taut and smooth.

02. Insert the skewer directly through the middle of the
meat. Then pull the skin over the skewer tip and
secure, pushing the skewer all the way through.

03. Push the oyster down, making sure it is tight in the
middle of the skewer.

04. Repeat with the second oyster.

05. Ensure that the skewer is centered through the
oyster muscle, and that the skin is very tight, this will
stop the skewer from turning while cooking.

06. Adjust the pieces on the skewer. Keep ¼ inch
(5 mm) of the skewer tip exposed.

Achilles

Akiresuken

This is actually the meat from the drumstick portion of the leg where the Achilles sits, so technically it is not just the Achilles, but "lower leg" doesn't sound as interesting. The tendons in this part of the leg are surrounded by pockets of fat, and when grilled slowly, result in very juicy meat and incredibly crisp skin.

Chickens needed:

Ingredients:	Amounts:
Achilles	1 piece (75–80 g)

01. Trim away any small pieces of tendon.

02. Lay the meat flat with the skin side facing up and the tendon lines running horizontally.

03. To leave room for a second skewer, insert the first skewer to the right of the center. Make sure the skewer pierces the skin at both ends so it stays tight while cooking.

04. Insert the second skewer about ¾ inch (2 cm) away from the first skewer. Likewise, make sure that this skewer pierces the skin at both ends.

05. The center of the Achilles should fall exactly half way between the two skewers. Keep 1 inch (2 cm) of the skewer tips exposed.

Soft Knee Bone

Hiza nankotsu

The soft knee bone is prized mostly for its texture, something that can take some getting used to. In reality, it is not the bone, but the cartilage that sits between the knee joint. There is also a super delicious pocket of fat and bits of meat surrounding it that result in a really delicious bite of chicken.

Chickens needed:

Ingredients:

Soft knee bone ....

Amounts:

5 pieces (45–55 g)

01. With the white cartilage facing up, insert the skewer directly down the middle, just below the cartilage.

02. Make sure the skewer is not exposed on either side.

03. Repeat for the next four pieces. Make sure the skewer is lined up down the middle, just below the cartilage.

04. Trim off any stringy pieces of meat along the length of the skewer, but keep the surrounding meat and fat.

05. Repeat on the other side in the same way.

06. Ensure the skewer is centered. Keep ¼ inch (5 mm) of the skewer tip exposed.

Neck
Seseri

This often-forgotten part of a chicken is almost always used for stocks or soups, but it's a real treat for those willing to put the effort of learning how to remove it properly. At first it might seem like there's not much there, but the more you practice the more meat you will get. The neck has a flavor and texture that really express the true essence of chicken.

Chickens needed:

Ingredients:	Amounts:
Neck	4-5 pieces (40–45 g)
Reserved wing trim (page 57)	2-3 pieces

01. With the fat side facing up, cut the neck meat into four pieces, each 1 ¼ inch (3 cm) wide.

02. With the skin side facing up, alternate two neck pieces with one piece from the bottom part of the wing.

03. Insert the skewer through the center of each piece. Make sure the skewer is not exposed on either side.

04. Repeat for all the neck and wing pieces.

05. Adjust the pieces on the skewer so they are tightly packed together, without overlapping.

06. Ensure the skewer is balanced and centered. Keep ¼ inch (5 mm) of the skewer tip exposed.

Wing
Teba

Wings are a great place to start if you don't feel like taking apart whole chickens. The way these are cut allows for the skin to be fully crisped on one side while also cooking all the way through much faster than an entire mid wing.

Chickens needed:

Ingredients: Amounts:
Wing .... 2 pieces (45–55 g)

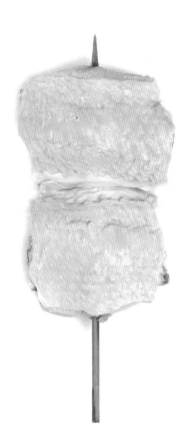

01. Insert the skewer just under the smaller bone of the wing, going all the way through the meat, between the skin and bone, without exposing the skewer.

02. Flip the second wing around. Insert the skewer through the small piece of meat, then just under the bigger of the two bones.

03. Continue just under the smaller bone all the way through.

04. Make sure that the skin side is as flat as possible and that the skewer is as sturdy as it can be, centered just under the bones.

05. Keep ½ inch (10 mm) of the skewer tip exposed.

Tail
Bonjiri

The tail, also commonly referred to as the Bishop's
nose, is one of the most succulent parts of the chicken.
When cooked properly, slow and low, the outside crisps
up fully, the fat renders, and you're left with an amazing
amount of collagen at the center. And with just one tail
per chicken this one is really worth the effort.

Chickens needed:

Ingredients: Amounts:
Tail .... 3 pieces (40 g)

01. Holding the knife blade at a 45 degree angle, cut
into the underside of the tail to remove the tail bone
and gland.

02. Flip the tail over and remove any gristle, remaining
feather, and soft bone.

03. There will be two slightly separate sides of the tail
with a loose piece of skin between them.

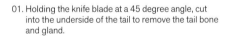

04. With the skin side facing up, pinch one tail piece
and insert the skewer at a 30 degree angle. Once
through, fold the skin over and continue skewering
the second side. Repeat for the rest of the tail.

05. Trim the non-pointed sides of the tail pieces along
the length of the skewer.

06. Ensure there are no loose pieces of fat. Keep ¼ inch
(5 mm) of the skewer tip exposed.

Wing Skin
Tebakawa

In most yakitori shops, the skin is the most readily available, using all different parts of the skin, first blanched then cooked. I found that in most cases this results in an uneven, kind of disappointing skewer. With this part of the wing you have the outer part of the skin on both sides and a very small amount of muscle on the inside. It gets super-crispy with just a bit of chew.

Chickens needed:

Ingredients:	Amounts:
Wing skin	6 pieces (40 g)

01. Line up six pieces of the wing skin with the smoother side facing down and the longest side of the triangle at the bottom.

02. Insert the skewer directly through the middle of the wing skin. Make sure that the skewer is not exposed on either side.

03. Repeat for all six wing skin pieces.

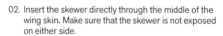

04. Adjust the wing skin pieces on the skewer, flattening them out as much as possible. Keep ⅛ inch (3mm) of the skewer tip exposed.

Wing Tip

Tebasakinosaki

For a long time we were just throwing the wing tips into our stock, until I stumbled on a book about arguably the best yakitori shop in the world, Torishiki. This skewer has all the crispiness of the skin skewer with a healthy dose of collagen for texture.

Chickens needed:

Ingredients:	Amounts:
Wing tip	7 pieces (40 g)

01. With the skin side facing up, insert the skewer at a 45 degree angle through the thicker end of the wing tip.

02. Fold the remaining piece of the skin and pierce through approximately ⅛ inch (3 mm) of it.

03. Keeping the meat smooth-side up, guide the skewer through the center, while pinching and weaving, making between two and three folds in the skin.

04. Repeat for the remaining pieces. Make sure all the pieces are facing the same direction.

05. Pinch all the skin together as much as possible. Keep ⅓ inch (7 mm) of the skewer tip exposed.

Thyroid
Kojosen

This is one of the tastiest parts of the chicken, and there is more of it than you would expect. After cooking it has a creamy intense chicken flavor. It takes some work to clean and get to, but it is well worth it.

Chickens needed:

Ingredients:
Thyroid ....

Amounts:
3–4 pieces (40 g)

01. Insert the skewer, pinching and weaving through the connective tissue but without piercing the actual gland.

02. Repeat with the remaining three or four thyroid pieces. Make sure all the meat is tight on the skewer.

03. Keep ¼ inch (5mm) of the skewer tip exposed.

Rib
Harami

As far as I'm concerned, the rib has the most interesting texture on the chicken. It's a very thin muscle, sandwiching a very thin layer of fat. It has an incredible chew and the chicken flavor really shines through, even with the tare and sansho.

Chickens needed:  or

Ingredients: Amounts:

Rib .... 5–6 pieces (45 g)

01. With the smooth side up, insert the skewer into the narrow end of the first piece.

02. Keeping the meat smooth side up, guide the skewer down the center of the rib, while pinching and weaving, making between two and three folds.

03. Repeat for the next four or five rib pieces, until the skewer has reached the desired weight.

04. Make sure all the pieces are facing in the same direction.

05. Adjust the rib pieces so they're tight together. Keep ¼ inch (5mm) of the skewer tip exposed.

Liver
Reba

The liver of any animal is always a great indicator of its health. Our livers have a clean, iron-rich, chicken flavor that's best when served medium rare. We marinate our livers in tare for a few minutes before we grill them, to speed up the caramelization process without overcooking them.

Chickens needed:

Ingredients:	Amounts:
Liver	4 pieces (45 g)

01. Separate the larger and smaller parts of the liver by cutting through the sinew.

02. Trim any remaining sinew and broken pieces of liver. Reserve all trim for the liver mousse, page 144.

03. Insert a wide, flat skewer directly through the center of the first piece. Skewer each piece only once; liver denatures quickly as it contains no muscle or tissue.

04. Repeat for the next three or four liver pieces. Make sure the pieces are balanced and the smallest piece is at the bottom of the skewer.

05. Gently adjust the skewer without twisting, so that it stays tight on the skewer.

06. Trim lightly along the length of the skewer on both sides, to help keep it balanced. Keep ½ inch (10 mm) of the skewer tip exposed.

Heart

Hatsu

The heart is the very reason that I fell in love with yakitori. Each one is the perfect combination of rich meat, crunchy fat, and intense chicken flavor. Once again, don't overcook the heart, it's the juiciness that really gives it its character.

Chickens needed:

Ingredients:	Amounts:
Heart	4 pieces (30 g)

01. Trim off the tops of the hearts, while keeping some of the fat cap attached.

02. At the thickest part of the heart cut 75 percent of the way down into the heart while leaving the tip intact.

03. With the uncut side facing down, flatten the heart on the cutting board. Insert the skewer through the center of the heart. Make sure no part of the skewer is exposed.

04. Repeat with the remaining three hearts. Make sure all the pieces are facing in the same direction.

05. Using a paper towel, remove any clotted blood from the heart pieces. Keep ¼ inch (5 mm) of the skewer tip exposed.

Ventricle

Hatsumoto

According to one of my customers, who happens to be
a doctor, this is actually a combination of the aorta, and
the ventricles that pump the blood around the chicken.
It also comprises of the fat that sits at the top of the
heart protecting it.

Chickens needed:

Ingredients:	Amounts:
Ventricle	4 pieces (35 g)
Heart	1 piece (7.5 g)

01. Cut a full heart into three even pieces.

02. Start with the tip of the heart that you just cut
into three.

03. Insert the skewer, with a weaving action, through
the first ventricle piece.

04. Once the skewer is half full with ventricle pieces
(about 15 g), add an upper piece of the heart.
Continue with the rest of the ventricle pieces.

05. Finish by skewering another ventricle tip directly
through the middle of the meat. Keep ¼ inch
(5 mm) of the skewer tip exposed.

Gizzard
Sunagimo

One of the most common questions that I get asked at the restaurant is, "What is the gizzard?" The gizzard is the muscle that crushes all the things that the chicken eats to make them digestible. This means it works extremely hard, which gives it a bouncy, almost crunchy texture.

Chickens needed:

Ingredients: Amounts:
Gizzard .... 5 pieces (40 g)

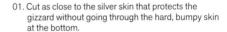

01. Cut as close to the silver skin that protects the gizzard without going through the hard, bumpy skin at the bottom.

02. Just before you touch the protective skin, turn your knife 45 degrees and cut along the bottom of the gizzard.

03. Continue at that angle, removing the silver skin from the other side.

04. Line up all the gizzard pieces, from smallest to largest, to face the same direction. Starting with the smallest piece, skewer the center of the flat side.

05. Repeat with the remaining gizzard pieces. Skewer directly through the center of each piece, all facing the same direction.

06. Adjust the pieces on the skewer so they are tightly packed. Keep ¼ inch (5mm) of the skewer tip exposed.

Meatball

Tsukune

The meatball is our most popular skewer by a long shot; we sell upwards of 200 sticks every day. This recipe took about six months to get right, you need enough fat, collagen, and meat to keep it together while it cooks, suspended over the grill. There's some minced soft bone in there for crunch, and fresh panko bread crumbs that bring it all together.

Chickens needed:

Ingredients:	Amounts:
Wing drumstick meat	300 g
Soft breast bone, finely chopped	70 g
White onion, finely diced, washed, squeezed dry	60 g
Fresh panko bread crumbs	25 g
Sea salt	3 g
Freshly ground black pepper	To taste

Yield: 450 g (enough for 9 skewers)

Method:

01. Debone the wing drumstick, making sure to leave a little of the soft bone/cartilage at the end of the bone. Place the meat and soft breast bone on a tray with the main component of the meat grinder and freeze for 25 minutes.

02. Set up the grinder and grind the meat and soft bone at a medium speed, then immediately grind a second time.

03. Set a large bowl on top of another bowl filled with ice and mix the minced meat in with the finely diced onion, fresh panko bread crumbs, and the salt, and pepper. Vigorously mix the meat until it becomes very tacky, then cover and chill in the refrigerator for 30 minutes, or until cold.

04. Using your hands, divide the meat mixture into 50 g balls and carefully form into oblong shapes on skewers. Chill until ready to cook.

01. Shape 50 g of the meatball mix into an oblong football, and insert the skewer directly through the middle of the meatball.

02. Gently squeeze the meatball, pinching the meat around the base and tip of the skewer.

03. Roll in your hand until it becomes smooth on the outside. Keep just the tip (1 mm) of the skewer exposed.

Duck Meatball

Kamo dango

The local fresh ducks that we use have a very different texture compared to European and American ducks, the breasts don't lend themselves well to being cooked rare as you would mostly do in Western kitchens. So we decided to mince the breasts, making meatballs, combining them with a classic Japanese flavor combination of kinome and sansho.

Ingredients:	Amounts:
Duck breast meat	600 g
White onion, finely diced, washed, squeezed dry	120 g
Smoked daikon, finely diced	35 g
Sansho pepper	1 g
Fresh panko bread crumbs	50 g
Duck skin	50 g
Salt	6 g

Yield: 750 g (enough for 10 skewers)

Method:

01. Separate the duck breast into skin and meat. Reserve 400 g of breast meat only, cut the remaining fat and meat into thick strips and place on a tray in the freezer for 20 minutes, until partially frozen. Hand chop the reserved breast meat until the size of an eraser at the end of a pencil. Once the duck meat is partially frozen, pass the skin and meat through the grinder on a medium die, twice (starting with the skin.)

02. Chop the onion and rinse under cold running water for 20 minutes. Strain, squeeze, and wring in a clean kitchen tea towel to remove any excess moisture.

03. Add all of the remaining ingredients and mix well.

04. Form into 20 g balls and keep on a tray in the fridge.

05. Blanch, 2 at a time, in boiling seasoned Chicken Stock (page 184) for 1 minute, then plunge into iced water.

06. Remove from the ice water and reserve on a paper towel-lined tray in the fridge.

01. When ready to grill, remove the blanched meatballs from the fridge.

02. Insert the skewer directly through the center of each meatball.

03. Adjust the meatballs on the skewer so they are tightly packed together. Keep ¼ inch (5 mm) of the skewer tip exposed.

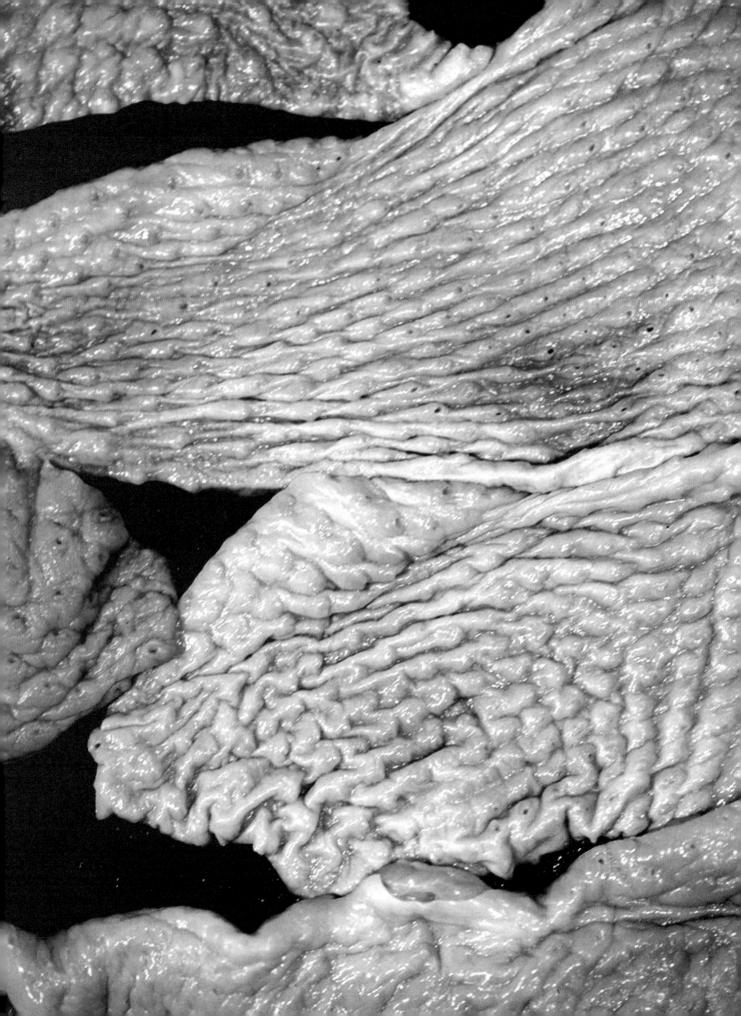

grilling

Cooking meat over charcoal is a challenge, but it is one of the most
satisfying things I can think of doing. The dry heat, the intense focus, and
the repetitive action is a form of meditation for me. Unlike cooking on gas
or electric, where the heat is consistent, when cooking over charcoal the
heat cannot be controlled by the flick of a switch, or the turn of a knob,
so it requires patience and skill.

Every charcoal is different. Over the years, we have tried many different types, but we have settled on binchotan, which is produced in China from the larger limbs of oak trees. Binchotan should be limbs of hard oak, burnt very slowly with a constantly decreasing supply of oxygen, suffocated with ash, which results in a very high-carbon, super-dense, smokeless, clean-burning coal. The high carbon content also creates a charcoal that burns with a very high infrared quotient. Whereas regular lump coal will smoke and flame, cooking the food as the charcoal rapidly combusts, binchotan penetrates the food with infrared rays and cooks with a dry intense heat. Binchotan charcoal is now readily available online; I definitely recommend that you try to get your hands on some. Binchotan is expensive but, unlike other charcoal, you can put it out in water and reuse it as many times as possible until it disappears to ash.

The next component in cooking yakitori is the grill. The primary difference between a yakitori grill and a regular grill is that with a yakitori grill the skewers are suspended between iron bars over the charcoal, so the heat of the binchotan is transferred directly to the meat. With a regular grill the heat is transferred to a flat grill and the meat is then cooked on that heated element. Given that you have just taken the time to balance a skewer properly, a yakitori grill allows for a more three-dimensional grilling opportunity: it allows you to cook a round meatball all over rather than just on two sides, like a burger.

Our yakitori grill is made by Kama Asa Shoten, another group of incredible people in Tokyo's Kappabashi district, with whom I have had the pleasure of working. My grill was designed with a few slight modifications from a purely traditional yakitori grill. I had drawers made to hold water just below the grate where the charcoal sits. This not only makes the clean-up easier at the end of each night, but it also helps to prevent the build up of fat, which can lead to flare ups, and gives a gentle steam to the otherwise unrelenting dry heat of the binchotan. Again, I don't expect you to have a grill like mine at home, but you can customize your current grill with a few cinder blocks and two square iron bars.

The next step is to light and distribute the charcoal. Binchotan takes a long time to light, so we begin the process at 4.15 p.m. with the intention of being ready to cook at around 5.45 p.m. We use an iron pot with grates over a strong gas fire until the coal glows hot, at which point we add it to the rest of the unlit charcoal with sufficient airflow and let the remainder of the charcoal slowly light. Binchotan is extremely sensitive to oxygen, so if you find you are having trouble lighting the charcoal, make sure that it is not being suffocated. You can use a fan to increase airflow.

After about an hour, we begin to arrange the distribution of the charcoal in the grill, creating varying zones of heat intensity for cooking the different skewers. A corner at the front right side of the grill is left with very little charcoal, relying on the ambient heat of the rest of the grill—perfect for cooking the very fatty pieces, such as the tail and skin, that need a lot of time to render and become crispy without burning or catching fire. Moving left, we maintain a section of moderate heat for skewers such as the oyster and Achilles, where you still need to render a fair bit of fat, but need to color and cook the meat side as well. Moving farther left, we keep a zone at the most intense heat, with charcoal piled up to the bottom edge of the bar, to cook those skewers that need the high heat to caramelize without overcooking, such as the heart, gizzard, inner thigh, wing, and neck. On the other side of the grill, we reserve about three quarters of the grill for all things cooked with tare sauce. This side is harder to maintain due to the constant dripping of the sauce, with sugar sticking to the charcoal and eventually extinguishing it. To maintain the correct temperature, it is necessary to shuffle and flip the charcoal constantly throughout the cooking process. It is important to remember that when cooking anything with sauce, as opposed to only sake and salt, it will burn faster, so be sure to pay a little more attention when flipping.

Our standard practice is to spray each skewer with sake and then season it generously from the top of the skewer to the bottom using moshio, a type of Japanese salt that is boiled with kelp from Awaji Island. We dry our salt in a dehydrator and use a restaurant-style salt shaker. I find this to be a much more consistent method of seasoning, rather than pinching from a box. Each skewer is then seasoned slightly differently; some with pepper, some with infused sakes, some with light brushings of different oils. Above each set of steps there is a list of seasonings used before grilling.

We spray sake on everything we grill as it allows us to season more liberally and still achieve the balance of flavors we are looking for. The alcohol in the sake evaporates almost immediately over the grill, but helps to keep all the seasoning stuck to the meat. Sake contains glutamic acid, from the koji mold used in the fermentation process, which helps to boost umami levels. It also contains a naturally occuring sugar. This sugar helps with caramelization, but there is not enough of it to burn.

Breast

Seasoning: olive oil, sake, salt.

01. Start with the smooth-side down over high heat, grilling until light brown, 2–3 minutes, 20 percent cooked.

02. Rotate ¼ turn, cook on each side until lightly colored, 1 minute, 60 percent cooked.

03. Once three sides are colored, finish cooking on the back until light brown, 2 minutes, 90 percent cooked.

04. Spray with sake and lightly season with salt to finish.

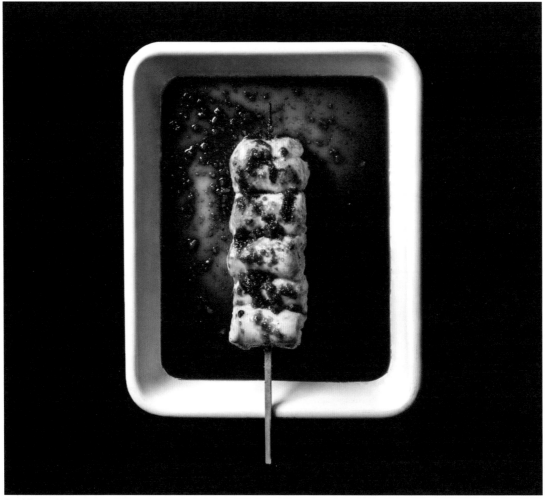

Garnish: wasabi, soy sauce.

Fillet

Seasoning: olive oil, sake, salt, pepper.

   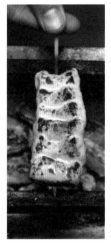

01. Start with the smooth side down over high heat, grilling until light brown, 1–2 minutes, 20 percent cooked.

02. Rotate ¼ turn, cook on each side until lightly colored, 1 minute, 50 percent cooked.

03. Once three sides are colored, finish cooking on the back until light brown, 1–2 minutes, 80 percent cooked.

04. Spray with sake and lightly season with salt to finish.

Garnish: yuzu zest, yuzu juice.

Green Miso Breast

Seasoning: olive oil, sake, salt, pepper.

   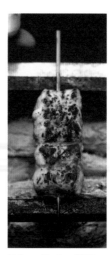

01. Start with the smooth side down over high heat, grilling until golden brown, 1–2 minutes, 25 percent cooked.

02. Rotate ¼ turn, cook on its side until lightly colored, 1 minute, 50 percent cooked.

03. Once three sides are colored, finish cooking on the back until dark brown, 2 minutes, 85 percent cooked.

04. Spray with sake and lightly season with salt to finish.

Garnish: lemon wedge.

Ume Shiso Thigh

Seasoning: sesame oil, sake, salt.

01. Start with the shiso leaf up over high heat, grilling until light brown, 1–2 minutes, 60 percent cooked.

02. Rotate ¼ turn, cook on its side until lightly colored, 1–2 minutes, 75 percent cooked.

03. Spray the shiso leaf with sake, turn and cook on the leaf side.

04. Once the shiso leaf starts to color, spray again with sake as this helps prevent the leaf from burning, 1–2 minutes, 95 percent cooked.

05. Spray with sake and lightly season with salt to finish.

Garnish: ume paste, black sesame seeds, chiffonade of shiso.

Thigh, Tokyo Onion
Seasoning: olive oil, salt, pepper. Dip: Tare (page 180).

01. Start with the smooth-side down over high heat grilling until both the onion and meat are light brown, 1–2 minutes, 30 percent cooked.

02. Rotate ¼ turn, cook on each side until lightly colored, 1–2 minutes, 60 percent cooked.

03. Turn to the back side, continue cooking, 2 minutes, 85 percent cooked.

04. Begin to dip into the tare, and color each side of the thigh until there is caramelization and small bits of char. Dip 2–3 times.

05. Dip one last time and lightly season with salt.

Inner Thigh

Seasoning: sake, salt, pepper.

01. Start with the smooth side down over high heat.

02. Cook until lightly colored with small amounts of char on the fatty bits, 2–3 minutes, 45 percent cooked.

03. Flip the skewer over to the back side and continue cooking until the same color is achieved, about 1–2 minutes, 90 percent cooked.

04. Spray with sake and lightly season with salt to finish.

Garnish: lemon wedge.

Oyster
Seasoning: sake, salt.

01. Start with the skin side down over medium heat, grilling until the skin browns and renders fat, 2 minutes, 25 percent cooked.

02. Rotate ¼ turn, cook until lightly colored, 1 minute, 40 percent cooked.

03. Turn to the other side until the skin is thoroughly caramelized, 1 minute, 65 percent cooked.

04. Turn to the back side until just slightly browned and cooked through, 2 minutes.

05. Lightly season with salt to finish.

Garnish: lemon wedge.

Achilles

Seasoning: sake, salt, pepper. Glaze: garlic thyme butter.

01. Start with the skin side down over medium heat, grilling until the skin browns and renders fat, 2 minutes, 15 percent cooked.

02. Rotate ¼ turn, cook until lightly colored, 1 minute, 40 percent cooked.

03. Turn to the other side until the skin is thoroughly caramelized, 2 minutes, 60 percent cooked.

04. Turn to the back side, cook until just slightly browned, 3–4 minutes, 95 percent cooked.

05. Brush with melted garlic thyme butter, season with salt and let rest for 3 minutes before cutting in half.

Garnish: garlic thyme butter.

Soft Knee Bone

Seasoning: garlic sake, salt.

01. Start with the white cartilage down over high heat, grilling until golden brown, 3 minutes, 40 percent cooked.

02. Once deeply colored, spray with garlic sake. Rotate ¼ turn, cook on each side, 2–3 minutes, 70 percent cooked.

03. Turn to the back side, continue cooking until all sides are deeply colored, 2 minutes, 95 percent cooked.

04. Spray with garlic sake, kiss the front side of the skewer one last time over high heat for 10 seconds.

05. Lightly season with salt to finish.

Neck

Seasoning: sake, salt, pepper.

01. Start with the fat side down over high heat, grilling until colored with small amounts of char, 3–4 minutes, 45 percent cooked.

02. The meat will begin to shrink considerably. Once this happens, turn over to the other side.

03. Spray with sake, continue cooking, 3–4 minutes, 95 percent cooked.

04. Spray with sake and lightly season with salt to finish.

Garnish: dabs of yuzu kosho.

Tail

Seasoning: sake, salt.

 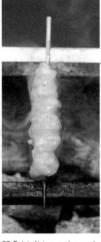  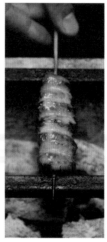

01. Start with the smooth side down over low heat, grilling until light golden brown, 1–2 minutes, 15 percent cooked.

02. Rotate ¼ turn, cook on each side until lightly colored, 1 minute.

03. Rotate ¼ turn every 30 seconds to 1 minute as it colors and renders fat.

04. After about 4 minutes, you should have achieved an evenly golden brown finish and the tail should feel crispy.

Wing
Seasoning: sake, salt.

01. Start with the skin side down over medium heat, grilling until dark golden brown.

02. After about 2 minutes the wing will begin to shrink and the skin will render.

03. Cook until the skin is deeply colored with flecks of char, 2 minutes, 70 percent cooked.

04. Spray the meat side with sake and season with salt.

Garnish: Shichimi (page 182), lemon wedge.

Wing Skin
Seasoning: sake, salt.

 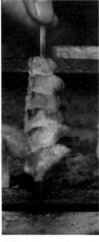 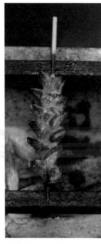  

01. Start with the skin side down over medium heat, grilling until golden brown, 1–2 minutes, 25 percent cooked.

02. Rotate ¼ turn, cook on each side until lightly colored, 1–2 minutes, 50 percent cooked.

03. Continue cooking on the back side until evenly colored, crispy and dark brown, 2–3 minutes.

04. Trim away any burnt bits with sharp kitchen scissors.

05. Lightly season with salt to finish.

Wing Tip
Seasoning: sake, salt, pepper.

   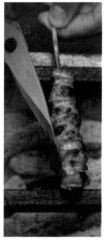 

01. Start on the smooth folded side over high heat, grilling until light brown, 1 minute, 25 percent cooked.

02. Rotate ¼ turn, cook on each side allowing to slowly render and lightly color, 1–2 minutes, 40 percent cooked.

03. Continue to rotate ¼ turn at a time until the color is nicely golden with some charring, 3 minutes.

04. It should be evenly colored and crunchy, 2–3 minutes. Trim the burnt bits with sharp kitchen scissors.

05. Lightly season with salt to finish.

Thyroid

Seasoning: garlic sake, salt, pepper.

01. Start over high heat, grilling until light brown, 1–2 minutes, 15 percent cooked.

02. Rotate ¼ turn, spray with garlic sake, cook on each side until lightly colored, 2–3 minutes, 50 percent cooked.

03. Continue to rotate ¼ turn at a time until golden with some charring, 4 minutes, 70 percent cooked.

04. Trim the burnt bits with kitchen scissors. Spray with garlic sake. Cook until darkly colored for 2–3 minutes, 95 percent cooked.

05. Lightly season with salt to finish.

Rib

Seasoning: olive oil, sake, salt, pepper. Dip: Tare (page 180).

01. Start over high heat, grilling until light brown, 1–2 minutes, 25 percent cooked.

02. Rotate ¼ turn, cook on each side until lightly colored, 2-3 minutes, 75 percent cooked.

03. Begin dipping the skewer in the tare, rotating the skewer so it doesn't burn, 30 seconds, 80 percent cooked.

04. Dip again into the tare and repeat the previous step.

05. Dip one last time to achieve the desired color, and lightly season with salt to finish.

Garnish: ground sansho pepper.

Liver

Seasoning: olive oil, sake, salt. Dip; Tare (page 180).

 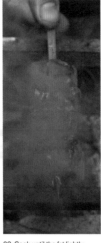 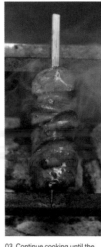 

01. Start with the smooth-side down over high heat.

02. Cook until the fat lightly caramelizes and is lightly colored, 1–2 minutes, 60 percent cooked. Dip in the tare and turn.

03. Continue cooking until the liver starts to firm up, dip in the tare again and turn for 30 seconds to 1 minute, 65 percent cooked.

04. Dip one last time and lightly season with salt to finish. We serve our liver at about 70 percent cooked.

Garnish: sansho pepper.

Heart

Seasoning: olive oil, garlic sake, salt, pepper.

01. Start with the fat-side down over high heat.

02. Cook until the fat lightly caramelizes and is lightly colored, 1–2 minutes, 60 percent cooked.

03. Cook on the back side until lightly colored, spray with garlic sake and cook for 30 seconds to 1 minute, 75 percent cooked.

04. Rotate ¼ turn and allow the fat to get slightly more caramelized, 30 seconds, 85 percent cooked.

05. Spray with garlic sake and lightly season with salt and pepper to finish.

Garnish: ginger juice, scallions (spring onions).

Ventricle
Seasoning: olive oil, sake, salt, pepper. Dip: Tare (page 180).

   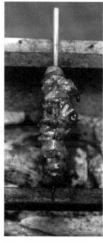 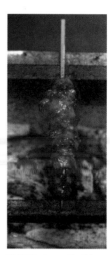

01. Start over high heat, grilling until light brown and the fat begins to caramelize, 1–2 minutes, 15 percent cooked.

02. Rotate ¼ turn, cook on each side until lightly colored, 1–2 minutes, 60 percent cooked.

03. Dip the skewer in the tare, rotating so it doesn't burn, 30 seconds to 1 minute, 80 percent cooked.

04. Dip the skewer in the tare again until lightly caramelized for 30 seconds to 1 minute, 90 percent cooked.

05. Lightly season with salt to finish.

Garnish: Kyoto shichimi (see page 226).

Gizzard

Seasoning: olive oil, garlic sake, salt, pepper.

  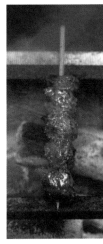 

01. Start on the less flat side over high heat.

02. Cook on each side until lightly colored and charred, spray with garlic sake, turn, 2–3 minutes, 50 percent cooked.

03. Spray again with the garlic sake, and cook until lightly charred, 1–2 minutes, 75 percent cooked.

04. Generously season with salt to finish.

Garnish: Garlic Chips (page190).

Meatball

Seasoning: sake. Dip: Tare (page 180).

  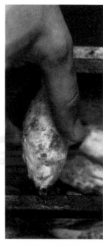  

01. Start with the meatball over medium-high heat, so that the meat at the tip is touching the bar (to keep it together.)

02. Rotate ¼ turn until lightly colored on all sides, 2–3 minutes, 75 percent cooked.

03. Pinch the meatball; it should feel bouncy and firm, not soft. If still soft, continue cooking while turning ¼ at a time.

04. Begin dipping into tare and turning to avoid burning. Dip up to 4 times, grilling for 2–3 minutes, 90 percent cooked.

05. Once you have reached a rich caramel color, dip one last time to finish.

To serve: Marinated Egg Yolk (page 193).

Duck Meatball

Dip: Duck Tare (page 193).

01. Place the duck meatballs over high heat.

02. Rotate ¼ turn, cook on each side until lightly colored, 2–3 minutes, 80 percent cooked.

03. Once firm, begin dipping into tare and turning to avoid burning. Dip 3 times, grilling for 2 minutes, 95 percent cooked.

04. Once the meatballs are a rich caramel color, dip one last time to finish.

Garnish: kinome leaves.

Vegetables

We use a mix of both local and Japanese vegetables at the restaurant; there is often a huge crossover between them. Just like the chicken, we treat our vegetables simply, doing our best to express their essence without too much fuss and with as little waste as possible. My focus when choosing vegetables is on vibrancy—I'm less obsessed with the titles they hold than with trusting my instincts that they still have potent life in them. In most major cities you will find the majority of the vegetables we use in either a Japanese or Chinese grocery, but in all likelihood you'll need to look in both.

01.

02.

03.

04.

05.   06.   07.

01. Mizuna (page 226)   03. Shungiku (page 227)   05. Shiso (page 227)   07. Myoga (page 226)
02. Mitsuba (page 226)   04. Sansho Pepper (page 227)   06. Kinome (page 226)

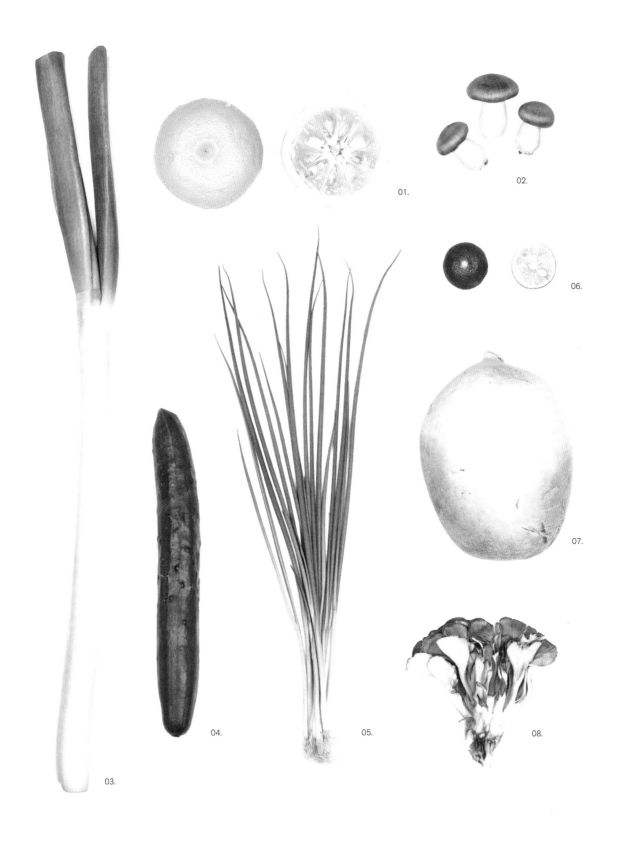

01.

02.

06.

07.

03.

04.   05.   08.

01. Yuzu (page 227)   03. Tokyo Negi (page 227)   05. Banno Negi (page 226)   07. Koshin Daikon (page 226)
02. Daikoku (page 226)   04. Kyuri Cucumber (page 226) 06. Sudachi (page 227)   08. Maitake (page 226)

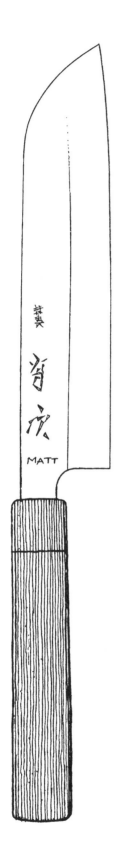

One of the main things that other chefs notice when they come to our kitchen is that almost all our vegetables are rinsed in cold water for a considerable period after they have been cut. Throughout the book, if a vegetable is being served raw (except tomatoes) you can safely assume that it has been cut using a mandoline, Japanese circular slicer, or a razor-sharp knife, washed for at least ten minutes in cold running water, air dried thoroughly, and packed interspersed with paper towel to absorb any excess water. The following is a quick guide to how we wash and cut each vegetable in our kitchen:

Basics
1. Always start with a knife that is as sharp as it can possibly be, the importance of a sharp knife when cutting vegetables is highly underrated. Using a sharp knife will extend the life of your vegetables, decrease any bitterness, and improve the texture. This is especially true when cutting anything in the onion family.
2. Cut with the grain of the vegetable. When I say the grain I mean the natural shape of the vegetable. For example onions have vertical lines starting from the bulb, and if you cut in the same direction as those lines you will end up with a much crisper, less astringent onion.
3. Wash, wash, and wash some more. Just to be clear, if we are trying to caramelize an onion we definitely don't wash them, but when we want an onion to have a crisp texture and a lighter flavor we rinse them in cold water for at least 15 minutes, or until the desired flavor and texture has been achieved.
4. Dry properly. My preferred method of drying is for the vegetable to sit in a fine mesh colander over a bowl, inside the fridge for at least an hour or until its dry and feels light. For salad greens, of course, you could use a salad spinner, but there will be instances where leaves get bruised.
5. Pack properly. Give the vegetable room to breathe, don't pack too much into a small container or you will undo all the effort that you have just exerted in steps 1 to 4. Intersperse layers of vegetables with an absorbent organic material, like a cotton towel or good quality paper towel.

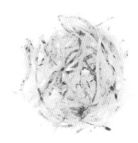

White/Red Onion (Salad)

Finely slice to desired thickness with the grain of the onion. The thicker you cut, the longer you will need to rinse for. With the thickness shown for our salads, rinse for about 30 minutes.

Scallions (Spring Onions)

Cut as fine as possible, starting from the base, wash for 15–30 minutes in cold running water.

Radish Mix

To make the radish mix we use a combination of a mandoline, a Japanese circular slicer, and a technique called katsuramaki, to achieve thin layers of radish, which we then julienne as thin as possible and rinse in cold water for 15–20 minutes, or until the sharp flavor dissipates slightly.

Mizuna/Mitsuba

The leaves are the best part of both these vegetables, so always start as close to the base as possible. Cut to your desired size, for all our salads we cut into 1¾ inch (4 cm) pieces. And try to keep the leaves about the same. Wash for 10–15 minutes in cold running water.

Myoga

Trim the base, cut in half lengthwise, and cut as thinly as possible starting from the tip. Wash for 3–5 minutes. Washing myoga is less about lightening the flavor and more about changing the texture and preventing the color from changing.

Cucumber

Cut the tip of the cucumber, then at a 45 degree angle cut about a 2 inch (5 cm) piece, then turn the cucumber 30 degrees and cut again at a 45 degree angle. The end should look like a crudely sharpened pencil.

The "smaller" section on our menu has dishes designed for snacking on at the beginning of a meal, and which can be eaten between many sticks of yakitori. The recipes included in this chapter are my takes on some classic izakaya dishes plus others that have become Yardbird staples.

Pickled Fennel with Yuzu

Ingredients:	Amounts:
Amazu (page 185)	1 liter
Yuzu skin, finely sliced	20 g
Large fennel	1

Yield: 500 g

Method:

01. In a medium non-reactive pot, bring the amazu up to a simmer with the yuzu skin. Set aside to cool to room temperature.

02. Rinse the fennel under cold water in a muslin (cheesecloth) lined bowl for 5-10 minutes. Allow to dry.

03. Submerge the fennel in the yuzu amazu. It will keep in the refrigerator for up to 1 month.

Pickled Cucumber

Ingredients:	Amounts:
Japanese cucumbers	4 pieces (120 g each)
Coarse gray sea salt (sel gris)	15 g
Pickling liquid from Young Ginger Pickles (page 193)	500 ml
Young Ginger Pickles, to serve (page 193)	20 g

Yield: 480 g

Method:

01. Wash the cucumbers and trim off the ends. Roll the cucumbers in the salt, gently applying pressure, using the salt as an abrasive to bruise the cucumbers. Place in a strainer (sieve) and leave for at least 1 hour.

02. Place the cucumbers in a container or bag. Pour the Amazu from the jar of Young Ginger Pickles over the cucumbers. Set the cucumbers aside for a minimum of two weeks.

03. When ready to serve, remove the cucumbers from the Amazu and slice into 1 ¼ inch (3 cm) rounds. Serve chilled with thin slices of Young Ginger Pickles.

Kimchi

Ingredients:	Amounts:
Napa (Chinese) cabbages, quartered and cut into 2 ½ × 2 ½ inch (6 × 6 cm) pieces	2 kg
Salt	25 g
Baby carrots, scrubbed and cut diagonally into 2 ½ inch (6 cm) strips	500 g
Garlic chives, cut into 2 ½ inch (6 cm) batons	200 g

For the kimchi base	
Green apples, cored	40 g
Cloves garlic, peeled	50 g
Ginger, peeled	40 g
Sugar	20 g
Salted shrimp	12 g
Korean chili pepper (gochugaru)	75 g
Fish sauce	8 g
Light soy sauce	8 g

Yield: approx. 2 kg

Method:

01. Place all the ingredients for the kimchi base with 25 ml cold water into a blender or food processor. Blend until smooth.

02. Evenly salt the cabbage pieces, place in a strainer (sieve), and leave for three hours. After this time, gently squeeze out any excess water.

03. Salt the baby carrots, then leave the baby carrots to stand for three hours. After this time, gently squeeze out any excess water.

04. Wearing latex gloves, thoroughly mix the kimchi base into the prepared vegetables. Place in a clean container or bag and leave to ferment for a minimum of three days.

Daikon and Red Shiso

Ingredients:	Amounts:
Daikon (mooli), peeled, quartered and cut into ½-inch (1-cm) thick slices	2 pieces (800 g each)
Salt	20 g
Red Shiso Vinegar (page 186)	1 liter
Red shiso leaves, roughly torn	30 g

Yield: 1.5 kg

Method:

01. Rub the salt evenly into the daikon slices, place in a strainer (sieve), and leave for at least one hour. After this time, squeeze out any excess water.

02. Place the daikon slices in a small bowl and cover with the shiso vinegar and shiso leaves. Set aside in the refrigerator for a minimum of two days.

03. When ready, serve chilled.

Cucumber Salad with Sesame, Miso, and Pine Nuts

Ingredients: Amounts:
Japanese cucumber .... 4 pieces (120 g each)
Coarse gray sea salt (sel gris) .... 2 g
Lemon wedge (⅛ of a lemon) 1
Sesame Dressing (page 188) .... 20 g
Ground sesame seeds .... 2.5 g
Olive oil .... 3 g

To garnish
Pine nuts, lightly toasted .... 10 g
Sesame seeds, lightly toasted .... 2.5 g
Yield: 2 servings

Method:

01. Roll the cucumber in the salt, gently applying pressure, using the salt as an abrasive to bruise the cucumber.

02. Trim away the ends of the cucumber, cut in half lengthwise, then into quarters lengthwise. Finally, chop into 2 inch (5 cm) batons.

03. In a mixing bowl, combine the juice from the lemon wedge with the Sesame Dressing, ground sesame seeds, and olive oil. Add the cucumber and toss until entirely coated.

04. To serve, put the coated cucumber pieces in a serving bowl, arranging them in a neat stack. Garnish with toasted pine nuts and sesame seeds.

Fruit Tomato Salad

Ingredients:	Amounts:
Fresh yuba	1 (120 g)
Fruit tomato	1 piece (80 g)
Shiso oil	1 tsp
Shiso leaf	1 piece
Coarse gray sea salt (sel gris)	2 g
Fruit Tomato Dressing (page 187)	To serve

Yield: 2 servings

Method:

01. To peel the tomato, prepare a small pot of rapidly boiling water and an ice bath.

02. Score a small X on the bottom of the tomato with a very sharp knife, just through the skin. Using a slotted spoon, gently place the tomato in the boiling water for 20 seconds, then remove and place immediately in the ice bath.

03. Remove the tomato from the ice bath after 30 seconds, and peel the skin gently starting at the X. If the skin does not peel easily, repeat the process.

04. Cut the yuba into 12 pieces at 10 g each, and absorb some of the liquid on a paper towel. Cut the tomato into quarters, and then cut those quarters in half, giving you 8 pieces.

05. Season each piece of yuba and tomato with two or 3 granules of salt.

06. Start with 3 pieces of yuba at the bottom of the bowl, then add 2 pieces of tomato. Repeat this pattern 4 times until neatly piled in the bowl.

07. Drizzle the dressing and shiso oil over the top of the salad , and garnish with the shiso leaf torn into 6 pieces.

Seared Yellowtail Salad

Ingredients:	Amounts:
Yellowtail loin	60 g
Yardbird Shichimi (page 182)	5 g
Yuzu Kosho Ponzu (see below)	20 g
Daikon radish, finely sliced	20 g
Watermelon radish, finely sliced	20 g
Mizuna	40 g
Olive oil	5 g, plus extra to dress the salad
Salt	for seasoning
Yuzu skin, microplaned	to garnish

For the Yuzu Kosho Ponzu	
Kabosu juice	100 ml
Yuzu juice	100 ml
Sudachi juice	100 ml
Soy sauce	160 ml
White sesame oil	50 g
Red yuzu kosho	10 g

Yield: 2 servings

Method:

01. First, make the Yuzu Kosho Ponzu. Combine all the juices, soy sauce, and red yuzu kosho together in a pitcher (jug), then add the white sesame oil.

02. Coat the yellowtail loin in the Yardbird Shichimi. Using a cook's blowtorch, sear the surface of the fish and then immediately put it in the refrigerator for 10–15 minutes.

03. Cutting against the grain on the diagonal, slice the yellowtail loin into ¼ inch (5 mm) slices. You will need 5–8 slices.

04. Spoon 3 g of the Yuzu Kosho Ponzu over the yellowtail slices and put back in the refrigerator while you assemble the salad.

05. Place the radish mix, mizuna, olive oil, and salt in a chilled metal mixing bowl. Add the remaining Yuzu Kosho Ponzu and then gently toss until all the ingredients are combined.

06. When ready to serve, remove the lightly marinated yellowtail slices from the refrigerator. In a chilled serving bowl, build the dish by layering the salad one third at a time and placing 2–3 slices of fish between each layer of salad.

07. Garnish with the yuzu skin and dress the salad with olive oil.

Eggplant Salad with Pickled Garlic and Ginger Tosazu

Ingredients: Amounts:

Japanese eggplant (aubergine) .... 1 piece

Pickled Garlic and Ginger Tosazu (see below) .... 25 g

Cucumber .... 50 g

Myoga, sliced .... 12 g

Vietnamese crispy shallots .... 14 g

Olive oil .... 4 g, plus extra to dress

Salt .... 1 g

For the Pickled Garlic and Ginger Tosazu

Tosazu (page 100) .... 1 quantity

Bonito pickled garlic .... 300 g

Ginger .... 75 g

Yield: 2 servings

Method:

01. First, make the Pickled Garlic and Ginger Tosazu. Combine all ingredients in a food processor and blend until smooth. This is a lot more than you need, but will keep well chilled for 1 month.

02. Using a cook's blowtorch, evenly sear the skin of the Japanese eggplants (aubergines). Only move from each spot that is burning when the skin glows like the end of a lit cigarette.

03. As you burn each eggplant, place in a metal bowl covered in plastic wrap so that they steam gently.

04. When ready to peel, place the eggplant on a paper towel and gently scrape away the skin.

05. Place the eggplant flesh into a vacuum bag or an airtight container, cover with the Pickled Garlic and Ginger Tosazu, then seal and leave to marinate until ready to use (a minimum of 2 hours.)

06. To cut the cucumber refer to page 127. Lightly salt the cucumber, then leave to sit in the refrigerator for 10–15 minutes until water is released. Gently squeeze any excess water out of the cucumber batons and return to the refrigerator until ready to use.

07. Combine 65 g of the marinated eggplant with the cucumber, half of the sliced myoga, 11 g of the fried shallots, the olive oil, and salt.

08. To serve, put the salad in a chilled bowl, layering everything neatly. Garnish with the reserved shallots and myoga, then dress with olive oil.

Mushroom Salad with Mizuna, Watercress, and Wasabi

Ingredients:	Amounts:
Pickled mushrooms (page 187)	15 g
Olive oil	3 g
Mizuna	20 g
Shungiku	20 g
Watercress	20 g
Red onion, finely sliced	10 g
Myoga	15 g
Lemon wedge (⅛ of a lemon)	1
Wasabi Dressing (page 187)	10 g
Salt and freshly ground black pepper	To taste
Lotus Root Chips (page 190)	9

Yield: 2 servings

Method:

01. Put the pickled mushrooms into a pan with 2 g of the olive oil and place over a medium heat until warmed through.

02. Put the mizuna, shungiku, and watercress leaves into a mixing bowl. Add the red onion slices and half of the myoga, then gently mix together using chopsticks.

03. When the mushrooms are warm, add them to the salad in the mixing bowl. Dress the salad with the juice from the lemon wedge, the Wasabi Dressing, and the remaining 1 g of olive oil. Season with salt and black pepper to taste.

04. Layer half the salad in the middle of a cold serving bowl. Place 4 of the Lotus Root Chips in the center. Add the remaining salad, then garnish with the remaining Lotus Root Chips and myoga.

Yardbird Caesar

Ingredients:	Amounts:
Napa (Chinese) cabbage	60 g
Mizuna	60 g
Lemon wedge (⅛ of a lemon)	1
Fried baby anchovies (shirasu) (see below)	15 g
Kizami nori, to garnish	5 g
Caesar Dressing (see below)	30 g

For the fried baby anchovies (shirasu)	
Boiled, salted, sundried baby anchovies (shirasu)	100 g
Olive oil	25 g
Canola (rapeseed) oil	25 g

For the Caesar dressing	
Egg yolk	1
Miso katsuo ninku	120 g
Anchovy fillets	60 g
Garlic cloves	4
Roasted Garlic (page 189)	100 g
Rice vinegar	100 g
Grated Parmesan cheese	140 g
Olive oil	250 g
Freshly ground black pepper	1 g

Yield: 2 servings

Method:

01. For the dressing, place the egg yolk, miso katsuo ninku, anchovy fillets, garlics, vinegar, and cheese in a blender. Blend on high until smooth.

02. Set the blender on a medium–low setting and start to pour in the olive oil in a slow, steady stream until the dressing is fully emulsified and thick.

03. Season with ground black pepper and add a splash of water to lighten the consistency.

04. Next, make the fried baby anchovies. In a shallow pan, heat the oils to 350°F/180°C. Fry the anchovies until they turn a light golden color, and any water has evaporated from them. As the anchovies will continue to cook slightly even when out of the oil, before the anchovies turn dark, remove them from the pan and drain on paper towels.

05. Allow the anchovies to cool and keep in an airtight container. They will keep for 1 week in the fridge.

06. Cut the cabbage into quarters, then slice as thinly as possible starting at the base. Next, cut the mizuna into 1 ¼ inch (3 cm) pieces, including the stems.

07. In a strainer (sieve) over a large metal bowl, thoroughly mix and wash all the leaves in cold running water for 5–10 minutes. Spin or leave to air-dry thoroughly.

08. Transfer the cabbage and mizuna into a cold mixing bowl. Dress with the juice from the lemon wedge, add 10 g of the fried baby anchovies, and gently toss.

09. To serve, layer the dressed leaves in the center of a chilled serving bowl. Garnish with the remaining 5 g of fried baby anchovies and the kizami nori.

Liver Mousse with Milk Bread and Crispy Fried Shallots

Ingredients:	Amounts:
Chicken livers	250 g
Butter	75 g
Freshly ground black pepper	2 g
Coarse gray sea salt (sel gris)	10 g
Crispy Fried Shallots, to garnish (page 190)	1 quantity
Scallions (spring onions) or chives, to garnish	12 g

For the Milk Bread

Milk (white sandwich) bread	15 g
Chicken fat, melted	40 g
Coarse gray sea salt (sel gris)	10 g

Yield: 5 servings

Method:

01. First, sterilize six 220 ml Mason jars —one jar for each serving of the mousse.

02. Make the liver mousse. Wash, rinse, and drain the livers, then dry with paper towels.

03. Melt the butter and set aside.

04. In a food processor or blender, blend the livers with the black pepper and salt on high until smooth. Pour in the melted butter in a slow, steady stream until emulsified.

05. Pass the liver mousse mixture through a fine mesh strainer (sieve) to remove any sinew, into a spouted measuring cup. Carefully pour 60 g of the liver mousse mixture into each of the sterilized 220 ml Mason jars. Close the lids to seal.

06. Cook the liver mousse mixture in the jars using either a bamboo or metal steamer or a water bath set to 176°F/80°C. Cook for 20 minutes or until set.

07. Cool the jars at room temperature, then chill until ready to serve.

08. Make the Crispy Fried Shallots as per the Basics recipe.

09. Cut the milk (white sandwich) bread into 2-inch (5-cm) thick slices. Gently brush one side of each slice with melted chicken fat and sprinkle lightly with salt.

10. About 20 minutes before serving, remove the jars of liver mousse from the refrigerator to bring them to room temperature. Garnish each jar with 2 g of washed and dried scallions (spring onions) or chives.

11. Toast the fat-coated side of the slices of bread until golden brown.

12. Place a jar of the liver mousse with all of the other elements on each serving plate. Encourage everyone to mix the Japanese scallions into the liver mousse, then spread it on the slices of toasted bread, and top with the Crispy Fried Shallots.

Miso Soup

Ingredients:	Amounts:
Miso Soup (see below)	200 ml
Mizuna	20 g
Daikon (mooli), quartered and sliced	5 g
Scallions (spring onions), thinly sliced	5 g
Yuzu skin	2 g

For the Miso Soup	
High-quality barley miso	1.25 g
High-quality rice miso	1.25 g
Mushroom Dashi (page 185)	200 ml

Yield: 1 serving

Method:

01. First, make the Miso Soup. Whisk the barley miso and the rice miso through a fine-mesh strainer (sieve) so that they will evenly distribute through the dashi. Add the whisked miso to the Mushroom Dashi.

02. Next, heat the Miso Soup in a stockpot or pan.

03. To serve, place the mizuna, daikon (mooli), scallions (spring onions), and yuzu skin in a warmed soup bowl. Pour the hot Miso Soup into the bowl over the other ingredients. Serve immediately. Eat while steaming hot.

Yardbird Soup

Ingredients:	Amounts:
Chicken Stock (page 184)	200 ml
Gobo (burdock), finely sliced	5 g
Mizuna, chopped	20 g
Napa (Chinese) cabbage, sliced	5 g
Myoga, chopped	5 g
Scallions (spring onions), finely sliced	5 g

Yield: 1 serving

Method:

01. Bring the Chicken Stock and gobo to the boil in a stockpot or pan.

02. To serve, place the mizuna, Napa (Chinese) cabbage, myoga, and scallions (spring onions) in the bottom of a soup bowl. Pour over the hot Chicken Stock. Serve immediately. Eat while steaming hot.

bigger

When we talk with our guests about the "bigger" section of our menu, we explain that they are not only bigger in size but bigger in flavor: most of these dishes are meant to be served toward the end of your meal. Many happen to be vegetarian, which tends to surprise people that come to the restaurant expecting to find chicken in everything. We sell as many balls of corn as we do meatballs on any given night.

Asparagus with Onsen Egg and Nori Dressing

Ingredients:	Amounts:
Asparagus	150 g
Olive oil	for brushing
Sake	for spraying
Onsen Egg (page 191)	1
Nori Dressing (page 188)	8 g
Furikake, to garnish	5 g
Seaweed Panko Bread Crumbs (page 190), to garnish	8 g
Salt and freshly ground black pepper	To taste

Yield: 2 servings

Method:

01. Trim the woody base and any small fronds from the asparagus spears. Using a vegetable peeler, peel off a very thin outer layer one-quarter of the way down each spear.

02. Brush the asparagus with olive oil, spray with sake, and season with salt and pepper.

03. Grill the asparagus over charcoal until colored but still with a little bite, 2–3 minutes.

04. Preheat a cast-iron skillet (frying pan) in the corner of a broiler (grill).

05. Remove the asparagus from the grill and cut each spear into 2 inch (5 cm) pieces. Place the asparagus pieces in a warm mixing bowl, add the Nori Dressing, and toss until completely coated.

06. To serve, carefully plate the dressed asparagus into the warmed skillet, leaving a space in the middle for the Onsen Egg to rest. Crack the egg onto a paper towel and remove any runny whites, then place the egg in the space left in the asparagus.

07. Garnish with the furikake and Seaweed Panko Bread Crumbs.

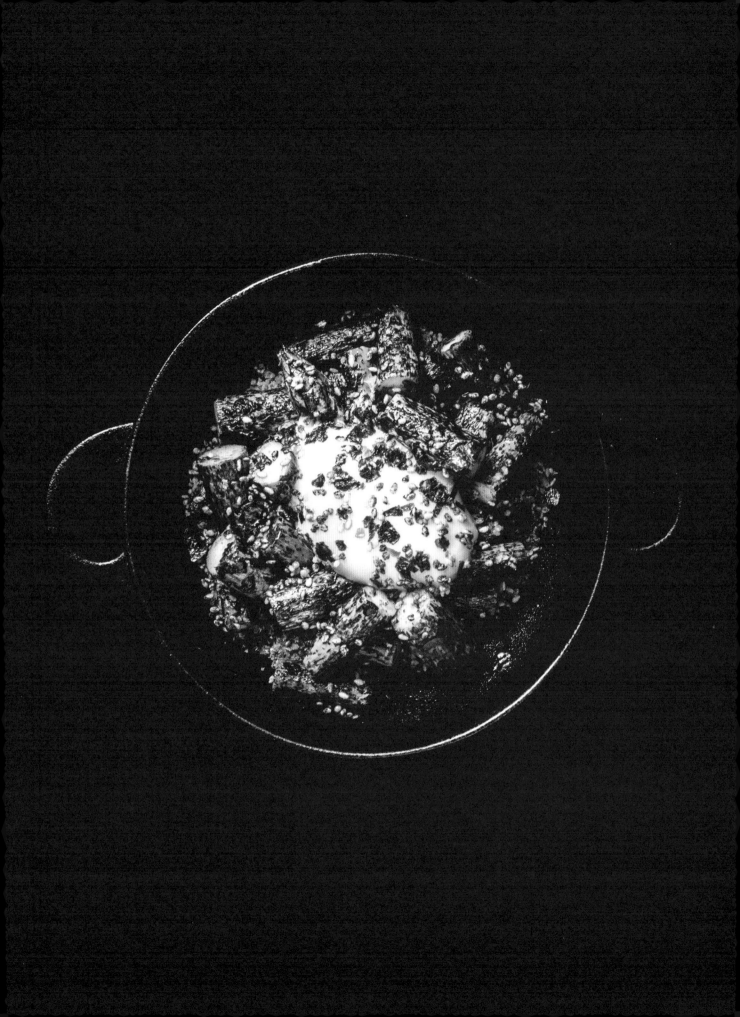

Brussels Sprouts with Black Garlic Sauce and Garlic Chips

Ingredients:	Amounts:
Brussels sprouts	250 g
Black Garlic Sauce (page 189)	15 g
Olive oil	3 g
Salt	2 g
Freshly ground black pepper	2 g
Lemon wedge (⅛ of a lemon)	1
Garlic Chips (page 190), to garnish	5 g

Yield: 1–2 servings

Method:

01. Peel the outer leaves from the Brussels sprouts, cut them in half, then wash and leave to dry in a strainer (sieve).

02. Marinate the prepared sprouts with 5 g of the Black Garlic Sauce and the olive oil. Ideally, do this in a vacuum bag so that the marinade can penetrate the inner leaves of the sprouts, however, if this isn't possible then a sealed container or plastic bag will also work. Leave to marinate for a minimum of 2–4 hours.

03. Once marinated, grill the sprouts over very hot charcoal in a wire basket. Allow the sprouts to become quite charred, but without overcooking—the time this takes will depend on the size of the sprouts, but roughly 4–5 minutes.

04. After grilling, toss the charrred sprouts in the remaining Black Garlic Sauce with salt, pepper, and the juice from the lemon wedge.

05. To serve, garnish with the Garlic Chips.

KFC (Korean Fried Cauliflower)

Ingredients:	Amounts:
Cauliflower, cut into 25 g florets	12 florets
Salt	20 g
Vegetable oil, for deep-frying	3 liters
White sesame seeds, to garnish	3 g
Lime wedge (⅛ of a lime), to serve	1

For the KFC batter	
Yardbird Chicken Flour Mix (page 191)	400 g
Tempura Batter (page 192)	400 g

For the KFC sauce	
Garlic cloves	100 g
Sugar	500 g
Mirin	50 g
Korean chili paste	150 g
Red yuzu kosho	250 g

Yield: 4 servings

Method:

01. First, make the KFC batter. Whisk all the ingredients with 480 ml ice-cold water until smooth. Chill in the refrigerator until ready to use.

02. To make the KFC sauce, blend the garlic with 1.5 liters almost boiling water until smooth. Place the garlic paste in a pan with the sugar, mirin, Korean chili paste, and red yuzu kosho, then mix well. Reduce over a low heat for 1–3 hours, stirring frequently, until the mixture has the consistency of a thick barbecue sauce.

03. Soak the cauliflower florets in 2 liters water and the salt for 1 hour. Just before cooking, remove the cauliflower from the saltwater solution and put in the batter, completely coating each floret.

04. Heat the vegetable oil in a deep fryer, or a deep saucepan, to 350°F/180°C. One by one, carefully drop the battered cauliflower florets into the hot oil, making sure that the pieces don't stick to the bottom of the fryer or to each other. Once all the florets are in the fryer, fish out any stray bits of batter. Fry the florets until they are deep brown in color, about 3 minutes.

05. Remove with a slotted spoon and drain on a wire rack, then on a paper towel. Transfer the cauliflower to a bowl. Immediately cover with a generous amount of room-temperature KFC sauce.

06. To serve, stack the sauce-smothered cauliflower florets in a serving bowl. Garnish liberally with the white sesame seeds and a lime wedge. Eat while hot.

Corn Tempura

Ingredients:											Amounts:

Corn kernels, cut from cobs .... 400 g (5-6 corn cobs, depending on size)

Tempura flour .... 100 g

Tempura Batter (page 192) .... 20 g

Vegetable oil, for deep-frying .... 5 liters

Sea salt and freshly ground black pepper .... To taste

Yield: 4 corn balls

Method:

01. After peeling the husk, and removing all the silk from the corn. Use both hands to break the corn in half as evenly as you can.

02. Over a medium mixing bowl, with one half of the cob in one hand, and your knife in your dominant hand, hold the knife parallel to the corn and begin to shave off the kernels in a turning motion cutting through only about 75 percent of the kernels. This allows water to be released during the cooking process, and prevents the corn from exploding in the oil and ruining your day. This cutting technique is called katsuramuki and there are a lot of demonstration videos available on the internet.

03. Place the vegetable oil in a medium pot and heat to 350°F/180°C.

04. In a large mixing bowl, add the corn kernels and the 10 g of tempura flour, mix the flour and the corn until every kernel is covered and there is a very small amount of dry flour left at the bottom of the bowl. If the corn feels wet at this point and is not covered, add more flour in small amounts.

05. Add tempura batter little by little, mixing vigorously with your fingers until you feel the gluten activate and the corn starts to become tacky. You should still be able to see individual kernels lightly bound by a very coarse batter. Little clumps of dry batter will form on your fingertips.

06. Rinse your hands of all batter. Dry them very well and dust the palms of your hands in the dry flour. At this point the palms of your hands and fingers should be covered in tempura flour.

07. Gently scoop up about 95–100g of the corn mixture, (which should be slightly smaller than a baseball) —it should feel sticky, but the flour on your hands will prevent it from sticking, and at the same time will coat the outside of the ball with flour.

08. Using both hands, begin to compress the corn kernels into a sphere, moving it from one hand to the other (the same way you would form a snowball; this method stops the formed balls sticking to your hand and allows it to be evenly covered in flour.) They should be packed enough so that they don't fall apart, but not so tightly that the center will not be cooked.

09. With the formed ball of corn in your hand, get as close to the oil as you can and very gently drop it into the oil using tongs and immediately pull your hand away, being very careful not to burn yourself. Repeat with the rest of the corn.

10. Fry for about 3 minutes, until some of the kernels are golden brown and the surface of the entire ball is crispy.

11. Remove the ball from the oil, and drain on a wire rack. Use a paper towel to remove any excess oil. Season liberally with salt and freshly ground black pepper.

12. Arrange the balls on a plate, in a pyramid form with 3 on the bottom and 1 on top. Serve immediately.

Method:

01. Peel the husk and break the cob in half as evenly as you can.

02. Begin to shave the kernels from the cob, only cutting through around 75 percent of the kernels.

03. Turn the cob as you go; this cutting technique is called katsuramuki, and will allow the kernels to release water and prevent them from exploding in the oil.

04. Add the tempura flour to the kernels.

05. Mix until every kernel is well coated.

06. Add the tempura batter little by little.

07. Mix well with your fingers until the mixture is tacky, and you can see individual kernels bound by thick batter.

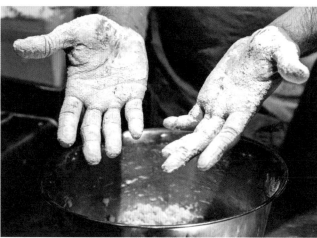

08. Wash your hands, shake them dry, then thoroughly dust in fresh flour to shape the corn balls.

09. Scoop 95–100 g of corn mixture and shape into something a little smaller than a baseball.

10. Start to compress the corn into a sphere.

11. Move it from one hand to the other, the way you would shape a snowball.

12. It should be packed well enough to not fall apart, but also not so tightly that the center won't cook.

13. Drop the corn ball into the fryer with your hand as close to the oil as possible, being careful not to burn yourself.

14. After around 3 minutes, remove the corn ball from the oil with tongs.

15. Drain on a wire rack and season with salt and pepper.

Fried Chicken with Garlic Kewpie Mayo

Ingredients:	Amounts:
Boneless, skin-on chicken drumsticks	10 pieces
Yardbird Chicken Flour Mix (page 191)	500 g
Vegetable oil	5 liters
Salt	1 g
Freshly ground black pepper	1 g
Lemon wedge (⅛ of a lemon), to serve	1

For the Garlic Kewpie Mayo	
Kewpie Mayo	250 g
Usukuchi (light soy sauce)	7 g
Roasted Garlic Purée (page 189)	35 g

Yield: 2 servings

Method:

01. First, prepare the chicken by cutting the boned-out drumsticks in half lengthwise, following the direction of the tendons.

02. Dredge the chicken drumsticks as lightly as possible in the Yardbird Chicken Flour Mix. Heat the vegetable oil in a deep fryer or deep saucepan to 350°F/180°C. Deep-fry the chicken drumsticks until very lightly golden, about 2 minutes—the insides should still be raw.

03. Place the chicken drumsticks on a slotted tray in a single layer to cool down. Once cool, place in the refrigerator until ready to fry again before serving.

04. To make the Garlic Kewpie Mayo, whisk all ingredients together until incorporated. This will make a lot more than you need, but will keep for 1 month in the fridge.

05. When ready to serve, finish frying the chicken. Heat enough vegetable oil in a deep fryer or a deep saucepan to 350°F/180°C. Remove the chicken drumsticks from the refrigerator and deep-fry until deep golden brown and the skin has a paper-like consistency, for about 4 minutes.

06. Remove with a slotted spoon and transfer to a paper towel-lined bowl. Season liberally with black pepper and salt.

07. To serve, place the chicken in a bowl lined with tempura paper or greaseproof paper, garnish with a wedge of lemon and the Garlic Kewpie Mayo on the side.

Duck Fried Rice

Ingredients:	Amounts:
Vegetable oil	20 ml
Duck leg meat, diced into 1 ¼ × 1 ¼ inch (3 × 3 cm) cubes (see below)	80 g
Garlic, chopped	10 g
Yukari Rice, cooked (page 191)	275 g
Welsh onion, sliced	10 g
Scallions (spring onions), chopped	10 g
Myoga, finely sliced	10 g
Yukari powder	2 g
White sesame seeds, toasted and ground	4 g
Salt	1 g
Green shiso leaves, finely chopped	7 g

Duck Legs	
Duck leg with skin on	2 pieces
Duck spice (see below)	40 g
Chicken fat	80 g

Duck Spice	
Yardbird Shichimi (page 182)	400 g
Salt	100 g
Sugar	100 g
Freshly ground black pepper	20 g

Ume Miso	
Water	500 g
Ume Paste (see page 189)	100 g
Sugar	500 g
Shiro miso	400 g

Yield: 2–3 servings

Method:

01. First, make the Ume Miso. Whisk all ingredients together. Cook over a low heat until reduced by one third and a thick paste. Reserve in the refrigerator until ready to use.

02. Season the duck legs all over with the duck spice and leave to cure in the refrigerator for 8–12 hours.

03. Once cured, pat the duck legs dry with paper towels. Place both the legs in a vacuum bag with the chicken fat. Sous vide in a water bath at 150°F/65°C for 7 hours. After 7 hours, ice down and chill.

04. Once chilled, remove the duck legs from the vacuum bag, pat dry with paper towels, and debone the legs trying not to shred the meat. Cut the duck meat into ¾ inch x ¾ inch (2 cm × 2 cm) dice.

05. Marinate in 10 g of the Ume Miso. Reserve in the refrigerator until ready to use.

06. Place a wok over a medium–high heat and add the vegetable oil. Once the oil is hot, add the duck leg meat and cook until the pieces start to color, 1–2 minutes.

07. Tip any excess fat out of the wok. Add the garlic and cook for 30 seconds; be careful not to burn the garlic.

08. Add the cooked Yukari Rice and fry, tossing frequently, until the rice is hot, fluffy, and broken up into individual pieces.

09. Add the Welsh onion, scallions (spring onions), and myoga and cook for 1 minute, until softened.

10. Add the yukari powder and half of the ground white sesame seeds. Toss and fry for another 30 seconds. Season with salt and half of the green shiso leaves.

11. To serve, tip the rice into a large serving bowl. Scatter over the remaining ground white sesame seeds and chopped green shiso leaves.

Takana Mushroom Udon

Ingredients:	Amounts:
Vegetable oil	20 g
Daikoku mushrooms, chopped	70 g
Takana pickles	60 g
Unsalted butter	25 g
Mirin	15 g
Sake	15 g
Mushroom Dashi (page 185)	140 g
Fresh udon or thick, white wheat noodles	160 g
Lemon wedge (⅛ of a lemon)	1
Freshly ground black pepper	Io taste
Korean chili pepper, to garnish	1 g

Yield: 2 servings

Method:

01. Heat a medium sauté pan over a medium heat. Add the vegetable oil and increase the heat to high, then sauté the mushrooms until nicely colored.

02. Add the takana pickles and butter to the pan. Continue sautéing until the butter starts to foam and becomes fragrant. Deglaze the pan with the mirin and sake.

03. Add the Mushroom Dashi to the pan, turn the heat up to high, then reduce the sauce by half.

04. In a separate pot of boiling water, cook the udon for 1 minute and 50 seconds, then remove and drain.

05. Add the noodles to the pan and toss until the sauce has the consistency of a thin gravy. Season with the juice from the lemon and some pepper.

06. To serve, place the udon in a warm bowl. Garnish with the Korean chili flakes.

Chicken and Egg Rice

Ingredients:	Amounts:
Chicken Fat Onion Paste (page 192)	80 g
Sweet Glutinous Mochi Rice, par-cooked (page 191)	220 g
Chicken Stock (page 184)	240 ml
Unsalted butter	20 g
Salt	3 g
Sweet peas (petit pois), shelled	30 g
Scallions (spring onions), chopped	10 g
Onsen Egg (page 191)	1
Crispy Chicken Skin (page 192), to garnish	6 pieces (80 g)

Yield: 2 servings

Method:

01. Heat a medium-sized sauté pan over medium–low heat. Add the Chicken Fat Onion Paste to the pan. Cook until slightly melted, about 2 minutes, then add the par-cooked sticky rice. Using a wooden spoon, stir until the grains of rice are mixed through—the rice should absorb some of the onion and fat at this point.

02. Increase the heat to medium–high. Add the Chicken Stock, about 50 ml at a time, stirring constantly so the rice does not stick to the bottom of the pan. Continue until the rice has absorbed all the stock and has the consistency of a loose risotto, still with a slight bite to the rice. Turn off the heat, then add the butter, salt, and the peas.

03. To serve, heat a small cast-iron skillet or frying pan. Starting at the center, ladle the rice into the skillet, letting the rice naturally mound in the middle. Make a small well in the center of the rice for the Onsen Egg.

04. Scatter over the chopped scallions (spring onions), then crack the Onsen Egg into the center of the well in the rice.

05. Garnish with the Crispy Chicken Skin on top of the rice. Serve immediately. Mix everything together at the table just before eating.

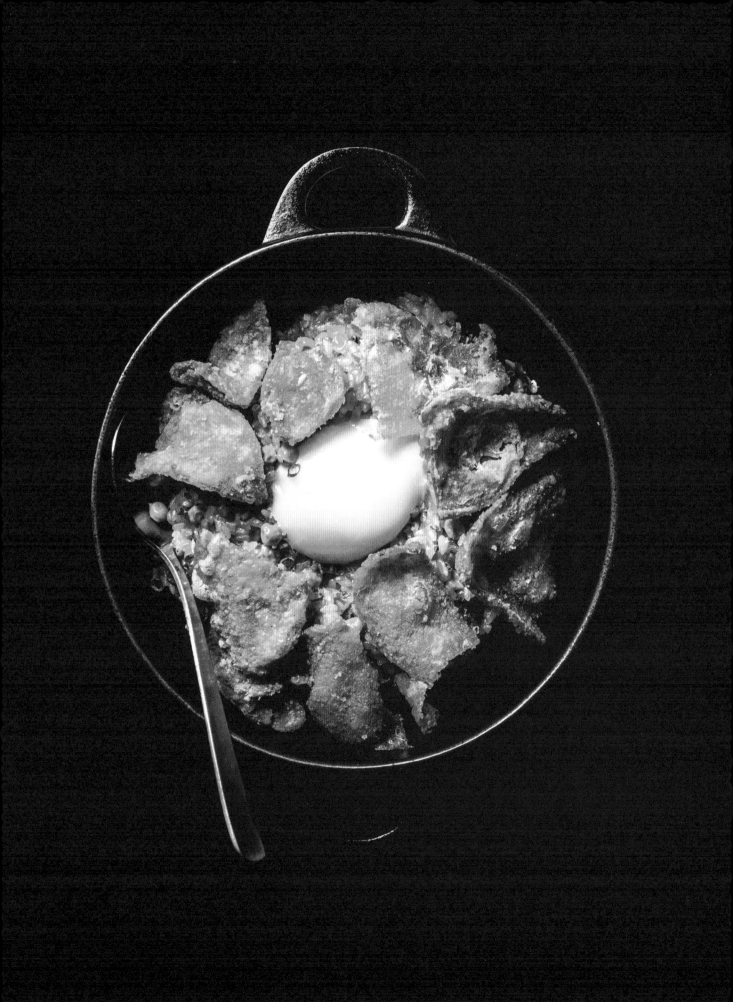

Mushroom Rice

Ingredients:	Amounts:
White onion, large	1
Fresh eringi king oyster mushrooms	6 pieces
Fresh shiitake mushrooms, stems removed	10 pieces
Fresh maitake (hen of the woods) mushrooms	1–2 heads
Unsalted butter, melted	5 tbsp, plus extra to serve
Usukuchi (light soy sauce)	2 tbsp
Sake	200 ml
Freshly ground pepper	A pinch
Sweet, glutinous, short grain mochi rice	500 g
Mushroom Dashi (page 105)	1 liter

To garnish	
Scallions (spring onions), finely sliced	15 g
Garlic Chips (page 190)	20 g

Yield: 4–6 servings

Method:

01. Finely dice one large white onion and rinse under cold water for about 15 minutes. Squeeze the onions dry and set aside.

02. Coat the mushrooms with 2 tbsp of the melted butter, 1 tbsp of the soy sauce, the sake, and a pinch of pepper.

03. Place the mushrooms under a broiler or overhead grill until lightly browned. Once cooled, dice all the mushrooms, except for the maitake, which can be hand torn.

04. Heat a large pan with the remaining 3 tbsp of melted butter and cook the chopped white onion over a medium heat, until slightly translucent. Add the mushrooms, 1 tbsp of the soy sauce, and then add the rice. Try to coat each grain of rice with the butter and soy sauce while slightly drying the pan—it's okay if the rice sticks to the pan a little, just don't let it burn.

05. As you would with a risotto, slowly start adding the Mushroom Dashi until the rice is cooked to your desired firmness. We cook our rice slightly al dente, which takes about 10 minutes.

06. To finish, add a small dab of butter for creaminess. We serve our mushroom rice in a very hot cast-iron pan, which allows for a slight crust to form as it is brought to the table.

07. To serve, garnish with the finely sliced scallions (spring onions) and Garlic Chips.

Scotch Egg with Cabbage, Tonkatsu Sauce, and Kewpie Mayo

Ingredients:	Amounts:
Eggs	8
Tare Sauce (page 180)	200 ml
Yardbird Chicken Flour Mix (page 191)	50 g
Fresh panko bread crumbs	200 g
White cabbage, thinly sliced	40 g
Lemon wedge (⅛ of a lemon)	1
Salt	10 g
Vegetable oil, for deep-frying	3 liters
Chicken Katsu (see below)	1 quantity
B+S Sauce (page 180)	20 g
Kewpie Mayo	6 g
Aonori	2 g

For the Chicken Katsu	
Chicken thigh meat, skin on	250 g
White onion, finely chopped, rinsed, and squeezed	50 g
Fresh panko bread crumbs	20 g
Salt	3 g

Yield: 5 Scotch Eggs

Method:

01. First, make the Chicken Katsu. (The amount given here is enough to make five Scotch Eggs in total.) Chill the chicken thigh meat and the elements of your meat grinder in the freezer for 20 minutes. Once chilled, pass the chicken thigh meat through the grinder twice, then put in a bowl. Add the onion, bread crumbs, and salt to the ground chicken, then mix together. Form the mixture into 60-g (2 ¼-oz) balls, place on a tray and then chill in the refrigerator.

02. Temper five of the eggs in warm water before cooking in rapidly boiling water for 6 minutes, gently stirring to center the yolks, until soft-boiled. Shock the eggs in an ice-bath to prevent further cooking.

03. Peel the shells from the eggs. Place the eggs in a bowl with the Tare Sauce; cover with a paper towel and allow the eggs to marinate in the sauce for 1 hour.

04. Once marinaded, remove the soft-boiled eggs from the Tare Sauce and place in a strainer (sieve). Once drained, roll the marinaded eggs in the Yardbird Chicken Flour Mix.

05. One at a time, remove the chicken meatballs from the refrigerator and press them into the palm of your hand until it is an equal thickness of about ¾ inch (2 cm) and a diameter of about 5 inches (12 cm).

06. Take the floured soft-boiled eggs and carefully wrap the chicken patties around them; make sure that there are no holes or pockets of air. Place the wrapped eggs on a floured tray and evenly roll them in the remaining Yardbird Chicken Flour Mix.

07. Crack the remaining three eggs in a separate bowl and whisk together to create an egg wash. Roll the wrapped eggs in the egg wash mixture and then cover with a thick coating of fresh panko bread crumbs. Keep the breaded Scotch Eggs in the refrigerator with the remaining loose panko until ready to fry.

08. In a mixing bowl, gently combine the cabbage with the juice from the lemon wedge and salt. On a serving plate, create a bed of cabbage for the Scotch egg to sit on.

09. Heat the vegetable oil in a deep fryer or deep saucepan to 340°F/170°C. Using a slotted spoon or ladle, carefully lower the Scotch egg into the hot oil. Deep fry until a deep golden brown, about 3 minutes.

10. Remove with a slotted spoon and drain on a wire rack. Season with salt and pepper, then leave to rest on a paper towel-lined tray for 1 minute.

11. Using a serrated knife, cut the Scotch egg lengthwise into quarters and add to the serving plate, on top of the cabbage. Drizzle with the B+S Sauce and Kewpie Mayo, then finish with a sprinkle of aonori.

Katsu Sando

Ingredients: Amounts:

Ingredient	Amount
White cabbage, thinly sliced, washed, and dried	20 g
Salt	10 g
Kewpie Mayo	5 g
B+S Sauce (page 189)	30 g
Lemon wedge (⅛ of a lemon)	1
Chicken Katsu (page 174)	90 g
Vegetable oil, for deep-frying	3 liters
Thick-cut milk (white sandwich) bread	2 slices

Yield: 1 sandwich

Method:

01. In a mixing bowl, lightly salt the cabbage, then leave to sit for for 2 minutes before squeezing out as much water as you can. Add the Kewpie Mayo and mix.

02. In a separate mixing bowl, add the B+S sauce and the juice from the lemon wedge.

03. Following the instructions on page 174, make the Chicken Katsu and then shape it into a patty that is a roundish square. Lightly press a dimple in the middle of the patty to help it cook evenly.

04. Heat the vegetable oil in a deep fryer or deep saucepan to 340°F/170°C. Using a slotted spoon or ladle, carefully lower the Chicken Katsu patty into the hot oil. Deep fry until a deep golden brown, about 6 minutes.

05. While the patty is cooking, place the bread in a toaster oven or salamander (overhead grill). Warm only one side of the bread—this will become the inside of the sandwich.

06. Remove the chicken patty with a slotted spoon and drain paper towel-lined tray. Roll in the B+S Sauce until glossy and coated all over.

07. Evenly spread the cabbage mixture on the toasted side of the bottom slice of bread. Place the sauced Chicken Katsu patty on top of the bread. Top with the second slice of bread, toasted-side down. Very lightly compress the sandwich, flipping it over twice so that it's evenly pressed.

08. Neatly cut the crusts from the slices of bread, then cut the sandwich in half. Turn the sandwich so that the cut-side faces upwards to show the cross-section and filling; insert a bamboo skewer through the middle of the sandwich to hold it together.

Rice Cakes with Mirin and Furikake

Ingredients:	Amounts:
Vegetable oil	15 g
Korean rice cakes	15 pieces
Butter	10 g
Mirin	50 g
Sesame and seaweed furikake	15 g

Yield: 2 servings

Method:

01. Heat a medium sauté pan on a medium—high heat and add the vegetable oil. Once the pan is hot, add the Korean rice cakes.

02. Fry for 3 minutes, until the rice cakes start to take on a golden color.

03. Add the butter and cook it until it starts to turn nut brown and fragrant.

04. Strain rice cakes through a strainer (sieve) to get rid of the excess butter, then return to pan and raise the heat to high and add the mirin.

05. Constantly move and toss the rice cakes until the mirin has evaporated and starts to turn into a light caramel.

06. Take off the heat and toss with the sesame and furikake to coat.

the basics

This next section is all about the sauces, batters, rubs, and randoms that make up the pantry at Yardbird. You will find many of the following recipes used in dishes throughout the book. When it comes to sauces and condiments such as amazu or tosazu, they keep indefinitely, and add acid and umami to whatever you happen to be cooking. If the quantity for any of these seems daunting, please feel free to scale down.

Tare

Tare sauce is one of the foundations of any yakitori restaurant. Every restaurant has a different recipe, method, and flavor, varying from ultra-sweet and sticky to subtle, thin, and soy driven. The end result depends on where in Japan you are, the chef's experiences, and how long the restaurant has been around. Very similar to a Chinese master stock, tare is traditionally never thrown away, never finished, and always evolving. The tare remaining at the end of one batch is boiled and added to the next batch, creating layers, nuances, and a sense of history. At Yardbird we still have some elements of the first tare we ever made, even though the recipe has been adjusted over time. We will always be able to taste where we originally started.

Ingredients:	Amount:
Chicken carcass and bones	400 g
Tokyo onion tops	100 g
Ginger, peeled and chopped	100 g
Sake	450 ml
Mirin	375 ml
Zarame sugar	250 g
Soy sauce	500 ml
Tamari soy sauce	150 ml

Yield: 1.475 liters

Method:

01. In an oven tray, roast the chicken carcass and bones on a bed of Tokyo onion tops and ginger at 425°F/220°C for 20 minutes, until the chicken bones are deep brown and the onion and ginger have softened.

02. Pour the sake and mirin into a deep cooking pot. Place over a medium heat and, when the liquid just starts to boil, using a blowtorch, carefully burn off the alcohol. There will be high flames, so make sure that your face and hands are not above the pot when you light the alcohol. Turn the heat to low until the flames die back.

03. Add the sugar to the pot and stir until it dissolves.

04. Add the roasted chicken bones, onion, and ginger to the pot and simmer over a low heat until everything turns a deep caramel color—this will take about 30 minutes.

05. Add the soy sauce and tamari to the pot and simmer over a low heat for 15 minutes, skimming off any excess fat from the surface. Remove from the heat and leave to cool.

06. Once the sauce has cooled, strain it through a fine mesh strainer (sieve) and place in the refrigerator. After it has chilled for a few hours, more fat will have solidified on the top. Skim that fat off. Reserve in the refrigerator until ready to use.

Yardbird Shichimi

When we decided to open a yakitori restaurant, I really wanted to make our shichimi memorable, not just some dried-out, pre-ground shit you find on the shelves of every Japanese grocery store. This recipe doesn't stray that far from the more common shichimi togarashi, except that we use Korean chili powder for some sweetness and add Szechuan pepper, a nod to our Hong Kong roots.

Ingredients:	Amount:
White sesame seeds	125 g
Black sesame seeds	125 g
Sansho peppercorns	20 g
Szechuan peppercorns	20 g
Korean chili pepper (gochugaru)	250 g
Dried yuzu	50 g
Aonori	14 g

Yield: 500 g

Method:

01. Toast the white and black sesame seeds in a dry pan over a medium–high heat until fragrant and lightly colored. Set aside.

02. Toast the sansho pepper and Szechuan pepper in a dry pan over a medium–high heat until fragrant. Tip into a blender and blend into a powder.

03. Combine all the ingredients and mix well. Serve the shichimi with your favorite Yardbird dishes.

Dashi

Ingredients: Amounts:
Dried kombu sheet .... 30 g
Katsuobushi .... 30 g
Yield: 3 liters

Method:

01. Place the dried kombu sheet in a stock pot. Cover with 3 liters cold filtered water and soak for 8 hours, or ideally overnight.

02. Place the pot over a medium–low heat and allow the kombu to simmer, but never boil, for about 15 minutes. Increase the heat and, when the dashi is almost boiling, remove the kombu.

03. Bring the dashi to a boil. Add the katsuobushi, wait for 30 seconds, then turn off the heat. Set aside for 1 hour to allow the dashi to steep.

04. Strain through a fine cloth strainer. Reserve in the refrigerator until ready to use.

NB: Dashi is best used on the day it's made. You can re-use both the kombu and katsuobushi by repeating the steps; this will result in a much duller dashi, called niban dashi, that works well as the base of a stew or other heavily flavored dishes.

Chicken Stock

Ingredients: Amounts:
Chicken neck and back bones .... 2 kg
Dashi (See opposite) .... 3 liters
White onion, chopped .... 200 g
Welsh onion tops .... 200 g
Ginger, sliced .... 150 g
Coarse gray sea salt (sel gris) .... 25 g
Light soy sauce .... 20 g
Yield: 2.5 liters

Method:

01. Bring a large stock pot of water to boil, add the chicken bones, and return to the boil for 3–5 minutes. Rinse the bones and drain in a strainer (sieve) to remove any impurities from the chicken bones.

02. Place the chicken bones and dashi in a clean stock pot. Bring to a boil and then reduce to a simmer. After 20 minutes of simmering, start skimming the surface of the stock with a ladle to remove any impurities.

03. Add the white onion, Welsh onion, and ginger to the stock pot. Continue cooking for 2 ½ hours, frequently skimming the surface of the stock.

04. After 2 ½ hours, strain the stock through a fine mesh strainer (sieve) into a suitable heatproof container.

05. Season the stock with salt and light soy sauce.

06. Reserve in the refrigerator until ready to use. It will keep, chilled, for 3 days. Alternatively, store in the freezer in a ziplock bag. It will keep, frozen, for 1 month.

Mushroom Dashi

Ingredients:	Amounts:
Dried kombu sheet	40 g
Dried shiitake mushrooms	60 g
Dried porcini mushrooms	30 g
Dried matsutake mushrooms	30 g

Yield: 2.5 liters

Method:

01. Place the dried kombu sheet and dried mushrooms in a pot. Cover with 4 liters cold filtered water and soak for a minimum of 8 hours, or ideally overnight.

02. Place the pot over a high heat and bring to the boil. Remove the kombu from the pot.

03. Lower the heat and simmer for 1 hour, constantly skimming the surface of the stock to remove any impurities.

04. Strain the stock through a fine mesh strainer (sieve) into a suitable container.

05. Reserve in the refrigerator until ready to use. It will keep, chilled, for 3 days. Alternatively, store in the freezer in a ziplock bag. It will keep, frozen, for 2 weeks.

Amazu

Ingredients:	Amounts:
Rice vinegar	1 liter
Superfine (caster) sugar	250 g

Yield: 1.75 liters

Method:

01. Place the rice vinegar and sugar in a pan and add 500 ml cold water. Gently heat while whisking until all the sugar has dissolved. Leave to cool. Reserve until ready to use.

Tosazu

Ingredients:	Amounts:
Rice vinegar	150 g
Mirin, alcohol burned off	75 g
Light soy sauce	125 g
Kombu	50 g
Katsuobushi	20 g

Yield: 550 g

Method:

01. Place the rice vinegar, mirin, and light soy sauce in a non-reactive pan. Add 300 g cold water and the kombu, bring to a simmer and then remove from the heat.

02. Add the katsuobushi to the pan and allow to cool slowly. Leave to sit for a minimum of 2 hours.

03. Once completely cool, remove the kombu and strain through muslin (cheesecloth), squeezing any excess liquid from the katsuobushi. Discard the contents in the cloth and pour the tosazu liquid into a non-reactive container. Reserve in the refrigerator until ready to use. It will keep, chilled, for 1 month.

Red Shiso Vinegar

Ingredients:	Amounts:
Pickled red shiso leaves	3 kg
Amazu (page 185)	2 liters
Salt	30 g

Yield: 2 liters

Method:

01. Wearing latex gloves, massage the pickled red shiso leaves with the salt in a large bowl, until a bubbly dark purple liquid begins to leach out.

02. Gently rinse the shiso leaves with cold water. Squeeze any excess water out of the leaves. Set aside the squeezed shiso leaves and rinse the bowl.

03. Place the squeezed shiso leaves back into the bowl. Slowly add the Amazu while squeezing the shiso leaves between your fingers as hard as you can. A deep pink color will emerge as you massage; keep on going until you have added all the Amazu and your hands have cramped from squeezing.

04. Submerge the leaves in the vinegar overnight in a non-reactive container. The following day, remove the red shiso from the liquid, squeezing them of any excess vinegar. Reserve the squeezed leaves for future use, e.g., the Yukari Rice, page 191.

05. Store the vinegar in a cool, dark place for up to 1 year.

Wasabi Dressing

Ingredients:	Amounts:
Sake, alcohol burned off	1 liter
Mirin, alcohol burned off	250 ml
Rice vinegar	500 ml
Soy sauce	500 ml
Tamari	100 ml
Kizami wasabi	250 g
Wasabi	50 g
Kombu	20 g

Yield: 2.3 liters

Method:

01. Combine all the ingredients together in an airtight container. Leave to stand overnight.

02. Store in an airtight container until ready to use. When ready to use, remove the kombu.

Pickled Mushrooms

Ingredients:	Amounts:
Shiitake mushrooms	40 g
King oyster mushrooms	40 g
Maitake mushrooms	40 g
Vegetable oil	5 g
Wasabi Dressing (see left)	150 g

Yield: 150 g

Method:

01. Line a tray with paper towels. In a hot pan, sear and color the mushrooms for 5 minutes until deeply caramelized. Drain on the paper towel-lined tray.

02. When the mushrooms are cool to the touch, slice the shiitake and king oysters lengthwise into ½ inch (1 cm) strips and pull the maitake apart into bite-size pieces.

03. Place all the mushrooms in a bowl and pour over the dressing to cover them completely. Marinate overnight.

Shiso Oil

Ingredients:	Amounts:
Green shiso	200 g
Vegetable oil	1 liter
Parsley	150 g

Yield: 200 g

Method:

01. Place all the ingredients into a blender and blend at high speed until it forms a smooth purée.

02. Transfer the purée to a pot and cook over a high heat for 2–3 minutes until it reaches 176°F/80°C on a thermometer.

03. Cook for 3 minutes, then tip into a strainer (sieve) lined with muslin (cheesecloth). Discard the contents in the cloth and pour the liquid into a non-reactive container. Keep chilled over ice so that it remains a vibrant green color. Reserve until ready to use.

Fruit Tomato Dressing

Ingredients:	Amounts:
Chinkiang black rice vinegar	200 g
Okinawan black sugar	50 g
ABC sweet soy sauce	70 g
White sesame oil	50 g
Black garlic	30 g

Yield: 350 g

Method:

01. Place all the ingredients in a blender. Blend on high until smooth. Reserve in the refrigerator until ready to use.

Sesame Dressing

Ingredients:	Amounts:
White miso	20 g
Rice miso	20 g
Mirin, alcohol burned off	30 g
Sesame paste	35 g
Dark sesame oil	2 g
Rice vinegar	12 g

Yield: 130 g

Method:

01. In a small pan, gently cook both misos with the mirin until soft. Blend with the rest of the ingredients in a blender or a food processor until smooth. Reserve in the refrigerator until ready to use.

Nori Dressing

Ingredients:	Amounts:
Roasted nori	30 g
Nama nori (fresh nori)	100 g
Rice vinegar	200 g
ABC sweet soy sauce	75 g
Olive oil	150 ml
Salt	To taste

Yield: 500 g

Method:

01. Combine the dry nori, nama nori, and rice vinegar in a blender. Leave to stand for 3 minutes to hydrate the roasted nori sheets.

02. Add the sweet soy sauce and blend until smooth.

03. While the blender is running, drizzle in the olive oil until it is well mixed. Season with salt to taste, depending on the salinity levels of the nori. Reserve in the refrigerator until ready to use.

Green Miso Pesto

Ingredients:	Amounts:
Italian basil	100 g
Flat-leaf parsley	50 g
Pine nuts	20 g
Olive oil	150 g
Miso Soup (Smaller, page 146)	200 g
Roasted Garlic (Basics, page 189)	100 g

Yield: 500 g

Method:

01. Place the basil, parsley, and pine nuts in a blender and blend at high speed until smooth.

02. While the blender is running, slowly add the olive oil, pouring it in a steady stream, until it is blended together. Add the Miso Soup and Roasted Garlic and blend again until smooth. Reserve in the refrigerator until ready to use.

Yuzu Miso Marinade

Ingredients:	Amounts:
Tsuru barley miso	500 g
Mirin, alcohol burned off	150 ml
Sake, alcohol burned off	130 ml
Frozen yuzu skin, chopped	50 g
White sesame oil	150 g
Dark sesame oil	15 ml
Light soy sauce	5 ml

Yield: 750 g

Method:

01. Place all the ingredients in a blender or food processor and blend until smooth. Reserve in the refrigerator until ready to use.

Roasted Garlic

Ingredients:

Ingredients:	Amounts:
Garlic cloves, skin on	1 kg
Salt	20 g
Olive oil	100 ml

Yield: 350 g

Method:

01. Preheat the oven to 425°F/220°C.

02. On a baking sheet, toss the whole garlic cloves in the salt and olive oil. Roast in the oven for 1 hour.

03. Allow to cool a little, then press the garlic out from the skin with your fingers. Pass through a fine mesh strainer (sieve) and reserve in the refrigerator for up to 1 week.

Black Garlic Sauce

Ingredients:	Amounts:
Sake, alcohol burned off	200 ml
Mirin, alcohol burned off	150 ml
Soy sauce	175 g
Maple syrup	150 g
Okinawan black sugar (or brown sugar)	150 g
Roasted garlic (See opposite)	100 g
Black garlic	75 g
Raw garlic	15 g

Yield: 750 g

Method:

01. Place the sake and mirin together in a pan. Over a moderate heat, reduce the sake and mirin by one third, about 2 minutes.

02. Reduce the heat to low and add the soy sauce. Cook for 2–3 minutes.

03. Add the maple syrup and sugar and then cook until the sugar has dissolved.

04. Place all the remaining ingredients in a blender. Slowly stream in the hot liquid, blend on high until smooth.

B+S Sauce

Ingredients:	Amounts:
Bull-Dog Sauce	500 g
Sriracha Hot Chili Sauce	50 g

Yield: 550 g

Method:

01. Combine the Bull-Dog Sauce and Sriracha Hot Chili Sauce. Place in a squeeze bottle. Reserve in the refrigerator until ready to use.

Ume Paste

Ingredients:	Amounts:
Umeboshi paste	300g
Frozen yuzu skin, chopped	20g
Sake, alcohol burned off	20g
Mirin, alcohol burned off	20g

Yield: 400 g

Method:

01. Place all the ingredients in a blender or food processor and blend until smooth. Reserve in the refrigerator until ready to use.

Lotus Root Chips

Ingredients:	Amounts:
Lotus root	1 kg
Vegetable oil, for deep-frying	3 liters

Yield: 600 g

Method:

01. Scrub the outside of the lotus root until pale beige in color. Using a mandoline, slice the lotus root into 3-mm/⅛-inch thick slices.

02. Rinse the lotus root slices in warm water for 10–15 minutes, then pat dry with paper towels.

03. Heat the vegetable oil in a deep fryer or deep saucepan to 325°F/160°C. Deep-fry the lotus root slices until very lightly golden and still slightly soft. Remove with a slotted spoon and drain on a paper towel-lined tray.

04. Place the fried lotus root slices in a dehydrator set to 149°F/65°C overnight. If you do not have a dehydrator, turn your oven to the lowest possible setting and allow to dry overnight. Store in an airtight container with foodsafe desiccant packs for up to 3 days.

Garlic Chips

Ingredients:	Amounts:
Peeled garlic cloves	500 g
Vegetable oil	3 liters

Yield: 150 g

Method:

01. Slice the garlic lengthwise on a mandoline 2 mm/⅛ inch thick. Rinse in running water for about 10 minutes.

02. Blanch for 30 seconds in boiling salted water. Dry on a paper towel.

03. Heat the vegetable oil in a deep fryer or deep saucepan to 300°F/150°C, 5-6 minutes.

04. Place the garlic chips in a dehydrator set to 149°F/65°C overnight. If you do not have a dehydrator, turn your oven to the lowest possible setting and allow to dry overnight.

05. Store in an airtight container with foodsafe desiccant packs for up to a week.

Seaweed Panko Bread Crumbs

Ingredients:	Amounts:
Unsalted butter	100 g
Olive oil	70 g
Aonori	10 g
Fresh panko bread crumbs	350 g
Salt	4 g

Yield: 500 g

Method:

01. Line a cookie (baking) sheet with paper towels and set aside. In a medium rondeau pot, heat the butter and olive oil over medium heat until the butter has melted.

02. Add the aonori to the pot and cook over a low heat, toasting and infusing into the butter and oil mixture.

03. Add the bread crumbs and cook over a low heat, stirring continuously and not letting the panko catch or color unevenly.

04. Sauté the panko until crispy and golden brown, about 20 minutes, then tip the bread crumbs onto the paper towel-lined tray. To keep the bread crumbs crispy, keep them in a warm place or in a food dehydrator.

Crispy Fried Shallots

Ingredients:	Amounts:
Banana shallots	500 g
Yardbird Chicken Flour Mix (page 191)	150 g
Tempura flour	100 g
Buttermilk	300 g
Vegetable oil	3 liters

Yield: 500 g

Method:

01. Cut the shallots into ¾-inch (1.5-cm) thick rings. Only use rings that are ¾–1 ½ inches (2–4 cm) in diameter. Rinse the shallot rings in cold water.

02. Marinate in the buttermilk for a minimum of 1 hour.

03. In a bowl, mix the Yardbird Chicken Flour Mix and tempura flour until evenly dispersed.

04. Strain the shallots from the buttermilk, leaving them slightly wet to help the flour stick to them. Dredge the shallots in the flour mix.

05. In a deep fryer or deep pan, heat the oil to 275°F/140°C. Working in three or four batches, fry until a very light golden brown, about 2 minutes. Drain on a paper-lined tray. Set aside in the freezer until ready to serve.

06. Reheat the oil to 350°F/180°C.

07. Working in three or four batches, fry the frozen shallot rings until golden brown, about 1½ minutes. Drain on a paper-lined tray. Season with salt.

Onsen Egg

Ingredients:	Amounts:
Eggs	4
Water	3 liters

Yield: 4 eggs

Method:

01. Set an immersion circulator to 145°F/63°C.

02. Fill a separate bowl with warm water. Gently place the eggs in the warm water for 5 minutes to prevent them from cracking when placed in the circulator.

03. Once the circulator reaches 145°F/63°C, gently lower the eggs into the water bath and leave for 1 hour.

04. After 1 hour, lower the temperature of the water bath to 55°C. You can reserve the eggs at this temperature for up to 1 hour.

Sweet Glutinous Mochi Rice

Ingredients:	Amounts:
Sweet glutinous mochi rice	300 g
Cooking sake	200 ml
Sea salt	2 g

Yield: 450 g

Method:

01. Rinse the rice thoroughly until the water becomes clear. Place the rice in fresh water and soak overnight.

02. The next day, drain the rice and let it air dry until it is bright white and dry to the touch; this will take about 30 minutes–1 hour.

03. Dissolve the sea salt in the sake. Then mix the salted sake into the rice.

04. Line a bamboo steamer with cheesecloth (muslin) and spread the rice evenly in the steamer—the layer of rice should be no more than 2½ cm (1 inch) deep.

05. Steam over a high heat until the rice is cooked through but not overly soft, about 6–9 minutes—each grain should separate easily.

06. Cool the rice on a tray. Reserve in the refrigerator until ready to use.

Yukari Rice

Ingredients:	Amounts:
Yukari powder (See page 193)	20 g
Japanese short grain rice	1 kg

Yield: 2 kg

Rice-cooker method:

01. First, make the Yukari water. Mix the yukari (red shiso salt) with 800 ml of cold purified water.

02. Rinse the rice thoroughly until the water becomes clear.

03. Place the rice in fresh water and soak for 8 minutes.

04. Drain the rice and let it sit for 15 minutes.

05. Add the rice to a rice cooker. Pour in 800 ml of the Yukari water, which should be slightly purple, and cook the rice.

06. Cool the rice on a tray. For fried rice, allow to dry overnight. Reserve in the refrigerator until ready to use.

Stove-top method:

01. Follow steps 1–4 in the rice-cooker method.

02. Add the rice to a pan, pour in 800 ml of the Yukari water, and bring to a boil over medium-high heat, with a tight fitting lid.

03. When it starts boiling, reduce the heat to low. Simmer for 7 minutes.

04. Remove from the heat, and let it rest for 15 minutes. Do not take off the lid.

05. After it has rested, take off the lid, and stir the rice lightly using a rice paddle.

06. Cool the rice on a tray. For fried rice, allow to dry overnight. Reserve in the refrigerator until ready to use.

Yardbird Chicken Flour Mix

Ingredients:	Amounts:
Japanese karaage flour	500 g
Potato starch	100 g
Tempura flour	250 g

Yield: 850 g

Method:

01. Mix all the ingredients together. Store in an airtight container or sealed bag until ready to use.

Tempura Batter

Ingredients: Amounts:
Egg yolk 1
Tempura flour .... 700 g
Yield: 1.25 liters

Method:

01. Mix the egg yolk with 1050 g iced water. Place the tempura flour in a large mixing bowl, then gently add the egg and water. Make sure you don't over-mix.

02. Keep the batter chilled at all times. Reserve in the refrigerator until ready to use.

Rendered Chicken Fat

Ingredients: Amounts:
Chicken fat and skin .... 1 kg
Yield: 500 g

Method:

01. Place the chicken fat and skin in a wide pot, then add just enough cold water to cover.

02. Over a medium heat, simmer the fat and skin until the water evaporates and the skin begins to curl up and stick to the pot.

03. Strain through a fine mesh strainer (sieve) in a container. Place in the refrigerator until the fat has hardened.

04. Scoop out the fat from the container until you reach the impurities and any remaining water at the bottom of the container. Reserve the fat in the refrigerator until ready to use.

Chicken Fat Onion Paste

Ingredients: Amount:
Rendered Chicken Fat (See above) .... 200 g
White onion, thinly sliced .... 4 kg
Sea salt .... 20 g
Yield: 2 kg

Method:

01. In a large wide pot, over a medium–low heat, melt the rendered chicken fat. Add the onions and salt to the melted fat and very slowly caramelize the onions, constantly stirring for about 2 hours, until a deep brown in color.

02. Allow the onions to cool in the fat, then purée in a food processor to a smooth paste.

03. Reserve in the refrigerator until ready to use.

Crispy Chicken Skin

Ingredients   Amounts:
Vegetable oil .... 2 liters
Yardbird Chicken Flour Mix (page 191) .... 200 g
Chicken breast skin .... 2 pieces (80 g each)
Chicken thigh skin .... 4 pieces (30 g each)
Yield: 200 g

Method:

01. In a wide pot, heat the vegetable oil to 325°F/160°C.

02. Lightly dredge the chicken breast skin and chicken thigh skin with the Yardbird Chicken Flour Mix. Remove any excess fat attached to the skin using the flour and your fingers.

03. Fry the chicken thigh skin for 4 minutes. Remove from the oil and set aside on a rack-lined tray. Then, fry chicken breast skin for 3 ½ minutes. Remove from the oil and set aside on a rack-lined tray.

04. Bring the oil temperature up to 350°F/180°C. Fry the chicken thigh skin a second time for 4 minutes. Remove from the oil and set aside on a rack-lined tray.

05. Fry the chicken breast skin for 1 ½ minutes. Remove from the oil and set aside on a rack-lined tray.

Young Ginger Pickles

Ingredients: Amounts:
Young fresh ginger .... 700 g
Amazu (page 185) .... 1 quantity
Yield: 700 g

Method:

01. Using a spoon or the back of a knife, lightly scrape the skin from the young ginger. Place the ginger in a preserving jar.

02. Place the Amazu in a pan and bring to the boil over a high heat. Remove the pan from the heat and pour the hot Amazu over the young ginger. Leave to cool completely.

03. Once cool, set aside in the refrigerator for a minimum of one week.

04. When ready to serve, remove the ginger from the Amazu, slice into thin pieces, and serve chilled.

Marinated Egg Yolk

Ingredients: Amounts:
Tare (page 180) .... 2 tbsp per skewer
Egg yolks .... 1 per skewer
Yield: 1 dipping sauce

Method:

01. Each meatball skewer is served with a tare and egg yolk dipping sauce. To make this sauce, dilute the original Tare sauce by 50 percent with room temperature water.

02. Drop in separated egg yolks (one per skewer), and let this sit for 2 hours in the refrigerator.

03. After 2 hours, put the semi-cured egg yolk into a small bowl and add 1–2 tbsp tare sauce. Mix the egg yolk vigorously in the tare sauce and dip the meatball inside.

Duck Tare

Ingredients: Amounts:
Duck bones .... 1 kg
Tare (page 180) .... 500 ml
Mizansho shouyu ni .... 50 g
Yield: 700 g

Method:

01. Roast the duck bones in a 350°F/18O°C oven for 20 minutes, or until deep brown.

02. In a medium saucepan, add the duck bones and the tare and bring to a boil. Immediately reduce to a simmer and cook for 5 minutes.

03. Allow the bones to cool in the tare. Remove the bones, skim any fat, and add the mizansho shouyu ni. This will keep refrigerated for up to 1 month.

Yukari Powder

Ingredients: Amounts:
Reserved red shiso leaves from Red Shiso Vinegar (page 186) .... 800 g
Yield: 800 g

Method:

01. Dehydrate at 145°F/65°C in a dehydrator overnight, or until completely dry.

02. Grind to a powder then store in an airtight container until ready to use.

Cocktails & highballs

We always knew that we wanted Yardbird to be as much about the drinks as it was about the food, and to be honest a separate book could probably be written about them. The reason we haven't highlighted our amazing sake producers is because Elliot Faber, our beverage director, has already written a book featuring all of them. In the early days of Yardbird, Raphael Holzer, Lindsay, Elliot, and I set out to create a cocktail list that would honor the simplicity of Japanese drinking culture, as well as the traditions of the Western bars that we grew up with. What emerged were versions of classic drinks using the ingredients that we have in the restaurant, as well as some straight-up Japanese classics. We tend to keep things simple, staying away from complicated garnishes, martini glasses, and anything overly labor-intensive. Our drinks are made to be consumed in quantity, with good food, and good friends.

Yaki Lime

Ingredients:	Amounts:
Lime, grilled and quartered	1
Muscovado sugar	2½ tsp
Fresh mint leaves	small handful
Flor de Caña Añejo Rum	60 ml
Soda water	to serve

Yield: 1 serving

Method:

01. Muddle the lime with the sugar in a shaker glass.
02. Lightly hand-press the mint leaves to release their oils, then add to the shaker. Add the rum.
03. Add ice and shake.
04. Top up with soda water and stir with a bar spoon, lifting as you stir.
05. Pour into a collins glass.

Rob Roy

Ingredients:	Amounts:
Sunday's NAS Malt & Grain Whisky	60 ml
Mancino Rosso Amaranto Vermouth	25 ml
Yardbird Cherry Brandy	7 ml
Cocktail cherry, to garnish	1

Yield: 1 serving

Method:

01. Chill a rocks glass in the freezer until cold, about 30 minutes.
02. Add the whisky, vermouth, and cherry brandy to a mixing glass.
03. Add ice and gently stir for 30 seconds.
04. Pour into the pre-chilled rocks glass.
05. Garnish with a cocktail cherry.

Whisky Lemonade

Ingredients: Amounts:
Lemon, cut into eight wedges 1
Okinawan Black Sugar .... 2 ½ tsp
Sunday's NAS Malt & Grain Whisky .... 50 ml
Fukucho Yuzu Lemon Liqueur .... 15 ml
Soda water .... to serve
Yield: 1 serving

Method:
01. Muddle the lemon with the sugar in a shaker glass.
02. Add the whisky and yuzu liqueur.
03. Add ice and shake.
04. Top up with soda water and stir with a bar spoon,
    lifting as you stir.
05. Strain over fresh ice into a collins glass.

Shino

Ingredients: Amounts:
Lemon, cut into eight wedges 1
Okinawan Black Sugar .... 2 ½ tsp
Elephant Gin .... 60 ml
Fresh shiso leaves 4
Soda water .... to serve
Yield: 1 serving

Method:
01. Muddle the lemon with the sugar in a shaker glass.
02. Lightly hand-press the shiso leaves to release their
    oils and add three leaves to the shaker. Add the gin.
03. Add ice and soft shake.
04. Top up with soda water and stir with a bar spoon,
    lifting as you stir.
05. Pour into a collins glass.
06. Garnish with the remaining shiso leaf.

Okinawa Express

Ingredients:	Amounts:
Helios Three-Year-Old Awamori	60 ml
Kokuto Shochu	25 ml
Fresh pineapple juice	60 ml
Lime, freshly squeezed	½
Okinawan Black Sugar	2 tsp

Yield: 1 serving

Method:

01. Add the awamori, shochu, pineapple juice, and lime juice to a shaker glass, then add the sugar.
02. Add ice and hard shake.
03. Strain over fresh ice into a collins glass.

Jolly Rancher

Ingredients:	Amounts:
Tantakatan Shiso Ume Shochu	60 ml
Sengetsu Kawabe Kome Shochu	30 ml
Watermelon	1 piece (80 g)
Lemon wedges, freshly squeezed	2
Simple Syrup (page 201)	a dash

Yield: 1 serving

Method:

01. Place all the ingredients in a blending cup and blend with a hand mixer.
02. Transfer to a shaker glass.
03. Add ice and shake.
04. Strain over fresh ice into a collins glass.

Bloody Kim Jong il

Ingredients:	Amounts:
Aylesbury Duck Vodka	50 ml
Lemon wedges, freshly squeezed	2
Bloody Kim Mix (see below)	1
Korean chili salt, for rim of glass	to taste

For the Bloody Kim Mix	
Tomato juice	6 × 163 ml cans
Tabasco Sauce	30 ml
Bull-Dog Sauce	50 ml
Yuzu salt	1 tsp
Simple Syrup (page 201)	15 ml

Yield: 1 serving

Method:
01. First, make the Bloody Kim Mix. Combine all the ingredients in a pitcher (jug). Reserve in the refrigerator until ready to use.
02. Rim a collins glass with the Korean chili salt.
03. Add the vodka and lemon juice into the glass.
04. Add ice and top up with the Bloody Kim Mix.

Wakayama Margarita

Ingredients:	Amounts:
Don Fulano Blanco Tequila	30 ml
Yoshimura Jabarashu	25 ml
Simple Syrup (page 201)	15 ml
Lemon, freshly squeezed	½
Lime, freshly squeezed	½
Simple Syrup (page 201)	a dash

Yield: 1 serving

Method:
01. Place all the ingredients in a shaker glass.
02. Add ice and hard shake.
03. Pour into a collins glass.

Bambino

Ingredients:	Amounts:
Fernet Hunter	25 ml
Iki Deluxe Barley Shochu	25 ml
Mancino Bianco Ambrato Vermouth	25 ml
Fee Brother Grapefruit bitters	1 dash
Grapefruit peel	2 pieces
Ice rock, to serve	1

Yield: 1 serving

Method:

01. Add the Fernet Hunter, shochu, vermouth, grapefruit bitters, and one of the grapefruit peel to a mixing glass.
02. Add ice and gently stir for 30 seconds.
03. Strain into a rocks glass over an ice rock.
04. Garnish with the remaining grapefruit peel.

El Chonie

Ingredients:	Amounts:
Yuzu salt, for rim of glass	to taste
Don Fulano Tequila	30 ml
Simple Syrup	15 ml
Lemon, freshly squeezed	½
Lime, freshly squeezed	½
Suntory Draught Beer	1 × 350 ml can

Yield: 1 serving

Method:

01. Rim a collins glass with the yuzu salt.
02. Add the tequila, Simple Syrup, and juices of the lemon and lime to a shaker glass.
03. Add ice and shake.
04. Top up with beer.
05. Strain into the glass and top up with beer foam.

Mezcal Mule

Ingredients:	Amounts:
Derumbes Santiago Mezcal	45 ml
Umeboshi paste	25 ml
Agave syrup	15 ml
Cucumber slices	4
Lime, freshly squeezed	½
Ice rock, to serve	1
Wilkinson Ginger Ale	1 × 190 ml bottle

Yield: 1 serving

Method:
01. Add the mezcal, umeboshi paste, agave syrup, lime, and three of the cucumber slices to a shaker glass and muddle.
02. Add ice and shake.
03. Strain into a mule cup over an ice rock.
04. Top up with ginger ale.
05. Garnish with the remaining cucumber slice.

Simple Syrup

Ingredients:	Amounts:
Sugar	700 g

Method:
01. In a small saucepan, bring sugar and 1 liter of water to a boil. Turn down the heat and simmer until the sugar has dissolved.
02. Remove from the heat and let cool completely.
03. The syrup can be refrigerated in a glass jar for up to 1 month.

Rockfish

Ingredients:	Amounts:
Sunday's NAS Malt & Grain Whisky (frozen)	60 ml
Wilkinson Soda Water	1 × 190 ml bottle
Long lemon peel, to garnish	1

Yield: 1 serving

Method:

01. Pour the whisky into a collins glass.

02. Top up with soda water.

03. Garnish with the long lemon peel.

Nikka Highball

Ingredients:	Amounts:
Nikka Black Deep Blend NAS Malt & Grain Whisky	50 ml
Wilkinson Soda Water	1 × 190 ml bottle
Lime peel, slightly burnt, to garnish	1

Yield: 1 serving

Method:

01. Pour the whisky into a collins glass.

02. Fill the glass with ice.

03. Top up with soda water.

04. Stir with a bar spoon, lifting as you stir.

05. Garnish with a slightly burnt lime peel.

Ichiro's Highball

Ingredients:	Amounts:
Ichiro's 'White Label' NAS Malt & Grain Whisky	50 ml
Wilkinson Soda Water	1 × 190 ml bottle
Fresh shiso leaf, to garnish	1

Yield: 1 serving

Method:

01. Pour the whisky into a collins glass.
02. Fill the glass with ice.
03. Top up with soda water.
04. Stir with a bar spoon, lifting as you stir.
05. Lightly hand press the shiso leaf to release
    its oil, then use to garnish.

Danryu Danball

Ingredients:	Amounts:
Kamimura Danryu Awamori	50 ml
Lime, freshly squeezed	½
Wilkinson Soda Water	1 × 190 ml bottle
Lime wedge, to garnish	1

Yield: 1 serving

Method:

01. Pour the awamori and lime juice into a collins glass.
02. Fill the glass with ice.
03. Top up with soda water.
04. Stir with a bar spoon, lifting as you stir.
05. Garnish with the lime wedge.

Yoichi Highball

Ingredients:	Amounts:
Yoichi NAS Single Malt Whisky	50 ml
Wilkinson Soda Water	1 × 190 ml bottle
Lemon peel, to garnish	1

Yield: 1 serving

Method:

01. Pour the whisky into a collins glass.

02. Fill the glass with ice.

03. Top up with soda water.

04. Stir with a bar spoon, lifting as you stir.

05. Garnish with the lemon peel.

HunterHi

Ingredients:	Amounts:
Fernet Hunter	50 ml
Wilkinson Soda Water	1 × 190 ml bottle
Fresh mint leaves, to garnish	2

Yield: 1 serving

Method:

01. Pour the Fernet Hunter into a collins glass.

02. Fill the glass with ice.

03. Top up with soda water.

04. Stir with a bar spoon, lifting as you stir.

05. Lightly hand press the mint leaves to release
their oil, then use to garnish..

Mars Highball

Ingredients:

Mars '3&7' NAS Malt & Grain Whisky ....

Wilkinson Soda Water ....

Orange peel, to garnish ....

Amounts:

50 ml

1 × 190 ml bottle

1

Yield: 1 serving

Method:

01. Pour the whisky into a collins glass.

02. Fill the glass with ice.

03. Top up with soda water.

04. Stir with a bar spoon, lifting as you stir.

05. Garnish with the orange peel.

KirinHi

Ingredients:

Kirin 'Fuji Sanroku 50°' NAS Whisky ....

Wilkinson Soda Water ....

Lime peel, to garnish ....

Amounts:

50 ml

1 × 190 ml bottle

1

Yield: 1 serving

Method:

01. Pour the whisky into a collins glass.

02. Fill the glass with ice.

03. Top up with soda water.

04. Stir with a bar spoon, lifting as you stir.

05. Garnish with the lime peel.

Hakushu Highball

Ingredients:	Amounts:
Hakushu 12 Year Single Malt Whisky	50 ml
Wilkinson Soda Water	1 × 190 ml bottle
Fresh mint leaf, to garnish	1

Yield: 1 serving

Method:

01. Pour the whisky into a collins glass.
02. Fill the glass with ice.
03. Top up with soda water.
04. Stir with a bar spoon, lifting as you stir.
05. Lightly hand press the mint leaf to release its oil, then use to garnish..

RainbowHi

Ingredients:	Amounts:
Rainbow Sansyu 12 Year Single Malt Whisky	50 ml
Wilkinson Soda Water	1 × 190 ml bottle
Grapefruit peel, to garnish	1

Yield: 1 serving

Method:

01. Pour the whisky into a collins glass.
02. Fill the glass with ice.
03. Top up with soda water.
04. Stir with a bar spoon, lifting as you stir.
05. Garnish with the grapefruit peel.

Chu Hi

Ingredients:	Amounts:
Sengetsu Kawabe Kome Shochu	90 ml
Pink grapefruit, freshly squeezed	1

Yield: 1 serving

Method:

01. Pour the shochu into a collins glass.

02. Fill the glass with ice.

03. Top up with the freshly squeezed grapefruit juice.

04. Stir with a bar spoon, lifting as you stir.

Yu-Gin

Ingredients:	Amounts:
Elephant Gin	50 ml
Kimino Sparkling Yuzu	1 × 250 ml bottle
Fresh shiso leaf, to garnish	1

Yield: 1 serving

Method:

01. Pour the gin into a collins glass.

02. Fil the glass with ice.

03. Top up with Kimino Sparkling Yuzu.

04. Stir with a bar spoon, lifting as you stir.

05. Lightly hand press the shiso leaf to release
    its oil, then use to garnish.

There are no words for how grateful I am to the people who work with us, past, present, and future. We are a posse, a gang, a crew; we are friends, we are professionals, but most importantly, we are family, and we have built this restaurant together. This section is dedicated to the many amazing humans who have put so much into making Yardbird what it is. There is no way for me to ever thank or name each one: those that know me, I hope, know how much I appreciate everything they have done.

super "CHOK"

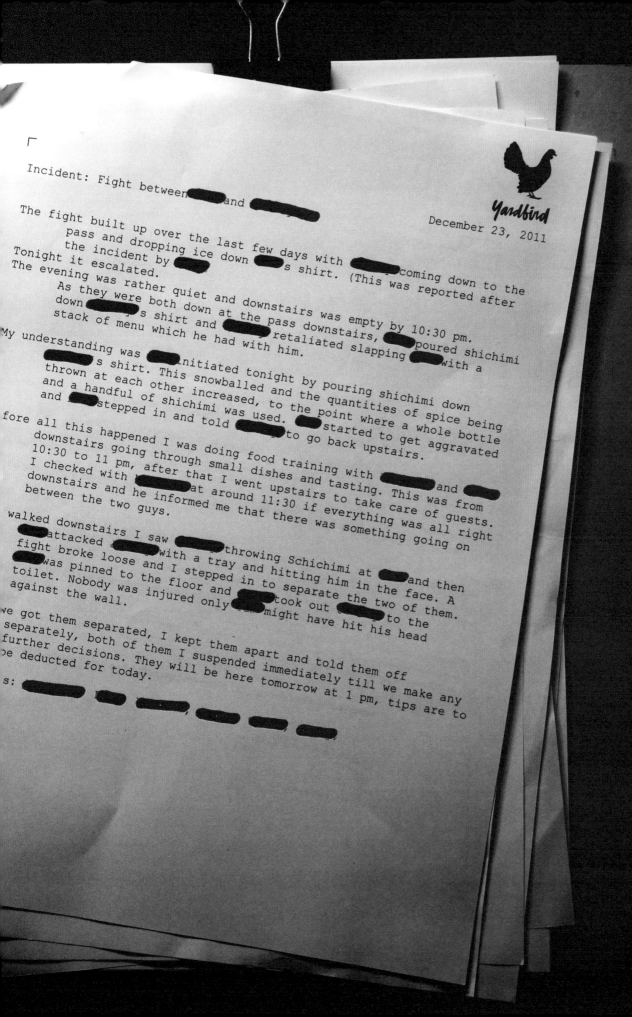

Incident: Fight between ▆▆▆ and ▆▆▆▆▆▆

Yardbird

December 23, 2011

The fight built up over the last few days with ▆▆▆▆ coming down to the pass and dropping ice down ▆▆▆s shirt. (This was reported after the incident by ▆▆▆) Tonight it escalated.

The evening was rather quiet and downstairs was empty by 10:30 pm. As they were both down at the pass downstairs, ▆▆▆ poured shichimi down ▆▆▆s shirt and ▆▆▆▆▆ retaliated slapping ▆▆▆ with a stack of menu which he had with him.

My understanding was ▆▆▆ initiated tonight by pouring shichimi down ▆▆▆s shirt. This snowballed and the quantities of spice being thrown at each other increased, to the point where a whole bottle and a handful of shichimi was used. ▆▆▆ started to get aggravated and ▆▆ stepped in and told ▆▆▆▆▆ to go back upstairs.

fore all this happened I was doing food training with ▆▆▆ and ▆▆▆ downstairs going through small dishes and tasting. This was from 10:30 to 11 pm, after that I went upstairs to take care of guests. I checked with ▆▆▆▆ at around 11:30 if everything was all right downstairs and he informed me that there was something going on between the two guys.

walked downstairs I saw ▆▆▆▆ throwing Schichimi at ▆▆ and then ▆▆ attacked ▆▆▆ with a tray and hitting him in the face. A fight broke loose and I stepped in to separate the two of them. ▆▆ was pinned to the floor and ▆▆▆ took out ▆▆▆▆ to the toilet. Nobody was injured only ▆▆▆ might have hit his head against the wall.

ve got them separated, I kept them apart and told them off separately, both of them I suspended immediately till we make any further decisions. They will be here tomorrow at 1 pm, tips are to be deducted for today.

s: ▆▆▆▆ ▆▆▆ ▆▆▆, ▆▆▆ ▆▆▆ ▆▆▆

Staff Q&A

Name: Dason Ying. **Role:** I was the training manager. **Origin:** I was born in New York, but I lived in six different cities growing up. Let's say I travel a lot. **Time at Yardbird:** Since 2012. **First encounter with Yardbird:** My best friend was the bartender here, and he was like, "I'm working at this restaurant—you should come by." So I came and we had dinner downstairs, right by where the toilet is, and it was just overall a really good experience. It was surprising and very refreshing for what it is—like, it's simple, but the vibe was fun, the staff were fun, food was great, drinks were great, and I just kind of fell in love. And then he suggested I work here for a little bit. It was supposed to be part-time. I was going to stay for probably three to six months. **Favorite dish:** Favorite dish? God. I can't answer you. Pork Takana Tofu—it's not on the menu anymore, but it's one of my favorite dishes of all time. **Favorite drink:** Whisky Lemonade. Actually, it's between a Whisky Lemonade and a highball: the Kako High. **Favorite swear word:** I'm going to be really unoriginal and say "fuck." **Most fun person at Yardbird to give shit to:** Wow, man! Most fun to give shit to? Normally I'm the one who takes the most shit. Yeah, I'm the one who gets the most shit. **Biggest night:** The five-year anniversary. **Dumbest Yardbird memory:** Every day. There is something dumb every day. We had our annual dinner this one year on a junk boat. We were of course drinking a shit-ton, getting completely pasted. We were dancing on one of the levels, and one of our ex-staff comes out of nowhere and pushes me. He wasn't going to push me off the boat—but I hesitated, and I tried to catch myself. I ended up falling down to the next level, hitting my thigh on the rail, and flipping over into the ocean. **Working at Yardbird has taught you:** Genuine care and attention to detail. **Languages you can speak:** Cantonese, Mandarin, English, of course, and a little bit of Japanese—that's about it.

Name: Paul Tsang. **Role:** Chopping up chicken. **Origin:** Hong Kong. **Time at Yardbird:** Four years. **Most fun person to give shit to at Yardbird:** Singapore Nick. **Worst person to work with at Yardbird:** Singapore Nick. **First encounter with Yardbird:** I worked with Matt before at another restaurant. **Yardbird has taught you:** I've learned a lot about the chicken—every part. **Languages:** Chinese and English. **Favorite Yardbird job:** Queueing the meatballs.

Name: Preeti Ghimire. **Role:** Caretaker, I would say. **Origin:** Nepal. **Time in Hong Kong:** Twenty years. **Time at Yardbird:** They opened in July and I started in October. So this October I'll have been there seven years. **Favorite dish:** Chicken fillet. **Favorite drink:** It really depends: when it's very hot, I love the El Chonie. And if it's winter, whisky. **Favorite thing to yell at work:** I always say, "What's the problem, maaaaaaaan?!" **Best person to make fun of at Yardbird:** I am very good with that—I make fun of everyone. **First encounter with Yardbird:** Through my cousin. At that time I wasn't working. My cousin, she used to work for Matt, so she used to come to my place and always talk about Yardbird, Yardbird, Yardbird. At that time I am thinking I should work, so I just said to her, "I want to work." I didn't mean it, but I said it, and then that day she talked to Matt, and she told me, "Okay, you need to come for a trial." I said, "What?!" Just to keep her word—because she had talked to her boss—I came for a trial. And I never looked back. I loved the first day; I felt like I was starting school. **Funniest Yardbird memory:** When Matt made an apple bong for me because I eat apples every day. **Working at Yardbird has taught you:** Many things. I can't even start. As a team, how you work. Being more positive overall. To be a better person, I would say. **Languages you can speak:** Nepalese, Hindi, and English.

Name: Tyler Huang Babrowsky. **Role:** Manager. **Origin:** New Jersey. **Time at Yardbird:** Two-and-a-half years. **How long you thought you'd work there:** Six months. **Favorite dish:** The ox tongue, which is no longer here. So I'm gonna go with the eggplant salad. **Favorite drink:** Favorite drink? Fuck. Like, cocktail? What are we talking here? Jumbo Ozaki. It's like a tea-based cocktail—really good. You should try it sometime. **Favorite swear word:** I think it's got to be "fuck." **Worst person to work with at Yardbird:** Honestly, it's jokes, but I'm going to say Preeti. **First encounter with Yardbird:** I was super-baked, came back from the States, and needed a job because I was going to live here for six months. I went to Sunday's Grocery, which was in Kennedy Town at the time, and just started talking randomly to Matt. I was just like, "Oh, could I get a job?" And he was like, "Yeah, you can start tomorrow." This is my first job in hospitality. **Biggest night:** There's too many. I really can't remember. Every fucking night we go out. Maybe a karaoke night. **Dumbest Yardbird memory:** I think when Geoff, on his birthday, fell asleep on a couch by the dumpsters and slept there all night. **Working at Yardbird has taught you:** It has taught me patience. **Languages you can speak:** Well, English, and I can speak a little bit of Mandarin, but honestly not really. **Good name for a dog:** Bubba.

Name: Tara Babins. **Role:** I'm the Communications Director for Yardbird, RŌNIN, and Sunday's Grocery. I also run the door at Yardbird. **Origin:** I'm from Calgary, Canada. **Time at Yardbird:** Since two months after it opened. I arrived here August 4, 2011, and I started working here that week. **First encounter with Yardbird:** Since before it was an actual restaurant. Matt and Lindsay were originally going to open Yardbird in Vancouver, and when I was in university, I was doing a communications course where I needed to create a website for a brand, and I knew that they had this concept in mind. When they decided to open here, the timing was good: with the point I was at in my life, and them opening, it was a good time for me to move. **Favorite dish:** Chicken Neck skewer. **Favorite drink:** Jumbo Ozaki. Wait—my favorite cocktail is the Jumbo Ozaki, but I do like highballs as well. **Favorite swear word:** "Bitch," probably. **Worst person to work with at Yardbird:** My boyfriend. **Loosest night:** Definitely one of my birthdays. The first birthday I ever celebrated here, I fell asleep on a table. Like, full-on passed out. Elliott had to assist me into my apartment. My legs were Jell-O. **Funniest Yardbird memory:** There are so many. Probably our first anniversary party; with all the shenanigans that went down, this place was literally a house party. People were everywhere. It was exciting, it was fun, and one of Matt's friends came to DJ for the first time. He's come back every year since. **Working at Yardbird has taught you:** What a strong work ethic actually means. How to be passionate about your job. And patience. **Languages you can speak:** English. I can speak a little bit of Hebrew. And I learned how to speak French growing up, but I really can't speak French. I can understand it. **When you're not at Yardbird:** I sleep. Sleep or eat.

Name: Justine Tai. **Role:** My official title is Content and Social Media Manager, but if there's anything that needs to be done with a computer, I can probably help. **Origin:** San Jose, California. **Time in Hong Kong:** Eight years in January. **Time at Yardbird:** Four years in January. **First encounter with Yardbird:** I met Matt and Lindsay as a customer at Yardbird. One visit turned into many visits, which eventually turned into a job. **Favorite dish:** Shiso Duck Fried Rice. **Favorite drink:** Kaku highballs for easy drinking, or Sunday's Coffee Shochu if it's one of those nights. **Most fun person at Yardbird to give shit to:** Elliot, because he takes everything with a smile. **Biggest night:** It was as a customer at their fourth anniversary party. It had a trailer-trash theme, with a watercooler full of blue jungle juice. People were dressed like they were shopping at Walmart. I had a lot of that blue stuff, so I don't really remember much else. **Dumbest Yardbird memory:** One year for Halloween, the staff dressed as skateboarders from the 1970s or something. Seeing our ex-GM Raph in a long, blond wig and Elliot with a ridiculous shaved beard was like a snapshot out of *Lords of Dogtown*. **Working at Yardbird has taught you:** That you can get paid to take photos of food. But in all seriousness, I've learned that a lot of things are out of your control, but if you can control your own emotions, that's already half the battle. **Languages you can speak:** English, Cantonese, and conversational French, if I have enough highballs. **When you're not at Yardbird:** I try to stay active or hike so I can be surrounded by greenery, or I hang out with friends and take photos of whatever we're doing that day.

Name: Danny Tse. **Role:** Sous-chef. **Origin:** China. **Time at Yardbird:** Four years. **Favorite dish:** Chicken Wing skewer. **Favorite drink:** Old Fashioned. **Favorite swear word:** Pok gai. **Worst person to work with:** No one. **Most fun person to give shit to:** Singapore Nick. **First encounter with Yardbird:** Worked with Matt at another restaurant. **Funniest Yardbird memory:** Every day is funny. **Languages you can speak:** Cantonese. **Favorite thing to do when you're not at Yardbird:** Sleep.

Name: Ka Lik Chan (Nick). **Role:** Head Chef. **Origin:** Hong Kong. **Time at Yardbird:** Since day one. **First encounter with Yardbird:** I worked at another restaurant with Matt for two years. **Favorite dish:** Chicken Neck skewer. **Favorite drink:** Our housemade umeshu (plum liqueur). **Most fun person at Yardbird to give shit to:** Whoever is making the balls (the Sweet Corn Tempura). **Biggest night:** One night we were so busy that we sold out every single skewer. **Dumbest Yardbird memory:** Once someone dropped the chicken-and-egg rice from the top of the stairs to the bottom. **Working at Yardbird has taught you:** That you can make a career out of chicken. **Languages you can speak:** I can speak most languages, but only the bad words. Cantonese, English, and Minnan. **When you're not at Yardbird:** I hang out with my wife, stay home, and play with my dog.

Name: Stacey Leigh Jang. **Role:** Finance and Administrative Director. **Origin:** Sherwood Park, Canada. **Time in Hong Kong and at Yardbird:** Off and on since 2009; permanently since May 2011. **How you ended up at Yardbird:** I'm Lindsay's sister, and she and Matt asked me to come "help" run Yardbird's office. I committed to three months to get them started; three months turned into six, and eventually we just stopped discussing it. It's been over six years now. **Favorite dish:** Liver Mousse. **Favorite drink:** Jumbo Ozaki— whisky and sweet tea, basically. **Working at Yardbird has taught you:** The importance of focusing on people's strengths. For a long time, all I could see were weaknesses, issues, and problems, and it consumed my thoughts and hindered my work immensely. At some point I switched to seeing people's talents, strengths, assets—and that changed everything. I learned how to work with people, not against them. And how to assist everyone and let them focus on their strengths. We have an incredible team with crazy talented people. I am grateful for the patience they showed me as I learned this lesson. **Languages you can you speak:** English.

Name: Mamta Singh Sunar. **Role:** RŌNIN Manager/ Mother of the House. **Origin:** Nepal. **Time in Hong**

Kong: Hong Kong is home. I grew up here. **Time at Yardbird:** Since day one. **First encounter with Yardbird:** Matt used to come for coffee at the place where I used to work. I was very surprised to see someone so passionate, excited, nervous, and happy all at the same time to open a restaurant. I'd never met an owner of a restaurant who was so involved in every little detail. Basically, Matt's passion made me so keen to be a part of his restaurant that I just told him that I would love to work with him. **Favorite dish:** It's hard to choose, but I always crave the Yardbird Caesar Salad and Sweet Corn Tempura. **Favorite drink:** Bloody Kim Jong il, Yardbird's take on the Bloody Mary. **Most fun person at Yardbird to give shit to:** I've been at RŌNIN for four years now, but back at Yardbird, Hussam/ Sam and Abu were the men who took all the shit from everyone and made everyone laugh at the same time. I miss those kids. **Biggest night:** Oh, there were so many crazy nights, but my favorite was our opening night. We all were so nervous and excited to open the door at 6 p.m., and at the end of the night we all sat down together and breathed in relief and talked about everyone's experience. I have never laughed so much. **Dumbest Yardbird memory:** I think this was a week after we opened: Abu and Sam got in some drunken, fun wrestling fight somewhere after work, and came to work the next day with swollen lips and broken hands. They both looked hilarious. I remember Matt was so mad but couldn't stop laughing. **Working at Yardbird has taught you:** Patience and tolerance, for sure. But also I have learned a lot about people's different personalities. Yardbird really set an example for a good working environment. One feels genuinely connected and cares for everyone here. **Languages you can speak:** Nepalese, English, and Cantonese. **When you're not at Yardbird:** I spend quality time with my husband and daughter. Sunday is all for them, so anything they love to do, I am there.

Name: Siu Yan Fung. **Role:** Senior Designer. **Origin:** Born and raised in Hong Kong, went to Canada for high school and college, then came back for good in 2008. **Time at Yardbird:** Since November 2013. **First encounter with Yardbird:** I first learned about Yardbird from an article online. A year later, a good friend of mine who also works at Yardbird told me that they had a job opening in their back office, so I applied and got the job. **Favorite dish:** Liver Mousse. **Favorite drink at Yardbird:** I don't drink, so I'll go with Wilkinson ginger ale. **Most fun person at Yardbird to give shit to:** The chefs (I love the chefs). **Craziest night:** There were a few times I worked at Yardbird events as a food runner. During the events, I had guests surrounding me like zombies, grabbing free food from my tray like they hadn't eaten for days—it was actually quite scary. **Funniest memory:** Going through a bunch of incident

reports which I put together for the Yardbird fifth-anniversary zine. It's fun to learn about how all the fights happened at Yardbird, like reading a book. **Working at Yardbird has taught you:** I need to SPEAK UP. I'm still working on it. **Languages you can speak:** English, Cantonese, and Mandarin. **If you weren't at Yardbird:** I'd like to become a painter or make a puppet movie.

Name: Fabien Mauzé. **Role:** Part of the management team and Junior Sommelier. **Origin:** Born and raised in France. **Time in Hong Kong:** Since March 2015. **Time at Yardbird:** Since October 2015. **First encounter with Yardbird:** I saw Matt and Lindsay on a video from i am OTHER—they were presenting Yardbird back when they'd just opened. That's how I decided to apply for a job at the company. **Favorite dish:** Hard question! The Liver Mousse or Katsu Sando. **Favorite drink:** If we're talking signature drinks, then I would say the Shino. **Most fun person at Yardbird to give shit to:** We are all a bunch of kids and we make fun of each other all the time, no exceptions. **Biggest night:** I think it's when we broke the sales record! I remember having a group in my section, right when we opened, that ended up spending HK $50,000 in less than two hours. **Dumbest Yardbird memory:** I remember a Korean couple getting so drunk that the guy fell asleep on the floor after puking in the toilet. His girlfriend was yelling at him in Korean while undressing him. We had to carry the fella up the stairs in his boxers. I called his hotel and sent him there in a cab. **Working at Yardbird has taught you:** Many things, from service style to being a host to giving me the chance to pass my sommelier exams! But, more generally, it has taught me how to grow a thicker skin. I used to be really sensitive about even small matters, but now I can handle everything way more easily. **Languages you can speak:** French, English, and Bahasa Indonesia. **When you're not at Yardbird:** Most of the time I go for a drink after work at our favorite dive bar. And when I'm off, I like spending some time with my partner—either Netflix-and-chill or going for a hike to escape the city!

Tyler Huang Babrowsky
Manager
Since 2014

Amy Ho
Accounts & Administrative Executive
Since 2017

Angela Cristina Page
Server
Since 2016

Satoshi Nakamura
Server
2011–2014

Billy Ka Ming Cheung
Chef
Since 2016

Dason Wun Hym Ying
Training Manager
2012–17

Doren Olayon Saa
Driver
Since 2013

Kinanti (Eka) Thomas
Chef
Since 2016

Elliot James Faber
Beverage Director
Since 2011

Fabien Mauzé
Assistant Manager
Since 2015

Siu Fung (Wasabi) Lam
Sous Chef
Since 2012

Gail Dorothy P. Lanorias
Bartender
Since 2014

Darren Gabilo Belgado
Server
Since 2017

Richard (Rich) Young Lee
Sous Chef
Since 2017

Caelan Robbie O'Rourke
Chef
Since 2017

Steven (Steve) Ross Mair
Server
Since 2017

Geoffrey (Geoff) Da-Yin Marett
Bartender
Since 2017

Gloria P. (Sairah) Paril
Chef
Since 2015

Pak Kwan (Harley) Ling
Bartender
Since 2016

Iona Holly Mathieson
Server
2017–2018

Iris Van Kerckhove
Server
2016–2017

Juntack (Jason) Oh
Chef
2017

Jeffrey (Jeff) Claudio
Chef
2017–2018

Ji Heng (Sing Nick) Sor
Chef
Since 2017

Stacey Leigh Jang
Finance and Administrative Director
Since 2011

Justin Lee Sonota Villanueva
Bartender
Since 2016

Justine Kate Tai
Content and Social Media Manager
Since 2014

Ka Lik (Nick) Chan
Head Chef
Since 2011

Nok Noah Hui
Server
Since 2017

Ka Ming Tse
Chef
Since 2013

Eduardo Jr. (Ed) Ecasama Maguad
Chef
Since 2018

Lila Parsad Gurung
Chef
Since 2012

Kenneth Wai Chan
Head of Operations
Since 2012

Kiyoshi (Yoshi) Edwin Hoshimi-Caines
Beverage Manager
Since 2013

Wing Kin Kwan
Sous Chef
Since 2015

Laura Sheng Tien
Junior Designer
Since 2017

Leo Inigo Verceles-Zara
Server
Since 2017

Lili Sunday Jang-Abergel
Future Employee
Since 2008

Yat Sin Lydia (Lyd) Tsang
HR & Administrative Executive
Since 2012

Mamta Singh Sunar
General Manager
Since 2011

Mason Yeaman
Inventory Manager
Since 2012

Mario Paring Capuyan
Steward
Since 2012

Yun (Nathan) Chen
Chef
Since 2017

Ofir Perlman
Server
Since 2017

Thomas Alexandre Etheve
Chef
Since 2018

Alex Tom Llewellyn
Server
Since 2018

Caroline Marie Claude Wiss
Server
Since 2018

Wai Lim (William) Fung
Chef
Since 2018

Po Fai Ng
Chef
Since 2017

Rod Erick Canafranca
Server
Since 2017

Ronin Abe Jang Abergel
Future Employee
Since 2011

Preeti Ghimire
Assistant Manager
Since 2011

Roy Yeung
Server
Since 2017

Samantha (Sammi) Mandy Yeung
Server
Since 2017

Siu Yan Fung
Senior Designer
Since 2013

Sun Jong (SJ) Kim
Server
Since 2016

John Michael (JM) Vitero Inot
Bartender
Since 2017

Tara Naomi Babins
Communications Director
Since 2011

Chun Ching (Paul) Tsang
Sous Chef
Since 2013

Kam Fung (Danny) Tse
Sous Chef
Since 2013

Raphael Holzer
General Manager
2011–2016

Min (Potsy) Shiu
Chef
Since 2015

Abubacar (Abu) Sibi
Server
2011–2014

Ling Chi (Chi) Wong
Chef
2011–2013

Wing Kay (Kay Kay) Leung
Chef
2012–2015

Kam Hin (Kenny) Tse
Chef
2011–2015

Nabin Rai
Chef
2011–2014

Nimrod Abergel
Bartender
2012–2015

Chun Wai (Ray Ray) Lam
Chef
2015–2017

Yardbird

EMPLOYEE ON-SITE ILLNESS/INJURY INCIDENT REPORT

(To Be Filled Out By Manager)

Employee Name ▓▓▓▓		Title ▓▓▓▓
Manager Name ▓▓▓▓		Title ▓▓▓▓
Today's Date 24 NOV 2013		Incident Time 10AM
Incident Date 24 NOV 2013		Incident Exact Location YARDBIRD

Please select one of the following: ☒ Accident   ☐ Incident   ☐ Spill

Details of injury/illness & treatment (e.g. body part involved, cut, strain, bruise, illness symptoms and date of onset, etc.):

CUT ON TOP OF HEAD

Was medical treatment received?   ☒ Yes   ☐ No

Was there any property/equipment damage?   ☐ Yes   ☒ No
If yes, identify property involved and description of damage:

Was the correct equipment/tool/material used? NA   ☐ Yes   ☐ No

What workplace conditions were contributing factors? (e.g. slippery floors, noise, lighting, etc.)

LEDGE ABOVE THE STAIRS

Was lack of personal protective equipment or safety controls a contributing factor?   ☐ Yes   ☒ No
If Yes, explain:

Were emergency equipment/services available?   ☒ Yes   ☐ No
If No, explain:

Was safety training provided?   ☐ Yes   ☒ No
If No, explain:

NO TRAINING REQUIRED TO WALK DOWN STAIRS

GIVING THANKS
2014
Yardbird Stüssy
HONG KONG

STÜSSY YARDBIRD
INTERNATIONAL
CHICKEN TRIBE
INTERNATIONAL
SHEUNG WAN
TAINT WHERE YA FROM, ITZ WHERE YA AT!
HONG KONGERZ

Table 1A—That Food Cray ♡

FOOD
CRUNCHY RAMEN COLESLAW
POTATO SALAD
TWICE FRIED CHICKEN
SWEET POTATO MASH

Yardbird

OPENING JUNE
33-35 BRIDGES STREET SHEUNG WAN, HONG KONG

Yardbird

ONE
YEAR ANNIVERSARY PARTY

FEATURING DJ

PUMP

JULY 21 2012

YARDBIRD ONE YEAR ANNIVERSARY PARTY
at CLUB FLY featuring DJ PUMP

FLY D/F, 24-30 ICE HOUSE STREET, CENTRAL, HONG KONG

YARDBIRD
5TH
ANNIVERSARY

sisters from different misters

It is no secret after spending a night with us in Yardbird that the real soul of the place is the people working inside it. I have been so blessed to work with my actual family and to develop the closest of friendships within the walls of the restaurant that they too have become practically family. Like many chefs I am not the most extrovert person, I don't participate in social media, and I generally don't go out of my way to make new friends. My business partner Lindsay is quite the opposite and often mocks me for this. One day while she teased me for having no friends in front of our then four-year-old son, Ronin, he piped up and said "yes he does! Everyone he works with is his friend." While that may not be 100 percent true, I would like to believe it's pretty close. When writing this book it has been my underlying fear to have people feel left out, unappreciated, or just forgotten. What I then realized is that this is inevitable, and to all those people: I love you and I'm sorry.

I want to start with the first person you see when you walk through the door, my baby sister and our door angel, Tara Babins. She came to Hong Kong six years ago with no experience in the f and b world and immersed herself immediately. Tara sets the tone of the restaurant, going to great lengths to exceed expectations, greet people as regulars even when it's their first time, and be the consistent sweet girl she has always been. It doesn't hurt that she has a mild case of OCD, her eye for detail keeps everyone on their toes, and our restaurant as organized as we can be. More than that she knows me better than anybody,

what I think often before I think it and how to deal with me in most situations, even when I can't deal with myself. A paragraph does not do her justice, Tara, I love you and thank you.

From the very first day I set foot in a kitchen in Hong Kong I have had the pleasure of working with Nick Ka Lik "garlic" Chan. I knew from day one that he was an incredible chef, but more important an incredible leader and human. He leads by example, with hard work, humility, and most of all humor. At least twice a week for the last nine years Nick will learn a new anecdote, acronym, and/or filthy word in English, which he then somehow commits to memory and spits out at the most inappropriate time, like when you are cooking thirty meatballs on the grill at once and the hood's not working properly, and the police are checking our license. No matter what, Nick can always make me smile. He has been the head chef of Yardbird since we opened and never have I doubted his capabilities, his commitment, or his friendship.

Next is a person you will probably never meet in the restaurant, Stacey Jang. This is Lindsay's sister, but she really is the best example of being my sister from a different mister. She is family through and through. Stacey is one of the most honest people I know; she speaks from the perfect combination of heart, mind, and gut. She is as selfless as they come and looks out for everyone's well-being both financially and otherwise. She is the ying to my yang; early on in our working relationship she realized all my shortcomings in being a creative, single-minded, selfish chef and has since the beginning supported me, and the restaurant, so that we can survive as a healthy business. Seven years on, it has been a pleasure to watch her flourish and grow—not only as a person but as the person really running the business end of this business.

brothers from different mothers

Up next is Raphael Holzer, the giant Austrian man who took a leap of faith and moved back to Hong Kong, after working with me for two years in Zuma, and opened Yardbird with me as our general manager. He has since moved on to follow his dream of creating his own liquor brand, Fernet Hunter, and I couldn't be more proud of him. Without Raphael's discipline and dedication Yardbird would not be what it is today. Every day was a juggling act of training, and babysitting the inexperienced waiters, mostly under the age of twenty five, and managing the almost immediately packed restaurant. Raph also managed to train all the bartenders, and develop the majority of our cocktails—after extensive testing, of course. To this day we still collaborate, hang out and enjoy the fruits of our labor on a regular basis.

"I will stay for three months," Elliot Faber told me when he came to help me with Yardbird's opening as our resident sommelier and sake expert. In those three months I almost fired Elliot three times, and realized how much I regretted not getting to know him better in the twenty years that our families had been friends in Calgary. Fast forward six years and Elliot is a certified sake educator, published author, and sake samurai. He is still heavily involved in the restaurants while running a few of his own projects, and is one of the best friends I have ever made in my life. Elliot is the man that will turn a twenty-one-year-old kid who has never even tasted sake into a passionate hopeful sommelier willing to voluntarily clean sake breweries just to be closer to the source of this magic liquid. He is an ambassador for the culture of drinking, always making new friends and connections, always managing to get as close as possible to the artisans producing whatever it is he is selling—and more importantly—consuming. Without Elliot, we would have never become what we are today, borderline alcoholics, and for this I salute him.

Kenneth Chan is famously known as the only person that I was not involved in hiring. There is very little that needs to be said between us for us to understand each other, because deep down we are both professional assholes. We like to keep to ourselves outside of the restaurant, and only value those who are truly close to us. If I was to rob a bank with one person, it would be Kenneth. He is steadfast, unafraid, smart and, most of all, loyal. To this day I am thankful that we somehow let an intern first interview this man, and I am most thankful to have him by my side every day, no matter what.

There are so many more people involved in the everyday workings of this business that will likely never get the praise they deserve. So to every single person that has ever worked with us, no matter for how long or how hard, I thank you and appreciate everything that you have contributed to this family.

Aka miso—red miso is the saltiest and most deeply flavored miso. It works really well with game meats, clams, and herbs.

Aonori—a type of fragrant seaweed that is dried and shredded. A component of shichimi, it's great with butter and has notes of truffle.

Banno negi—Japanese scallions, or green onions, that are slightly smaller and milder than their western counterparts. If you can't find these, use the smallest, freshest scallions (spring onions) available.

Binchotan—a highly carbonized oak wood charcoal that burns very cleanly, with very little smoke, and a very high infrared value.

Black garlic—a slowly fermented garlic with an intensely sweet, raisin-like flavor.

Bulldog Vegetable and Fruit Tonkatsu Sauce—a fruity Worcestershire-style sauce often served with fried pork cutlets. You could make it yourself but it's like making ketchup: it's never going to be as good.

Chin Kiang vinegar—a Chinese black vinegar made from glutinous rice and various spices; it has a rich sourness that pairs well with Okinawan black sugar.

Daikoku mushroom—a type of mushroom that looks like a cross between a Shimeji mushroom and a King Oyster mushroom. They are quite juicy and have a strong flavor. If you can't find them, try a Crimini or brown mushroom.

Daikon—a long white radish, commonly used in Japanese, Korean, and Chinese cuisine. Poor translations of the word often lead to it being called a turnip, or white carrot.

Eringi mushroom—an alternative name for a King Oyster mushroom, readily available in most Asian stores.

Furikake—a rice seasoning that consists of many different ingredients, most commonly nori, sesame seeds, bonito flakes, and a healthy dose of MSG.

Gobo—otherwise known as burdock root.

Gochugaru—a sundried, Korean chili pepper flake.

Goma abura—a dark-roasted sesame oil.

Kabosu—a green citrus fruit somewhere in between sudachi and yuzu in both size and flavor. The juice leans more towards an unripe orange, and the skin more along the lines of South Asian limes.

Karaage ko—a Japanese flour blend specifically designed for frying. It's often a blend of wheat and potato starches.

Katakuriko—a Japanese potato starch used primarily for frying and thickening sauces.

Katsuobushi—a boiled, fermented, smoked, and dried bonito fish, used primarily for making dashi.

Kecap manis—an Indonesian sweet soy sauce that's sweetened with palm sugar.

Kewpie mayo—a delicious Japanese mayonnaise that's good with everything.

Kinome—the leaf of the prickly ash tree. See sansho pepper entry.

Kizami nori—finely sliced and roasted seaweed. It is cut using a machine similar to a paper cutter; if you can't find kizami nori, you can cut nori yourself with scissors.

Kizami wasabi—the preserved stems of the rhizome known as wasabi.

Kombu—a seaweed also known as kelp that's most commonly used in its sundried form to make the stock known as dashi.

Koshin daikon—a radish native to both Japan and China, also known as watermelon radish.

Korean rice cakes—small store-bought cakes made from steamed glutinous rice.

Kubi kushi—square skewers that Yardbird uses almost exclusively for yakitori.

Kyoto shichimi—similar to shichimi, but more heavily roasted, with a higher sansho pepper content. This can easily be purchased online.

Kyuri—a Japanese cucumber that is denser, crunchier, and has fewer seeds.

Maitake mushroom—a meaty, fragrant mushroom also known as hen of the woods.

Matsutake mushroom—a pine mushroom that is only found in the wild, primarily in Japan, parts of central China, and the Pacific Northwest.

Milk bread—a sweet soft-style white bread fortified with milk.

Mirin—a sweetened cooking wine, an essential part of Japanese cuisine.

Miso katsuo niniku—garlic that has been marinated with katsuobushi and miso.

Mitsuba—otherwise known as Japanese trefoil. This is a slightly medicinal, watery herb found throughout Japanese cuisine.

Mizansho shouyu ni— whole sansho peppercorns that have been braised in soy, sake, and mirin.

Mizuna—a Japanese mustard green with a slightly peppery leaf, and a refreshing crunchy stalk.

Mochi gome—a Japanese short-grain glutinous rice.

Mugi miso—miso that has fermented with barley groats as a component.

Myoga—an edible flower bud from the ginger family. Only this part, and not the root, is used.

Nama panko—fresh panko; it is the only panko we use in our restaurants. If you can't find nama panko, buy the least sweet white bread from your local Asian bakery, take off the crust, and pulse in a food processor until you have very coarse bread crumbs.

Neri ume—salted umeboshi paste that's blended with the red shiso leaves it has been cured with.

Niniku miso zuke—garlic cloves that have been pickled with miso until they are crunchy and sweet. The variety we use also has bonito flakes.

Nori—roasted, edible, red algae seaweed.

Nama nori—fresh, edible, red algae seaweed.

Okinawan black sugar—a type of sugar made from mineral-rich sugar canes on the southern Japanese island of Okinawa. It is the only sugar to have high levels of calcium, potassium, and folic acid. It imparts a slightly bittersweet flavor to many of our dressings and cocktails.

Onsen egg—an egg cooked in its shell at a constant temperature of 145°F/63°C, giving the white a slightly coagulated texture while the yolk remains mostly liquid.

Rice vinegar—a Japanese vinegar made from rice spirit.

Salted shrimp—shrimp that have been fermented with salt to preserve and intensify the flavor.

Sansho—a type of peppercorn that has citrus notes, and gives a slightly numbing feeling. It's related to the Szechuan peppercorn.

Sel gris—a moist, coarse, gray French sea salt.

Shio kombu—kombu that has been sliced and cooked, most commonly with soy sauce, sake, and mirin, then dried.

Shirasu/jako—salted, boiled, and sundried baby anchovies. When fried, they add great texture and saltiness. When left uncooked, they add a subtle, salty, fish flavor.

Shiro goma abura—unroasted sesame oil.

Shiro miso—white miso; it is the most common type of miso. Do your best to find one that has no additives.

Shiso—a herb also known as perilla, it is commonly used in both Japanese and Vietnamese cuisine.

Shungiku—the edible green leaves of a type of chrysanthemum.

Sudachi—a small, green citrus fruit prized as much for its fragrant, slightly soapy skin as it is for its bright limey juice.

Takana—a cooked and pickled mustard green, most often cooked with soy sauce, chili, and sesame. There are many types of takana but the one that we use is from Kyushu. It is slightly spicy and very addictive.

Tamari—a dark soy sauce most commonly brewed with soybeans and very little wheat. The west has adopted tamari as a gluten-free soy sauce, but this is not always the case with tamari, so do check the ingredients. Its rich flavor and color are key elements of tare sauce.

Tempura flour—a fine, bleached wheat flour designed to make tempura batter.

Tokyo negi—a type of long onion, commonly used in Japanese cuisine. It is also known as Welsh onion and naga negi.

Tosazu—a bonito flake flavored soy vinegar. The prefix "tosa" refers to the old name for the Shikoku region in Japan, where the production of katsuobushi was historically centered.

Udon noodles—thick wheat noodles from Japan.

Usukuchi—a light soy sauce, with a high wheat and salt content.

Wasabi—a rhizome, in the same family as mustard, cabbage, and horseradish.

Welsh onion—see Tokyo negi.

White sesame seeds—always refer to Japanese roasted sesame seeds.

Yukari—salted and dried red shiso leaves.

Yuzu—a citrus fruit that is yellow in the winter and green in the summer. It is mostly used for its skin when yellow, and more for the juice when it's green.

Yuzu kosho—a fermented condiment made of salted yuzu skin and chili. There are many different types found throughout Japan, most commonly the green and red varieties.

Zarame sugar—a type of coarse crystallized brown sugar, also known as coffee sugar. It also plays a crucial part in the making of tare, allowing a slower caramelization process before burning.

index

Salt is always sea salt, unless otherwise specified.

Butter should always be unsalted, unless otherwise specified.

All herbs are fresh, unless otherwise specified.

Eggs and individual vegetables and fruits, such as onions and apples, are assumed to be medium, unless otherwise specified.

All sugar is white caster (superfine) sugar and all brown sugar is cane or Demerara, unless otherwise specified.

Cooking times are for guidance only, as individual ovens vary. If using a fan (convection) oven, follow the manufacturer's instructions concerning oven temperatures.

Exercise a high level of caution when following recipes involving any potentially hazardous activity, including the use of high temperatures, open flames, using a cook's blowtorch, and when deep-frying. In particular, when deep-frying, add food carefully to avoid splashing, wear long sleeves, and never leave the pan unattended.

Some recipes include raw or very lightly cooked eggs, meat or fish, and fermented products. These should be avoided by the elderly, infants, pregnant women, convalescents, and anyone with an impaired immune system.

Using the grill as we do, we don't need to soak our skewers because they don't go near the flame. However, if you are using a barbecue or grill at home, it is probably best to steep your skewers for 20 minutes in cold water before using so they don't catch fire or char and affect the taste of the finished dish.

At Yardbird we use a specialised grill designed for yakitori (pages 94–5). I would recommend using a similar type to get the best results from these recipes and small yakitori grills for home use can be purchased online. However, the skewers can also be cooked on a home barbecue or grill, just be mindful that the grilling may not be as even and the skewers may stick a little.

Exercise caution when making fermented products, ensuring all equipment is spotlessly clean, and seek expert advice if in any doubt.

When no quantity is specified, for example of oils, salts, and herbs used for finishing dishes or for deep-frying, quantities are discretionary and flexible.

Exercise caution when foraging for ingredients; any foraged ingredients should only be eaten if an expert has deemed them safe to eat.

All herbs, shoots, flowers, and leaves should be picked fresh from a clean source.

Making a book has been one of my lifelong dreams. That being said, this has also been one of the most stressful and difficult projects I have ever worked on. As a chef, what we do is temporary, our craft is ever evolving and we have the luxury of making mistakes every day to make us better at what we do. In my experience it is all the mistakes I have made in life that have brought me closer to the things and people I most love. This book is our legacy, and it is permanent.

I have led an incredibly fortunate life. I have loyal and generous people that I get to call my family, friends, colleagues, and customers. I have been supported from every angle, allowing me to be free to design, manage, and cook the way that I thought was best for what was meant to be my dream restaurant. It is my family that has always been there to support me. I take liberties when I talk about family: in this modern world we live in my family is not necessarily related to me by blood (yet often is). We are connected by a force of nature that is inexplicable, one that brings us together in such a way that we become a single entity striving for the same goal.

Lindsay Jang is my partner in life. We have two incredible children together, and have built our business together on a foundation of a love for what we do, what we stand for, and the people we do it with (and for). People often comment how difficult it must be to run businesses and a life with the former love of your life, and maybe on paper it should be, but we have struck an incredible balance between us that I am grateful for every day. Through thick and through thin, with the help of many, we are in a very happy place, each of us with our own lives, free to follow our separate passions as well as our shared ones, and most importantly we share two of the most beautiful, warm and socially adept children I have ever had the pleasure of being partially responsible for making. Without Lindsay this book would not be.

This book is dedicated to my family, both blood and extended, living and missed. Especially my mother, who knows no limit to the love she gives and the support she has always given me. Above all, this book is for my incredible children, Lili Sunday and Ronin Abe.

CONTRIBUTORS
Cody Allen, Tara Babins, Tyler Babrowsky,
Michael Carter, Ka Lik Chan (Nick),
Kenneth Chan, Jeff Claudio, Elliot Faber,
Siu Yan Fung, Mark Gainor, Raphael
Holzer, Stacey Jang, Mike Jennings,
Jason Michael Lang, Richard Lee, Alex
Maeland, Justine Tai, Tsang Chun Ching
(Paul), Tse Kam Fung (Danny)

THANK YOUS
Eli Abergel, Avi Abergel, Nimrod Abergel,
Amit Abergel, Eric Babins, Bonny Gold-
Babins, Bertha Gold, Abe Gold, Nick Kim,
Atsushi Kono, Jimmy Lee, Wayne Parfitt,
Savva Pavlov, Angela Reynolds, George
Ruan, Toki San, Masayoshi Takayama,
Kodai Uno

Phaidon Press Limited
Regent's Wharf
All Saints Street
London N1 9PA

Phaidon Press Inc.
65 Bleecker Street
New York, NY 10012

phaidon.com

First published 2018
© 2018 Phaidon Press Limited

ISBN 978 0 7148 7645 0

A CIP catalogue record for this book
is available from the British Library and
the Library of Congress.

Commissioning Editor: Ellie Smith
Project Editor: Eve O'Sullivan
Production Controller: Lisa Fiske
Step-by-Step Photography: Alex Maeland
Food and Atmospheric Photography: Jason
  Lang and Siu Yan Fung
Design: Michael Carter
Illustration on page 38 by Michael Carter and
  Mark Gainor, all others Evan Hecox

Printed in China

The publisher would like to thank: Vanessa
Bird, Madeline Coleman, Sam Cook, Freddie
Janssen, Lisa Pendreigh, Gregor Shepherd,
and Kathy Steer.

LANDSCAPE OF DREAMS

THE GARDENS OF ISABEL & JULIAN BANNERMAN

LANDSCAPE OF DREAMS

THE GARDENS OF ISABEL & JULIAN BANNERMAN

ISABEL & JULIAN BANNERMAN

FOREWORD BY HRH THE PRINCE OF WALES

PIMPERNEL
PRESS LTD
www.pimpernelpress.com

This book is dedicated to our first client Mrs Green,
all the other brave souls who have commissioned us,
and all the gifted artisans who have worked with us.

'First on the wal was peynted a forest
In which ther dwelleth neither man ne best,
With knotty, knarry, bareyne trees olde,
Of stubbes sharpe and hidouse to biholde,
In which there ran a rumbel in a swough
As though a storm shoulde bresten every bough.
and dounward from an hille, under a bente,
Ther stod the temple of Mars armypotente.'

Geoffrey Chaucer *The Knight's Tale*

Pimpernel Press Limited
www.pimpernelpress.com

Landscape of Dreams
© Pimpernel Press Limited 2016
Text © Isabel and Julian Bannerman 2016
Photographs © Isabel and Julian Bannerman
and Dunstan Baker 2016,
except as noted on page 296.

A catalogue record for this book is available from
the British Library.

Designed by Dunstan Baker
www.greygray.co.uk
Typeset in Minion Pro

Page 2: Meadow, ash tree and caravan,
Hanham Court.

ISBN 978-1-910258-60-6
Printed and bound in China
by C&C Offset Printing Company Limited

9 8 7 6 5 4 3 2 1

Contents

CLARENCE HOUSE

"So I awoke, and behold it was a dream" (John Bunyan 1628 – 1688)

Julian and Isabel Bannerman's creative genius, as they themselves acknowledge in this remarkable book, seems to be based in large part on the intuitive harmony of the dream world they both inhabit. This extraordinary gift of theirs transforms the otherwise mundane and unexceptional into, quite literally, a fragment of Elysium; an echo of some long-lost part of ourselves.

For me, they are the worthy heirs of William Kent, one of the greatest and most creative of early eighteenth century "designers" who, like Julian and Isabel, managed to combine the arts of architecture, landscape and interior design in one seamless, unified theme. To do this believably, and with such original élan, is a mark of their unique contribution to posterity. So is the sheer quality of the workmanship they deploy through their incredibly talented team of craftspeople.

There is no doubt that this flair for visionary creativity can sometimes bewilder the client with its scope and brilliance, but the end result always astonishes and inspires, as those of us fortunate enough to have benefitted from the "Bannerman touch" can confirm.

The photographs in this book clearly demonstrate the true gift of exceptional beauty bequeathed by two rare souls working in harmony with Nature – or, as the Bushmen of the Kalahari might describe it, with "the dream that is dreaming us."

[signature]

Wonderland

'Alice opened the door and found that it led into a small passage ... she looked down and looked along the passage into the loveliest garden you ever saw. How she longed to get out of that dark Hall, and wander among those beds and bright fountains ...' *Alice's Adventures in Wonderland*

Julian woke this morning and, as he has done many times before, relayed to me the marvellous dream just dreamt: in the dream he finds a lost, unloved house in an overgrown garden, not to be found on any map. We both have this dream, recurrently; it differs, but the crux is the same, our being the hunter and the lost house the quarry. We dream waking and sleeping about architecture and landscape, derelict houses and shattered gardens, imagined and actual, real disappearing places, like Mavisbank or Edwinsford, that slipped through the system. This curious searching brought us together. We seek these places out and imagine detail for detail what we would do to them. It is an addiction, induces delusions, providing great highs and great lows; the consequences can be tremendous, but it has never been boring.

Part of the fascination of Alice's world is that illusory, hallucinatory quality, the super-real. The lure of the garden is dreamlike, primarily about things just beyond our grasp, in the making and also in literature, poetry, painting and photography. In his book *A Gardener's Labyrinth* Patrick Kinmonth puts it thus:

'In the end perhaps no garden can be as perfectly beautiful as the one that hovers out of reach, beyond description, the garden of promise that lies coiled in a patch of untouched brambles, dormant in un-scattered seeds or glinting from a pair of brand new secateurs.'

Books have always been part of the process, the way to free the imagination and think. And through books and places, history provides this too, particularly the by-ways of offbeat visionaries.

Along with getting lost in the car and trespassing in abandoned properties we turn to books to provide a portal. Books also people the house with great characters. Looking across the shelves here there sits a broad range of heroes: John Aubrey; Inigo Jones; Charles Bridgeman; Thomas Wright; Batty Langley; William Blake; Eric Ravilious; Barbara Jones; and Hylton Nel. Books about all the decorative arts as well as architecture and gardening have been pivotal in shaping the way we both think, along with, of course, observing the real world closely at all times. Observation is the key. Julian and I were lucky enough to grow up in middle England, in professional, educated, secure and enormous extended families. We are both at the bottom of large families, the youngest of five by a gap of over six years, which makes us both almost only children, but our siblings were like four extra parents. We sucked in information from every source around us, as everyone does, and were blessed by the encouragement of others, not just family, who took trouble to share their wonders. We share a curious kind of baking in our upbringing, hard to distil especially from such close quarters, which led to a particular aesthetic: picture making and garden making. Inevitably one would think that the formative years of freedom, childhood, have informed the decisions we take at the branching moments in life and the way the world looks to us for the rest of our lives.

Alice escapes thanks to the 'Drink Me' potion, but the relief is immediately countered by bewilderment at her finding, in the garden beyond, a pair of men painting the red roses white. My childish mind was consumed by the riddle of paint on petals. This was, I think, my first encounter with the idea of the garden as an artificially made thing. Julian concurs that among the many strong things about childhood to which we should cling as much as possible in grown-up life is a blurring of the separation between real and imagined, the impossible and the possible and, most importantly for him, the strangeness of scale. A child being so small, so close to everything, lives in a world that

is scaled at one to five. Everything appears huge in the first ten years of life and one's memories are stored in the proportions in which they were experienced. When you go back to a childhood haunt you find it sadly diminished: cats are no longer the size of Cheshire, and caterpillars do not sit on table-sized mushrooms smoking. Childhood is more psychotropic than being grown up and proximity to nature heightens experience: to play in a stream, as a child, is to swim the Orinoco. Many of us desire to keep contact with this exaggerated reality. These very early images remain a fixed part of the mental geography, they are lodestones, and they are part of who we are and why we do what we do. Ostensibly very middle Britain are the influences of *Martin Pippin in the Apple Orchard*; *The Wind in the Willows*; *The Secret Garden*; *The Midnight Folk*; *The Flower Fairies*; *The Borrowers*. But wherever they come from there is no doubt in my mind that the journeys and the landscape, which often concern Mervyn Peake, Tolkein, C.S. Lewis, T.H. White, John Buchan, Kipling and Robert Louis Stevenson, the travels on foot, sometimes hunted and sometimes at night, all help connect us to the thrill of the natural world. These, along with Johnnie Morris, Jacques Cousteau, and Eric Thompson's *Magic Roundabout,* created my imaginative early perception of the natural world.

In childhood, magic, danger, wonder, threat, opportunity, all lurk outside. I, being at the end of the line, was a pale and almost silent introspective sort of changeling, who either sat at the piano for interminable hours or rootled around outside. Of course I 'got away with murder' according to my siblings. I certainly climbed out of my bedroom window on the second storey of the Old Rectory, East Hendred, a spring line village on the Berkshire Downs, to which we moved from London in 1967. Outside at night I continued my garden games in the twilight, a particularly important time of day altogether, and still so and especially in the garden. If the others were home for the holidays they would all be 'up', eating and drinking outside and I listened to them argue. Bored by that, I would make for my special haunts and, believing myself to be a witch, to the centre of my witchy operations, the place where two towering wych elms (it is hard to believe now just how giant elm trees were) glowered at the very far end of the garden, overlooking a well. The lid of the well was littered with tawny needles from the three inky yews that grew round it. It let out a cold breath as one struggled to lift it. Unfathomable and profoundly silent, the power of the well gods could be invoked by dropping a stone and holding breath for an intense eternity to receive the lost splash relayed back as it hit the water far below. An alternative shrine was the tree house, with commanding views over the village. This my sister Frances and I had assisted our brother Charlie in building. As apprentice assistant to Charlie, eight years older, I learnt not much about engines or mechanics sadly, but a lot about building in wood, brick, salvage, and going to 'Challow Dump' to find things for our creations. (Much later I discovered that Challow was also the favourite haunt of our friend Candida Lycett Green when looking for things for her houses and gardens, places which have been a powerful influence on us both and which she made with miraculous panache and practically no money.) Charlie made a blast furnace using a cast iron stove and an old hoover, melting glass, brass, lead and even silver and I assisted. Beyond the garden there were long walks

Above: Magic Lantern slides of John Tenniel's 1870s illustrations for *Alice in Wonderland*.

Below: Isabel's grandmother's house Burrow's Hill, Shere, Surrey.

or bike rides on the downs, up along the Ridgeway, the Vale of Oxford below, the cooling towers of Didcot and the Harwell Atomic Research station to the east, while to the west was the Neolithic, equally powerful world of Wayland's Smithy and the Uffington White Horse. We made all sorts of dens and headquarters, furnished with Challow finds and a lot of army surplus – billy cans, gas masks and Sam Browne belts, our father's kit from the war. In the outhouses frosted with furry saltpetre walls we got a 'Cosystove' going and toasted toast, stored apples that went fascinatingly mouldy, brewed beer and fermented filthy wine with plums and apples from the garden. We caught, skinned, cured and ate rabbits. We collected dead things and their nests, eggs and young and tried to rear them. We ate lots of raw vegetables and rhubarb because we were always hungry and there were no snacks to be had, except at Esme's house down the road which was 1920s Arts and Crafts – like Bag End in *The Hobbit*. My father grew marrows and fabulous small artichokes he got as 'slips' from the Italians who lived at Rowstock Corner. Once I was allowed to go camping with my father and the others – my mother loathed all things outdoors – at Talybont on the Usk in Wales. I had never been happier.

I found when I went to boarding school just before I was ten that I loved the camaraderie of school life, loved routine, loved making things, making up plays, making music, making clothes, making toast on an iron, and making coffee with an element that you put in the mug. The latter two things were forbidden and hence deeply exciting, and I learnt to be rebellious about received ideas, to think strategically about how to outwit the nuns. I also learnt to love the smell and the peace of the library and to escape from the hurly burly of bells and screaming girls by getting outdoors. We were made to go for very long walks at weekends to keep us quietly exhausted and out of mischief. Den-making was done in rhododendron groves like mangrove swamps: smoking dens, drinking dens and dens to dream in, for that is what dens are for. As a refuge from London there was also my paternal grandmother's house. Burrows Hill was in Surrey. The gardener was called Dickinson; I think he had 'war wounds' because he seemed always in pain and was very tall and stiff and cross – rather as Julian and I find ourselves now. He inspired such terror in us children that the gratification of stealing raspberries from the fruit cage and tomatoes from the greenhouse was magnificently intense. Charlie's first tree house was the one here in the strawberry tree or arbutus; it was a fine vantage point for spying on Dickinson's movements. Once a redoubtable memsahib in Calcutta, Grandmamma was also passionate about her dahlias, which had a bed solely for their glory, spiked with bamboos wearing flower pots for the collection of earwigs and looked upon by a rather green bust of Dante. She gardened in a tweed skirt; an apron; heavy tights; the chic-est of Italian loafers; and her gardening watch was an early silver Rolex. We were all happy to garden with her because she was a great sport, although less so when it meant afternoons

picking out weeds and moss from the crazy paving with broken dinner knives. There was a white-pillared veranda where lunch was eaten every day from April until October. There was a very good wisteria all over the side of the house facing south, and at the edge of the crazily paved terrace was a small retaining wall with a narrow bed on top. Another area about which, like her hair, she was fiercely anxious, this bed was planted out with lipstick-red geraniums every summer, held in with miniature hurdles. Beyond the croquet lawn was the wood, bordered by rhododendrons and millions of naturalised *Crocus tommasinianus* – source of immense pride to her. Beyond this were several acres of Surrey woodland whose canopy was, like the sandy soil beneath, light, being mostly birch and hazel, the floor spangled and the clean air scented with myriad lily of the valley in May. It was exciting and filled with dangerous burrows, mushrooms and stinkhorns.

In London I found myself doing A levels at St Paul's, which to begin with I found alarming in its sophistication. Country bred, I read *Country Life* with more relish than *Cosmopolitan* and indeed had done so since before I could read. I liked it because it was not reading, it was looking at pictures mostly, and the pictures were of houses and that fascinated me. Both my parents had been gripped with a thing about houses, pictures and furniture, and Julian's parents similarly loved to take him to the country-house sales that abounded in the 1960s. My mother eventually turned this passion into a job by opening an antique shop in Wallingford, which prompted my happy exile to boarding school and, later when she succeeded in moving us back to London, in Chelsea, and together we went on buying trips round the country in her yellow Volvo estate and would stop to look at houses, market towns and the odd church. She liked to share a smoke and a gin in the evenings and tales of the 'trade'. My Dad, who had been involved in the setting up of the Open University throughout the seventies, was by now working for a quango called the Centre for Environmental Studies, researching regeneration and the built environment, and he and I would set off at weekends for urban walks round Thamesmead and other social housing developments, as well as to Columbia Road to buy plants for his pots, and on excursions to look at the paintings of Claude and Poussin for whom he had a great admiration. In 1975 'The Destruction of the English Country House' exhibition happened at the Victoria and Albert Museum, masterminded by people who would later become Julian and my heroes and friends: Roy Strong, John Harris and Marcus Binney. It found me already recruited, I think, into the cult of the country house. It was followed by a companion exhibition 'The Glory of the Garden'.

I went to Edinburgh to read History and History of Art, cherry-picking Early Islamic Architecture and the Development of the English Country House. I loved Edinburgh from the moment I alighted at Waverley Station: the city, the architecture, the Scots, the university, the friends, the theatrical productions, the junk shops, the parties, were all beyond my greatest expectations. Students spent a lot of time drinking in bars

Above: Hardwick Hall and Wardour Old Castle (the grotto by Joseph and Josiah Lane in the foreground) by David Vicary, early 1960s.

Below: Antoni Gaudí, Parc Güell, 1900–1914 (top); Niki de St. Phalle, Tarot Garden, Tuscany, Italy, 1998 (bottom).

and Bannerman's was close by the university, in the Old Town, and did particularly good lunches. I met the eponymous owner at a party in my second term. At the end of the party everybody went back to Bannerman's for a 'lock-in', and within months I had decided to 'lock in' for a life with Mr Bannerman.

Julian's very earliest childhood memories are of officers' quarters in Fordell House, an eighteenth-century mansion at RAF Pitreavie on the Firth of Forth, a time from which he remembers wild strawberries, cannons in the garden and the trams in Princes Street, Edinburgh. In the golden age before he was seven he gardened alongside his mother Hilda at the Butts, his grandparents' house in Stanhope, within the confines of the walled garden beside the River Wear. He played in the rotating rustic summerhouse, whose gables were adorned with split logs, and which smelled strongly of creosote and the hibernating tortoise. He remembers the scent of grape hyacinths, gathering petals for the making of rose water, and supplementing his pocket money by picking hips and haws in the hedgerows, which could then be sold to the Chemist for rosehip syrup. He would smell the silence when the river was in flood, knowing that the water was rising right against the outside of garden wall and over the dangerous stepping-stones at the wide ford. Julian and Hilda would visit High Force, a powerful waterfall on the River Tees, and picnic among the 'velvet paths' of the moor above Stanhope. The moor was very special, all foxholes and heather, and Julian would use the shooting butts to make dens with branches of bracken. A great aunt at Cockermouth had done her own archaeological dig in her garden, finding a Roman trough and burnt Roman corn. This awakened an interest in archaeology, which developed at school and has stayed with Julian. Whitehaven nearby was where his grandmother Anne Ismay's family, who founded the White Star Line, came from. Anne is buried in the churchyard at Stanhope near the fossilised tree stump.

All at once they moved to Clifton in Bristol, and prep school interrupted everything. Wellbury Park, Hitchin, was on the chalk, on the Icknield Way in Hertfordshire, down a two-mile drive. It was incredibly isolated and a perfectly beastly place lorded over by a psychotic, but the boys were able to run wild in the lilac- and mock-orange-filled shrubberies, swing from ropes of wild clematis like Tarzan, and jump from top to bottom of giant beech trees cosseted by the freshly leaved layers of branches. They were allowed to make gardens, and prizes were awarded. Julian remembers his first garden, scattered from a Suttons seed packet with a lushly drawn thatched cottage on the outside, but recalls with vivid envy Campbell's garden next to his. Campbell's father was in the Navy and naturally he made his garden the shape of a battleship bordered with inky-black Victorian rope edgings. It was planted with naval restraint solely with blue irises. While his first foray

Above: Cliffs at Lulworth, Dorset Coast, by David Vicary, early 1960s.

Left, from far left: 'Bannerman's Bar from Niddry Street, South' by Richard Demarco, 1981; Etching by Robin Tanner: 'Christmas', 1928-1929. The artist's eye offers a fresh vision of village and stumps.

Above, from left: Endellion Lycett
Green: 'Hemelsleutel, Sedum
'Matrona' and Echinops', 2013, and
'Eryngiums, Ferns and Perovskia',
2016; a Greek village painted by a
restaurateur. Thinking about planting
and planning in terms of painting is
part of the process and painters like
Endellion's use of plants and form is
always instructive.

into design may not have been garlanded with success, Sutton's seed packets were always
a comfort and protector to which he turned in the dark nights of misery at boarding
school. Formal learning at school was a constant trial to someone who would clearly
be diagnosed as dyslexic today, and his struggles were not helped by his father, Hugh,
who misinterpreted this as the fault of the school and therefore moved him repeatedly
through a succession of mildly ghastly establishments. After a couple of years of torture
at Wellbury he was sent to a totally different geological and botanical world, a school in
East Sussex at Crawley Down which smelled of azaleas, overgrown lakes and bamboos.
An equally dismal crammer at Seaford, East Sussex, followed this; back on the chalk he
remembers glow-worms and bicycling to Alfriston through cow parsley in May.

Hilda made a real garden at Hurle Crescent in Bristol in the early sixties with lots
of herbaceous borders, sister Christine introduced 'groovy' Italian loungers, and Julian
helped when he was not making what he describes as 'a shantytown of a tree house' in
someone else's garden. Down the road were the Zoological Gardens, designed in their *fin
de siècle* heyday as a proper pleasure and botanical garden, with a giant *Prunus* 'Tai-haku'
or great white cherry, seared into Julian's consciousness along with other fine specimen
trees dotted around the '*Barbar*-esque' cast-iron cages and aviaries. Julian loves Bristol
because the topography is nearly as good as Edinburgh; the handsome crescents and
squares of Clifton are halted suddenly by the downs and the gorge, the tidal reaches of
the Avon. Only twenty years after being blitzed it was still a very painterly place, just
then being destroyed by town planners, and still thronged with shipping, the city-centre
docks crammed with cargoes of Scandinavian timber bearing strange hieroglyphic
stamps. There were bombsites everywhere, each with burgeoning buddleia. Hilda and
Julian hated buddleia forever more. Hilda Bannerman, brought up in Newcastle, always
missed the beauty of Northumberland, the coast, and holidays on The Holy Island of
Lindisfarne where they would arrive in a carriage across the causeway at low tide. She
could never come to terms with the dreary Bristol Channel, but she loved the Mendips
and took the family to live in Wells, Somerset, in the mid-sixties.

The smallest city in the country, Wells is a market town settled at the foot of the
Mendip Hills. The town ends abruptly on the edge of the mysterious Somerset Levels,
where Glastonbury floats over the vaporous dykes. A city where the Vicars' Close and
Library were utterly medieval, manuscripts still chained to the benches, its heart lay with
the moated Bishop's Palace, and the Bishop's beautiful daughters. The gardens behind
New Street were all long and thin and walled, following the medieval pattern of the town.
They are very silent, completely blocked from the bustle of the street by the houses. There
were peonies and *Lilium pyrenaicum* growing there when Hilda got to work and floods
of scillas under the curtains of the weeping ash. She planted philadelphus, kerria, lilac
and roses, which grew up the walls, with herbaceous beds along the base. Hugh looked
after the small kitchen garden purchased from next door at the end of the garden, where
there were roses, lily of the valley, raspberries, potatoes, broad and runner beans aplenty.

Threadlike lanes connected the backs of all these gardens, belonging to opticians, doctors and vets. There were second-hand book and antiques dealers, even a picture gallery where Julian worked upstairs, learning how to re-line pictures amidst the smell of hot wax and marijuana. He learnt a lot about painting here. Remarkable pictures were pressed onto the vacuum table: Frank Brangwyns, Augustus Johns and Vanessa Bells. From Batcombe down to the Bristol Channel the landscape with its mumps and barrows was formative for Julian, puttering about on his NSU Quick 50 moped. It was an Eden of pink lime-washed houses and huge apple trees in the cider orchards, but sadly these magnificent orchards were being grubbed up and burnt, an inferno of apple-wood incense, all done in return for tawdry payments from the big cider producers.

Julian spent a lot of his childhood holidays at Tours-sur-Marne in France, staying with the Chauvets who ran a small Champagne house, as he always says, 'opposite Laurent Perrier'. His father had been billeted there during the 'Phoney War' and remained friends with Madame Chauvet and Monsieur Paillard. Hilda thought it wise to educate her daughters as Europeans by way of Catholic convents overseas; James somehow missed out, but Julian was lucky and got to fly regularly to Le Bourget in a Dakota and thence to Epernay and the 'Petit Maison'. He learnt much from the Chauvets apart from French: about collecting huge snails along the Marne in the early morning, about *la chasse*, about champagne and about the cyclical and studied way that they lived. Their business was entirely integrated into their daily lives, the standards, such as Pupette's cooking, and routine of which never faltered. French was a doddle therefore. Maths, on the other hand, was torture and the O level eluded him nine times, and this put paid to his ideas of becoming an architect.

To get away from the claustrophobia of home, Julian took to spending time in the lollipop hills on the edge of Dartmoor near Drewsteignton, at Broadmoor Cottage, where lived the father-in-law of his eldest sister Susan. Brigadier Marindin was part of a now vanished rural world peopled by those that had retired from the services and the colonies. They lived in great discomfort but equally great contentment, on tiny pensions. The 'Brig' was endlessly clearing brambles and market gardening, trying his hand at soft fruit production to make a little extra income; he had terrific eyebrows, and had taken a Japanese surrender in Burma. He was a kind of 'Rogue Male'; devoted to his black labrador, he frequently muddled the dog's condemned and dyed mince with his own. Dartmoor was a homecoming for Julian; he felt happier in the honeysuckle-filled lanes and bouldered streams, amid the mossiness and fern-furled, primrose-rich, feral life of Devon.

Antiques and building restoration were a haven for those in the 1960s and 1970s who did not fit into other conventional paths through life and who were prepared to graft and use their guile. Film-making, set-building, painting and decorating, gardening, architecture and photographing landscape and old buildings like Durham

Above: Edwin Smith photographs always offer something new and amazing, like these from *The English Garden*, Thames and Hudson, 1964.

16

Cathedral were what appealed to Julian when he left school. He went to Peru for a year and made a documentary about Benedictine Monks growing bananas there. When he came back he applied to the Ruskin School of Art in Oxford and was accepted but not given a grant. He paid his way by working nights at the Randolph Hotel, and almost certainly by not paying his rent to Cha Bridgewater his landlady in Rawlinson Road, who, along with her entire family, was to come back into our lives later and in a big way. He enjoyed painting in the painting well, meeting Henry Moore who told him he had the hands of a sculptor not a painter, and David Hockney who wore dashing odd socks. But the night-portership took its toll and he drifted into painting and decorating with Derek Richards, a friend from Bristol, while living in Fiztrovia. Some time later he coasted up to Edinburgh which had myriad family connections, getting a job with Richard Demarco at his contemporary art gallery.

Richard Demarco had been instrumental in founding the Fringe at the Edinburgh Festival, starting the Traverse Theatre, where it all began, bringing in artists and developing exhibitions and eventually a gallery there, which then became a separate entity. An extraordinary man, a ticking bomb of energy fuelled by mars bars and flying saucer sweets, open to all ideas and pursuits, the fact that Richard is rarely judgemental leaves him open to the accusation of lacking judgement. But of those who cross his path only a very few do not come away energised and altered by his undiluted passion for life and people. He always placed himself in the centre of a vortex of British and European contemporary art and above all he promoted cultural links with Eastern Europe. During the dim days of the Iron Curtain, he presented artists such as Paul Neagu and Marina Abramović, and organised exhibitions of contemporary Polish, Romanian and Yugoslav art. Julian says: 'Ricci's amazing thing was including a wealth of broad ideas and diverse people, some of whom were maddening, but he was determined that we should all explore the outside world, and it was not about making money.' Richard's involvement with the artist Joseph Beuys led to Julian's working with him and also particularly with Tadeusz Kantor's Cricot 2 theatre group. David Gothard and Julian raised the money to make a huge theatre in the Art College for Kantor and Cricot to perform in the Festival where Beuys had done 'Strategy', and afterwards they took the company with their show to open the new Riverside Studios in Hammersmith to universal critical acclaim. Beuys had a profound understanding of landscape, and a preoccupation with Rannoch Moor where Richard had taken him as he took endless groups round Scotland and Europe.

Right: The Sacro Bosco Gardens of Bomarzo, Viterbo, Italy, commissioned by obsessive Pier Francesco Orsini upon the death of his wife and lost in the 19th and for most of the 20th centuries. The park remains as surprising and seminal as when Julian first climbed in to an overgrown and almost unknown spot in 1968. We attempted to copy these magnificent urns for Arundel in 2008.

Throughout the 1970s, Richard's 'Edinburgh Arts' embarked on a series of journeys 'The Artist as Explorer', starting in Edinburgh. These journeys radiated out across Europe, underpinning the internationalism of this unique Scots-Italian artist's own extraordinary voyage. Julian organised for a polyglot collection of people from all over, from the Kansas City Art Institute to interested bods, painters, writers, actors, to see and do the things which Richard thought were expressions of human artistic endeavour outside the conventional understanding of 'Art'. They travelled from Ħaġar Qim in Malta, to the trulli houses of Puglia, the nuraghe of Sardinia back through the Celtic fringe of Western Europe to Maeshowe in the Orkneys. On one of these trips they sailed a replica of Darwin's 'Beagle' round the coast of Cornwall and Devon. Richard is, among other things, entirely inclusive about everything important, seeing no special merit in academe or the establishment; he is a champion of art outside the gallery, architecture without architects and the 'University under the Tree'. Together with Ian Hamilton Finlay he fought an ongoing battle with the apparatchiks of the Scottish Arts Council from whom he was unable to get funding. Being with Demarco was a remarkable kind of 'Open University' for anyone, and Julian loved it. But when he borrowed five thousand pounds from his father to buy three storeys of derelict building on the Cowgate in Edinburgh's Old Town to live in, he also found himself getting a loan from Allied Brewery and opening Bannerman's Bar. More astonishingly he found himself in possession of a instant success. Opening the first week of the 1980 Edinburgh Festival, the then Director, John Drummond, quickly gravitated there making it his informal HQ along with Sheila Colvin, and stars of stage and screen followed.

For Julian the bar was exhausting, consuming his life utterly and unexpectedly. Luckily he wound up with a beautiful Catalan girlfriend, Isabel Figueras, known as 'Bet', who was doing postgraduate Landscape Architecture at Edinburgh. Like Richard Demarco, Bet shared with Julian her European vision, modernism and internationalism. In landscape and architecture, she introduced him to the ideas of Dan Kiley, Ricardo Bofil, Frank Gehry and Renzo Piano and he introduced her to the British landscape world that he loved, from front gardens to Neolithic barrows and henges. She had only ever been to suburban Surrey and Hampshire and thought England was something of a joke. Bet's grandfather had invented the string bag for oranges and had had a house designed by Gaudi called Casa Figueras. Gaudi and Parc Güell made a huge impression on Julian when they spent time in Barcelona, as did her grandparents' beautiful house on the coast where they picked armfuls of wintersweet flowering in hedgerows in

Above, left: Richard Demarco standing in front of two collage portraits of himself, JB in background.

Above, right: This Robert Smithson Spiral Jetty, Great Salt Lake Utah (mud, precipitated salt crystals and water), is an example of the sort of seventies land art that JB was discovering through Ricci.

Below: Martin Stokes and JB outside The Ivy, 1981.

Above: JB and Bet Figueras.

Below: Standing stones at Avebury and Scorhill, Dartmoor, by David Vicary.

January, and where the pool was a tank carved in Roman times from the limestone hillside. When Dan Kiley came to Edinburgh to give a lecture at the University, Bet and Julian asked him back to Bannerman's Bar afterwards. Born in Boston in 1912, Kiley was one of the greatest landscape architects of the twentieth century along with Russell Page. Together they talked of Kiley's passion for his Morgan car and how he liked to get home in it, following the long ridgeway drive to his house in Connecticut. This drive he had long ago planted with lilac bushes either side so that when they flowered in May it resembled a puffing purple steam train – an image never forgotten by Julian who has a compulsion for lilac. But Bet went back to Barcelona, where she became the preeminent Catalan landscape architect, working on the 1992 Olympics, the Parc de Cervantes and the restaurant elBulli, but most particularly as the landscape architect for the Barcelona Botanical Garden with architects Carlos Ferrater and Josep Lluís Canosa. She was a great teacher, teaching at the Technical School of Architecture in Barcelona and all over Europe, and she was pivotal in opening up Julian's mind to the idea that he could do whatever he wanted to do.

While they were still together what he wanted to do was buy a very derelict place, The Ivy, in Chippenham, Wiltshire. A capricious architectural starlet of a house, built in 1727, it was a Baroque moment of ultimate 'show-off' when the West Country, particularly, had a flowering of crazy mannerist architecture executed by the likes of the Bastard brothers of Blandford and William Halfpenny in Bath and Bristol. It is not known if the latter designed The Ivy but it certainly apes the Italian mannerist swagger of houses he is known to have worked on. It sparked in Julian and, later, me a crush on the formal gardens of England, Holland and France in the seventeenth century, the canals and terraces seen in Kip's bird's-eye engravings, which were heartlessly, ruthlessly rooted out by Capability Brown and his acolytes. Leadless and lightless, The Ivy was boarded up, peeling, mushrooming, and left to crumble in the hope that houses could be built on the land. It appealed to all Julian's natural love of underdog and glamour when Derek Richards took him and Bet to see it. His mother Hilda called him a foolish boy when he chose to keep both the bar and the ruin and was soon struggling up and down the M5 to meetings with English Heritage. Once he was late for an informal meeting with James Lees-Milne; Julian having driven four hundred miles from Edinburgh, the waspish diarist notes that 'not much good would come of that young man'. Jim Lees-Milne was a writer and expert on country houses who worked rescuing houses for the National Trust from 1936 until 1973, and he was brought to The Ivy by David Vicary who became our dearest friend and mentor, and was to open up another university under the tree, or rather in our kitchen.

DV, as he was affectionately known, had turned up at the house in the early days when Julian was camping out in the stables, and he was found unclipping his bicycle clips, bearing the *Daily Mail* and a bottle of 'Val Polly' (Valpolicella) – his favourite tipple. A magical scarecrow of a man, beautifully turned out in his uniform of dark brown alpaca long waistcoat – a sort of subfusc outfit after Doctor Johnson – David had a mop of excellent hair, definitive nose, and wry vivacious eyes. He was always on a riff, streaming with laughter at his own jokes before could get them out, spoke and, even better, wrote in his own onomatopoeic code, and had names for everyone and everything. He had been everywhere and remembered every detail of houses and families and furniture, and he would rail in a giggly way at television costume dramas on frequent postcards sent to Edinburgh: 'My diarghs ... they go to bed at Holkham in Knorrfolk and wake up at seven in Devon! There they are at Saltram on the Plym for breakfast when the night before they were dining on the Wash.' David had been part of the letter-writing fraternity of architectural campaigners who had kept The Ivy from being pulled down. DV introduced us to Candida Lycett Green, who lived in the next door town of Calne and was instrumental in the campaign to save The Ivy amongst many such triumphs; it is she among others whom we have to thank that the three acres we know as Covent Garden was not demolished in the 1970s. DV took the trouble to introduce us to his very dear friend, who he had also mentored, garden designer and writer Rosemary Verey, herself fast becoming a legend in the gardening world at that time, and also to many congenial arty locals. DV thought Julian desperately 'im*pul*sive!' in all his habits from lavish shopping at Sainsbury's to mending The Ivy, saying it was 'so impetuous for the impecunious' to go planting '*two* avenues of lime trees' when there was barely a flushing lavatory on the premises. This was ironic given that DV was living in his own ravaged ruin, stuffed with wonderful things which he would not shed even to get the electricity reconnected. But DV admired and adored Julian for his determination to save the house, and for the fact that, not having the money to do the things that English Heritage required for the provision of grant aid, he just got on with it any way he could, mostly by physically doing it himself and with the help of friends.

In March 1982 I walked into Bannerman's to buy a sausage and in July I caught a train to Chippenham carrying two enormous baskets each containing a brass chandelier which Julian and I had bought together in Paris some weeks earlier. Even with my arms thus extended I fell instantly in love with The Ivy, and its master I had already decided to marry. When we came to live there it was in similar straitened circumstances to DV. We rigged up a bucket with taps, a plug and a waste using a treadle Singer sewing machine with another bucket on the pedal beneath which you threw out the window.

DV suffered from something one can see is a condition like that of Alan Bennett's *Lady in the Van* – which DV read with great joy and amusement: a breakdown of some sort had occurred which made it impossible to start again. But his ability to adapt was

Below, clockwise from top left: Birch House, Gatchina Palace, St. Petersburg, 1780; The cover of Barbara Jones's *Follies and Grottoes* which she wrote and illustrated herself, 1953; La Glacière, Désert De Retz 1781; Peter Snow, 'Homage to Bonnard', 1966; Barbara Jones, design for a lino floor in the entrance hall of Customs and Excise Southend-on-Sea, 1950s.

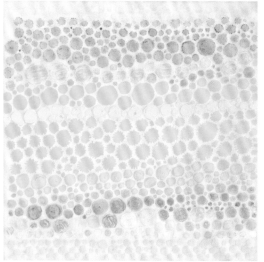

Top: The Ivy, Chippenham, Wiltshire, in state of dereliction in the early 1980s.

Above: Roses in The Ivy's garden and on the drawing room mantelpiece.

phenomenal. His fine sensibilities were untouched and the irony of his rebukes to us – 'get *on*, mend poor Trailing Ivies please!' – was entirely dismissed, despite his living truly like Miss Havisham or worse. His determination was such that he managed, when well into his sixties, to climb into his house through a hole in the bramble thicket outside and thence through the top panel of his front door which had been conveniently smashed in by burglars. He had seen Sissinghurst in its heyday and met Vita – his old friend Ursula Codrington had been literary secretary to Vita, L. P. Hartley and others of that kind. He had bought paintings by Keith Vaughan and John Craxton, and widened our world to include the likes of Angus McBean, Oliver Messel, and Oliver Hill. He taught us to look at everything, from door hinges to saplings and seedpods. As he was mostly without a car – the flashy red BMW that he had permanently 'borrowed' from Rosemary Verey soon had a tree growing through the sun roof – he would get us to take him far and wide to look at houses and gardens – Mapperton, Dixter, Chatsworth – and to then secret and lost places where he had stayed in the past like Erddig, Godolphin and Calke Abbey. Though he died twenty years ago, he is a constant companion as mentor, master, eye-opener and encyclopedia. He was astonishing in the way he led such an observant life, and was such a mine of architectural, horticultural, historical and social knowledge. He taught that nothing is new, nothing is original, and nothing comes wholly formed from the imagination. It is all observed and logged and then drawn on and altered, adapted or amended to a particular situation. Whilst opinion and conviction are essential drivers for the passionate endeavour, for dealing with the world about us, be it visual or political or

whatever, an open mind, curiosity and constant observation are prerequisites for coming up with solutions to the problems we are being asked to solve. Because, as Dan Kiley put it most succinctly: 'The design we are looking for is always in the nature of the problem itself; it is something to be revealed and discovered.'

It is obvious from this story that for us an important part of observation is history. History is a giant story about people, stretching back like a magic carpet taking you into the past, questioning why, how, and how beautifully people, largely nameless people, did things in the past in architecture, agriculture and horticulture, and it is never boring. Understanding the wider story, the culture, the landscape, the painting and sculpture, the stone masonry, the geography and geology, the botany, all the varied ingredients of history are endless. And then there is the natural history aspect of gardens: the ecology, the 'fit and graceful patterns' of nature, culture, pre-history, are not necessarily evident in the gardens one makes, but they are paramount, as everything is informed by them, everywhere. Then there are the plants: a bit like bee-keeping, you can never know enough about plants. The knowledge is endless and endlessly fascinating, the language is beautiful and the business of knowing and growing them is trial, torture and of course hugely rewarding. The ambition is to work with this fertile balance of tensions and naturally create something beautiful; something with soul; that works on many or at least another level. When, as we later describe, Helen Kime burst into tears upon entering the Temple Grove at Highgrove it was a revelation; it showed that something we did was working, that there was an emotional charge there that someone else had caught, that someone else shared our responses to the resonance of the place. Mary Keen writes that 'getting under the skin of a place is what matters'. Understanding the landscape doesn't show in the photographs in this or any other book, but it is a pivotal thing; 'For nature, who abhors mannerism, has set her heart on breaking up all styles and tricks,' says Ralph Waldo Emerson. The vagaries of style and fashion are hard to avoid entirely. Everyone gets caught up in a zeitgeist or a mood, which is often a reaction to the domination of stale old ideas. But it should not be about tricks. Tricks become joyless very quickly. Joy is important, and solid, and timeless. Everyone feels it when they go to the Villa Lante, to Ninfa, to Kyoto or sees a photograph of a place created by Luis Barragán. Julian and I have never been to a Barragán garden but even from poring over photographs one can get his dictum that 'a garden must combine the poetic and the mysterious with serenity and joy' and see that he succeeded. Such places are Himalayas of achievement one can only peer at, ever distant, but striving in that direction in some small way is worth doing.

Gardening is essentially problem solving, and those who do this for a living are very lucky. For us life, gardening and design are about 'doing', about the need to reconcile oneself with one's surroundings, but the fun is in the problem solving. The results must be practical and born of common sense because this makes environmental sense, and usually it makes economic sense too. The practical aspects of design and the search for function are more rewarding than any imaginative flights of fancy. It is far from satisfying to create a thing which does not work on a practical level. For instance, if one introduces a stone object into a lawn, it is just annoying for the person who maintains it if it is so designed that the lawn has to be cut by hand or with a strimmer every week because a mower cannot get right up to the edge of the stone. This is bad design.

We like the kind of dreamy 'left alone' quality that allows the garden and the person in it to be. As Mary Keen says, gardens are places to be in, not things to look at. But Julian and I also like order, we are reasonably tidy and live in an orderly fashion, and we like the detective work and logistical nightmares that make gardening gripping year after year. Energy and stamina are needed in bucketloads. Often a struggle, gardening and bitter graft do have their rewards. They can keep at bay the wolves of melancholy. The endless knock-backs that nature inflicts can help to keep self-pity in perspective. Ambition is frequently thwarted. Jealousy is a constant companion in horticulture, as in many things, but nature offers endless re-inventions and chances to try again. It offers tiny victories, which bolster the soul and help one to deal with all manner of setbacks. Gardening is a many-levelled board game: chance conditions, community-chest budgets,

Opposite: A selection of David Vicary's 1960s photographs inherited by us after his death in 1995, among them an unknown folly, the Pavilion at Westbury Court in Gloucestershire, Wardour near Shaftesbury, Sissinghurst Castle, a thatched folly around a tree in Kent, a French chateau, the front door of Peterstone Farmhouse in Burnham Overy, and Goldolphin House in Cornwall.

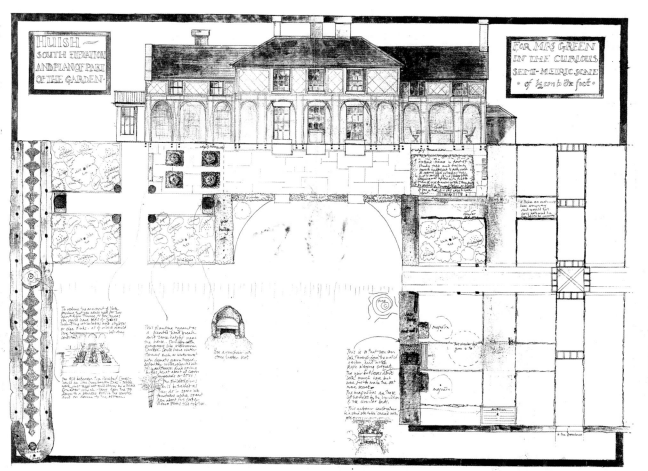

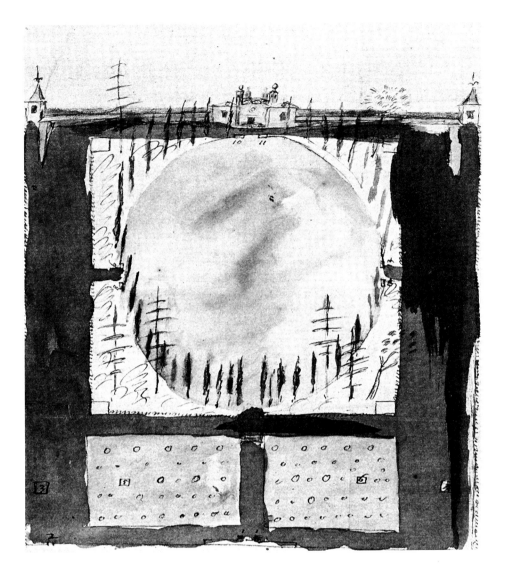

three dimensions, four seasons, twelve hardiness zones, with pestilential snakes and laborious ladders. Kim Wilkie describes landscape as a 'riddle; it changes with every cloud and wood and yet is timeless and stationary'.

This infinity and adventure is all around us, outside the back door or in a London basement area like my father's pot gardening. The point is that you can make a garden that speaks to the soul with no money and in the smallest of spaces. The thing that is important, as Kiley says, is not so called 'design'; it is how you live life, it is life itself, and with luck, if you design things, beauty may be the result, not a preconception. Adventures in gardening can be tiny, as tiny as the thrill of pushing sweet pea seeds into compost in February, but, like Alice, they can make you feel huge.

Leeds Castle and Beginning to Make Things

By the end of the 1980s Julian and I were living at The Ivy. It was marginally modernised, and I had worked in Bath at 'Coexistence' a pioneering retailer of contemporary design and furniture. Meanwhile Julian had cut out the dry rot, dosed both it and himself with terrifying chemicals, tackled the structural problems and leadwork on the roof, found Lee the Tree to electrify the house, plumbed it with my help, and laid out a formal garden. Most of this was subsidised by the building of the 'mounds' to hide the development and new ring road on the edge of the grounds. We were paid for taking in earth which ironically was being dug up to enable the concrete footings of the new houses we were trying to hide to be built. DV was in residence most days and

together we would entertain or be entertained by people he introduced us to, such as Joan Small and her daughters and Simon and Judith Verity and their family. Simon, a virtuoso stone-carver and letter-cutter, and Judith, equally an artist, making lino-cuts and hand-pressing prints and poems, lived in an Arts-and-Crafts school house at Rodbourne nearby. Together we all became fascinated by follies and grottoes. When Simon was asked to decorate a grotto in the belly of a new maze at Leeds Castle in Kent, he put together a team and called upon us to help him decorate a chamber beneath its middle and a tunnel, the underworld, that led from there straight back to the outside world. It was the work of architect Vernon Gibberd, a sort of concrete Pantheon at the centre of the yew maze. Simon was a Puck-like pied piper and his gang for the summer were beautiful, young and very varied, a band of artisans, jewellers, writers, travellers, anarchists, builders and a poet. Many stayed during that summer with us at Horserace House at Sissinghurst, which we had rented from Vanessa, daughter of Ben Nicolson and granddaughter of Harold and Vita. It was deliciously primitive, full of curiosities and almost engulfed in woodland, foxgloves and *Rosa filipes* 'Kiftsgate'. They were fun, feral

Above: The Giant of Warmley, Bristol, part of a fantasy garden built by a brass magnate in the mid-18th century (left); a rustic embrasure with a bench inscribed 'Here loungers linger, here the weary rest', Badminton, Gloucestershire *c.*1750 (right).

Below, from left: Thomas Wright's illustration of the Universe, 1750; Wright's illustration from *Arbours and Grottos*, 1756; an IB pen and ink rendering of the Wright-designed ceiling of the Badminton hermitage – burr elm gothic vaulting with moss infill *c.*1750.

times, living rather rough and dancing round bonfires to the car radio. It was a time of discovery, poking about old grottoes, reading up about them, finding materials – ghost flints in quarries below the Pilgrims' Way, Bristol Diamonds or Mendip Potatoes (geodes full of glitter and agate from the Doulting quarries near Wells) – and the beginning of our rootling about for roots and stumps.

When the grotto and tunnel at Leeds were finished, Julian and I stayed on, building a sort of wooden hermitage clad in all sorts – anthracite, nuts, bark, moss, and sweet chestnut nodules from the park at Knole nearby. Outside this building, which we tucked beneath a very boring timber entrance bridge to the maze, a stair led out – the exit from the maze – between two retaining walls. The whole thing was a bit like the exit to a tube station and together with Simon we suggested to the Trustees of Leeds Castle that we could improve it. We chose to do this by cladding the walls with dead elm tree trunks, burred and bubbled with epicormic growth, which you see in a living tree as masses of 'water shoots' around its base or from a burr which is like a wart on the trunk. We brought these across the country from the spring line above Llanthony Priory behind Hay-on-Wye. In one of life's stranger confluences we had fallen in love with Llanthony partly through reading Bruce Chatwin; staying at the Priory, we had found these dead elm trunks and somehow got into conversation with Colin Passmore, who owned the land there, and persuaded him to let a few fallen heroic trunks go. For generations, in winter, farmers had fed their sheep the bark from these coppiced wych elms when there was nothing else. Then the beetle did for the Elms in the 1970s, since when they had stood in bucolic isolation, bizarrely beautiful, too tough and twisted to rot. One night in October the great storm blew, sending a thunderbolt down the chimney at Horserace, and in the morning the whole of southern England was like a table of spillikens and splintered wood. Just at the moment we became fascinated by all things rustic, several million trees blew over.

Our interest in stumps started with Thomas Wright, the Wizard of Durham (1711–1786), and our fascination with him came from Eileen Harris. Eileen turned up with her equally eminent architectural historian husband, John Harris, to see what was going

Above: A pen and ink sketch of the Badminton hermitage, IB 1989.

on when we were working at Leeds Castle. Our friendship with John and Eileen was to prove formative and encouraging; they call us the 'Grotty People' – a hangover from when we got fed up with being labelled 'Grotto-builders'. The authority on Robert Adam, Eileen is also fascinated by the garden buildings of the eighteenth century, and she was amazed to find that we were making things that looked like the engravings in Wright's *Arbours and Grottos* of 1755. Instrumental in the re-printing by the Scolar Press of a limited edition of facsimile copies of Wright's book, she instantly and very generously gave us a copy. Thomas Wright came from County Durham as did Julian, and there the comparison should probably end. Wright was an astronomer and mathematician who explained to Kant, among others, that the appearance of the Milky Way was 'an optical effect due to our immersion in what locally approximates to a flat layer of stars'. Wright spent much of his life in the houses of aristocrats, particularly in the West Country, inventing gardens and buildings with enormous intelligence and lightness of touch, making musical instruments, designing arbours and grotesque architecture and, sometimes, tutoring the children of the house. Whilst living at Lord Halifax's house at Horton, Northamptonshire, he designed the 'Menagerie', a building which was being rescued in the late 1980s by Gervase Jackson-Stops.

After Horton, Wright took over from William Kent at Badminton, working particularly for the Duchess of Beaufort there, and at Stoke Park in Bristol, finishing the house, drawing up a serpentine garden, designing eye catchers and a cottage orné in the village as well as the most bizarre hermit's cell in the park, still extant. DV had dragged us out to see it, saying '... it looks like an old Gladstone bag dumped in the Park' and with the permission of David Somerset we went on to study the crumbling hovel designed *circa* 1750. It is titled 'Urganda's Cell' on a small gouache in a bedroom at Badminton shown to us by Caroline Somerset. Urganda was an enchantress from the bestselling Chivalric Romance *Amadis of Gaul*. Inside it is a 'salon' but it is clothed in a

Above, from left: Eileen and John Harris in front of the entrance to the tunnel at Wormsley; the concrete 'tube exit', Leeds Castle, Kent, before and after rustic cladding; inside this building, with moss-covered walls and grotesque archways.

Below, from left: 'Pigeonerie Tree', a pen and ink drawing by IB for Andy and Polly Garnett, Cannwood Farm, Somerset, 1990; the finished article, with sheep; Simon Verity, Leeds Castle, 1987.

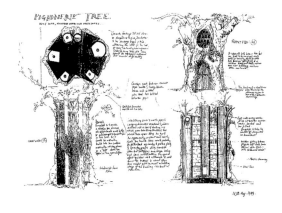  

Above: Grotesque archways at Leeds Castle and the twisting underworld tunnel.

Below: Another living root house sketch, IB 1990.

thatched-log-built exterior and is a very rare survivor of the taste for wooden artifice in the landscape about which Eileen was quietly amassing information. Queen Caroline commissioned William Kent to make the most fabled of these types of building, Merlin's Cave at Richmond Lodge in the 1730s. The Hermit's Cell at Badminton, despite looking like a suitcase on the outside, was once thoroughly sophisticated inside and is the closest thing any of us will ever see to Kent's Merlin's Cave, although much dilapidated, painted over and just lost. The top of the burr-elm table only went missing about forty years ago, although the bubbly elm trunk pedestal remains, with its amazing wooden castors which would have allowed the massive table to be moved aside by servants. There was still evident a box bed, baroquely detailed with rococo shapes in more burrs of elm, the frame to a mirror and a picture which by rubbing we discovered appeared to have had the figure of Urganda presiding over an altar scratched out on the boards. The shutters had burr decoration and the roof was a gothic vault, ribs made from slips of burr elm joined together. Moss had been glued between the ribs and initially it must have been an extraordinary trysting place. Even the floor was made of carefully laid end-on blocks of wood and inscribed with constellations of stars and mathematical formulae in copper-headed pins. Outside at the back is an embrasure with a rustic twig bench inscribed with the same little copper pins laid out to spell 'Here Loungers Linger, Here the Weary Rest'.

We studied the fallen bodies from the great storm whilst researching and talking to Eileen about historic garden buildings made from wood. The artisans who built things like this on estates all over Britain were deeply rooted, powerfully inculcated in the domains that were their world. Woodmen, foresters, gamekeepers, joiners, plasterers, masons all knew their locality inside out and way back through their forbears. They knew the individual trees in the woods and in the parkland – the branches in fact, and what they would one day be useful for, or might be made useful for by the hanging of stones upon them to bend and train them. They coppiced, they wasted nothing and the wood lore that they handed down told them exactly what bit of a tree is good for what purpose. Even today the butt of a shotgun or pistol is made from the densest wood in the heart of the ball of a tree, often a walnut tree, partly for the figuring, but also because, being at the tree's base, its life was spent entirely underground and under pressure from the whole weight of the tree making this bit extraordinarily dense. Thus certain parts of certain species of tree have certain qualities, which those who live among them know and understand. In an oak the 'stag wood', the dense dead fingers that poke at the sky, leafless but not rotten, are known to burn slow and hot like coal. The estate workers who made, for instance, the bark temple at Exton in Rutland, a fragment of which remains today, understood how to make the most durable buildings out of wood. We have only been able to stumble along trying to figure out how they did this by trial and error. After the storm, most upturned roots were very hairy and crumbled into a fibrous compost astonishingly quickly, ash and lime particularly. Oak is longer lasting, but sweet chestnut has a great propeller-like rootstock that, left underground, rots back to the enduring heartwood and makes the most fantastical and seemingly indestructible shapes.

The breakthrough came only shortly before we embarked on the temple grove at Highgrove in 1995, seven years later, when we found Donald McDonald, the head forester on the Cowdray Park Estate, and he led us to our Shangri La, the softwood forests round Midhurst, where immense sweet chestnuts had been felled during the Second World War, their roots left in situ. The woods had been overlaid with fir-tree plantations, but the foresters knew where the sweet chestnuts were. Rootling around with a digger and with Donald, we would find a sort of wooden, mossy fairy island, a wavy slightly elevated shape, the sawn-off stump of what must have been several-hundred-year-old sweet chestnut trees, and, with a flick of the digger bucket a whole starfish of rotted back roots would ease out of the light sandy soil, like a molar at the dentist. They were astonishing things, six or seven feet across sometimes. Our hearts soared as we realised just what we could do with them. They interlocked like children's 'Jacks' or sea defences; you could build with them, you could plant in them, and you could make sort of waves of them with sunken paths between. We were on to something.

Waddesdon Dairy

It was January 1990 when we clambered around the lost, almost buried rock and water garden around the dairy buildings at the bottom of Waddesdon hill with Beth Rothschild. Beth was in her early twenties but already a serious botanist, a graduate of Kew, conservationist and trustee of Botanic Gardens Conservation International. Her father, Lord Rothschild, wanted his children involved at Waddesdon Manor, now part of the Rothschild Foundation, and at Beth's suggestion he invited us to come to look at the 'caves', purportedly made for goats, in the fanciful late-nineteenth-century rock and water garden beside the, now derelict, model dairy. As part of an estate entirely conceived in the French manner, *le style normand*, the dairy was the epitome of this Francophile taste very closely associated with the Rothschild family, a vogue which one might argue originated with the Hameau de la Reine at Versailles built in 1783. Everything at Waddesdon is executed at a level of quality, perfection and bravura, which one can only admire. The ruined rock and water garden had been the height of fashion when it was built a hundred years earlier, and the collection of barns old and new, asbestos and brick, had been the perfect model dairy. In its heyday this had been the final port of call on a tour of the estate: after the collection, the parterres, the aviary, the stables, the Crystal Palace of glasshouses, the acres of kitchen gardens, came the rock garden and finally the dairy and the buttery. Here the pedigree herd of Jersey cows lived in immaculate stalls wearing Meissen name-tags, and guests would be presented with butter pats, stamped with the Rothschild 'Five Arrows' symbol, from the exquisite sunken, marble and tile-lined buttery.

There were old photographs of bedding-out round the buttery and a couple of murky ones of the rock garden, but no plans. The Great War did for this garden and the dairy; the men who had tended it did not return to Buckinghamshire, the glasshouses fell apart, the ponds silted up. In the seventies the sunken paths and canyons were used as a tip for the broken glass, which was bulldozed into the ponds along with dead cows and machinery. It was a sorry mess and nobody could really imagine how delightful it could be made again.

James Pulham and Son was a family firm of landscapers and terracotta-makers in London, and in the second half of the nineteenth century they combined these crafts to make a false rock material, Pulhamite, which would survive outdoors without cracking and laminating as most Portland cement renders do. Pulham's rock faces were extremely real; he gave them little pockets in which to grow ferns and Julian, no lover of this kind of gardening when we set out on this mission, thinks he was clever. When the Waddesdon garden was built, rock gardens were all the rage, lurking in public parks and the houses of the newly wealthy, as at Prior Park in Henley-on-Thames where there is still a mini-Matterhorn and underground caves with lakes. The Rothschilds had a Pulhamite rock garden at Halton as well as Waddesdon. This kind of garden had never been our métier, but Beth was determined to start restoration work and convinced us it would be fun to excavate and work out what was there. And indeed it was. Julian happily embarked on a feast of clearing and archaeology, diggers dug and, with the help of Beth's younger sister Emmy and a small budget from the Alice Trust, we uncovered an elaborate garden worth putting back together. At the same time Lord Rothschild had engaged a fiercely cool architect, Ron Herron and his firm Imagination, to come up with a revolutionary way to resurrect the dairy buildings.

The excavations proved so much fun that everyone got increasingly excited by the project. It was suggested that we produce a proposal for the work to be done, in competition with Clifton Nurseries, and present it at Spencer House, Lord Rothschild's headquarters in London, to a scary 'committee of taste'. The eminent gardener and writer Mary Keen was among them and claims to this day that we might not have won the contract had it not been that it was a very hot day and I was wearing Bermuda shorts. In fact we had simply made the most gigantic effort with our presentation, providing

Opposite: The boathouses at the dairy seen through fronds of *Matteuccia struthiopteris*.

leather-tooled books, collages and using an early version of photoshop to show how things might be, and a video with a voice-over and music. Clifton had assumed that the job belonged to them. More importantly, we produced a fully costed budget for the garden, to which, once awarded the contract, we stuck solidly and successfully.

We started and progressed quickly with the process of reconstructing the garden. Ron Herron meanwhile was also having fun. He settled an imaginary grid over the garden and suggested that we think of it in modular form, two-metre squares at a time. This and his proposals for the dairy buildings everybody found puzzling. One weekend Lord R appeared with interior designer Piers von Westenholz who was advising him on all sorts of projects including this one, and, as always, he was pleased to find us working at weekends so that he could catch up with developments. We walked around the site together discussing ideas and possibilities for the buildings now that the garden was coming back to life. The asbestos had by now been removed from the dairy buildings, while to protect us as we were working in the empty lake the engineers had decreed that a massed concrete abutment be built to stop the dairy buildings from slipping.

Top: An aerial view in 1993, looking north, of the finished dairy building, the boathouses and water garden.

Above, left: An aerial view in 1990, looking south, the derelict dairy building and water garden mid-restoration.

Above, right: A c.1900 photograph of the garden and buttery.

Opposite, top: The buttery garden box cubes and balls in Jim Keeling pots with 'Five Arrows' insignia.

Opposite, bottom: The dairy inner courtyard espalier pear trees and ivy clipped in a diamond pattern.

Previous pages: The dairy on the left, with an added oak balcony to Lord Rothschild's office upstairs, and the buttery and box garden on the right, in spring.

Above: The internal courtyard, showing the entirely new western wing with the central porter's lodge and loggias either side.

Right: Simple squares of grass in the courtyard; the 'Five Arrows' glass door is open on the left.

Opposite, top: The boathouse with dining table (left); ivy softens the waterside steps (right).

Opposite, bottom: Seen from across the water, the steps with ivy risers, planted pots and the roof with diaper-work tiling in the *style normand* (left); the loggia with vines (right).

It was a monumental piece of civil engineering in the water garden, and we all called it 'Queen Mary Dock'. But repairs to the main buildings and new extensions had not even approached the planning application stage.

The approach we suggested for the derelict buildings was to get on and restore them, saving everything possible and extending them to make a workable space in the same majestically detailed style, but with modern functionality. By adding a fourth side to the 'u' of buildings a porter's lodge could be made at the entrance, and a kitchen, and the resulting private inner courtyard could be used for glamorous entertaining. To the side we suggested a 'Winter Garden' and to the lakeside a boathouse for outdoor eating under cover. Piers just said to Lord Rothschild 'Why don't *they* do it?' Having worked for eighteen months with Beth and Fabia Sturridge we knew how Waddesdon worked, had won some spurs, and now unexpectedly we found ourselves commissioned to design the dairy buildings as Lord Rothschild's office and a gathering place.

A garden or building is only as good as the client who commissions and backs it in the end. Lord Rothschild's faith in our abilities when he asked us to carry out our ideas first in the garden and then with the dairy itself has never ceased to amaze us. We tested his patience often, but it paid off, and through his own efforts and intense commitment he got something 'really good'; which, as designer David Mlinaric said, he always does. The building has won many awards including a Europa Nostra Award in 1994.

We employed an architect friend from Edinburgh days, Rory Duncan, and Pauline who was masquerading as our nanny at the time but was a fully fledged architect from New Zealand, and we installed them in the gardener's cottage, which became the site office. The dairy is hardly an agricultural building; it is, instead, a mass of intricate detail, all of it important and which we strived to preserve – tuck pointing, Honduras pitch pine sarking and rafters which had to be brought up to 'regs' standards – and we fought the planners to save the cast-iron ventilated 'cow' grilles as windows rather than replacing

Inside the drawing's title block:

BANNERMAN
THE IVY
CHIPPENHAM
WILTSHIRE
SN15 2AE
CLIENT
LORD
ROTHSCHILD
44 ST JAMES'S
PLACE
LONDON SW1A 1NP
JOB TITLE
WADDESDON
DAIRY
WATER & ROCK
GARDENS
DRAWN SCALE
JH   1:200
DWG NO DATE
WD/2 6/01 JUNE 00
DRAWING TITLE

them with timber framed windows. We were allowed to experiment and flex some design muscles, making doors from 'planks' of bevelled glass held together with great bronze hinges in a form which made oblique reference to the Rothschild crest of 'Five Arrows' which appears everywhere throughout the Manor and the village of Waddesdon; even the pub is called the 'Five Arrows'. It is a reference to the five sons of Mayer Amschel Rothschild who set out from Frankfurt to make their fortunes in the capitals of Europe. We experimented with heating and insulation, which was a huge problem in an agricultural building whose georgic roots we wanted to maintain. Using a high Ancaster-stone dado we created 'under-floor' heating but up the wall, and we also ran all the services and communications behind the stone skirting which made them easy to access and alter. To this we added huge slab Ancaster-stone and wide elm-boarded floors. We designed lights and desks, and every detail had to be of the highest quality and finish. With the help of my mother's cousin, the architect Philip Jebb, we worked out how to have two fireplaces in one long room and get both of them to work.

The design for the formal garden round the buttery was very simple: rectangular box-edged beds and green lawn, with box balls in pots centred on stepped, square plattes of box. Sadly the box succumbed to blight and has been removed. The central courtyard

Above: The plan showing the water garden, Ron Herron's grid and various tented structures.

Opposite, top: *Rheum palmatum* (left); wisteria on the rock bridge above the water (right).

Opposite, bottom: An archway of real rock, with honeysuckle and *Rosa* 'Félicité Perpétue' (left); a cascade of Pulhamite rock, *c*.1890, with philadelphus, *Rosa* 'Rambling Rector', white valerian and ferns.

was also calm and understated: a lawn intersected with cross paths surrounded by box-edged beds, with espalier pear trees on some walls and diamond patterns of clipped ivy on the other, echoing the Normandy patterns of diaper brickwork and tiles on the roof. Giant steps with ivy-covered risers softened the sheer walls of Queen Mary Dock, which meant that the terrace felt more connected to the water and people can sit on the steps and enjoy the garden. The informal rock and water garden has certainly gone the way we intended – wild and Robinsonian. The Victorian style of the Pulhamite rock garden was fascinating but uncongenial to the level of labour available in the late twentieth century and to the aesthetics of today. Whilst the newly uncovered rocks were to be naturalised with special tiny ferns in the pockets provided by Pulham, the cascades made to flow again and wisteria to hang over the arches, it was agreed that the whole garden could afford to feel more of a lost domain, spangled with wild flowers and bulbs, a wild garden on steroids, mysterious, rich in planting such as ferns, hellebores, fritillaries and martagon lilies. It would be scented at dusk with lilac, philadelphus (one of the only survivals from the original planting) and *Primula florindae*. Mary Keen continued to be on the committee of taste and became a good friend and ally, and Sue Dickinson, the world-class head gardener at Eythrope, Lord Rothschild's private garden, helped enormously with her knowledge, advice, encouragement and support. They both, like us, felt that what was needed was excellence and rarity, enough of any variety of plant to make an impact and draw gasps, and also something of the spirit of Ninfa, the historic Italian garden of ruins and water. We all wanted it to have rampant rambling roses growing up the trees and hanging over the water, drifting myrrh across the lake, which now, twenty-five years later, they really do.

Above: JB mending the Pulhamite cascade.

Right: *Rosa* 'Hillieri' on top of the rock face.

Wormsley

Wormsley, the house and the garden, was the 'Beaux stratagem' of Christopher Gibbs who set himself the mission of finding a country hideaway near enough to London in which his friend and client Paul Getty could house both his family and his extraordinary library. Set in a long deeply engraved crack in the chalk of the Chilterns, barely forty miles from Hyde Park Corner, it was the seat of the regicide Adrian Scrope and, by descent from the end of the seventeenth century, the Fane family, whose fortunes waxed and waned there until 1986. Christopher suggested to Paul and Victoria that they buy the then deliciously crumbly estate, and then masterminded the entire restoration with an array of notables: Nicholas Johnston was chief architect; Penelope Hobhouse designed the walled garden; and Chester Jones and David Mlinaric designed indoors, along with Jane Rainey, chief amanuensis to Christopher himself. Circumventing many complications that circumstances threw up, mostly to do with safety and security for the family, the team conjured a vibrant, eclectic world and we were lucky enough to play a very small part and sometimes hang around backstage. Julian and I were talking recently about the fact that there are people whom you spend a lifetime trying to please, and Christopher is one of them. When his eye glints and he takes a mint from you and sucks it smiling, remembering the days when we all smoked Rothmans, the world lights up. He has been our chief antiquarian mentor along with David Vicary and John and Eileen Harris, and a minder too, opening up a continent of curiosities, erudition, intuition, religion and sedition. He is both patrician and tactician, a man of vision and mission, a magician, a magus, a Merlin, and a Gandalf.

Christopher lent us his copy of *A descriptive account of the mansion and gardens of White-Knights: a seat of His Grace the Duke of Marlborough. By Mrs. Hofland. Illustrated with twenty-three engravings, from pictures taken on the spot by T.C. Hofland. 1819.* Commissioned by the Marquess of Blandford, but never paid for, this is a record of a now-lost garden in Reading. The Hoflands were a husband-and-wife alliance, later to be asked to do the same for his museum by Sir John Soane. Christopher suggested that we imagined such a garden at Wormsley. Christopher had no idea where it would lead, but at worst it would live in great company in the Getty library and an idea or two might just tickle Paul's fancy. We wrote and illustrated in indelible ink on rag paper a fantasy of follies and grottoes, water tricks, towers and kiosks. These ideas were intended to link the whole estate together in a coherent way, using treats to find and places to go. They were appreciated but not immediately taken up. We were asked instead to design a satellite tower, an eye-catcher on the high horizon in which to hide huge satellite dishes. Surveillance was everywhere on the estate, understandably; cables deer could not cross without setting off alarms, cameras menacing in glass globes amongst the shrubberies.

Opposite: The Campo Santo in the beech woods.

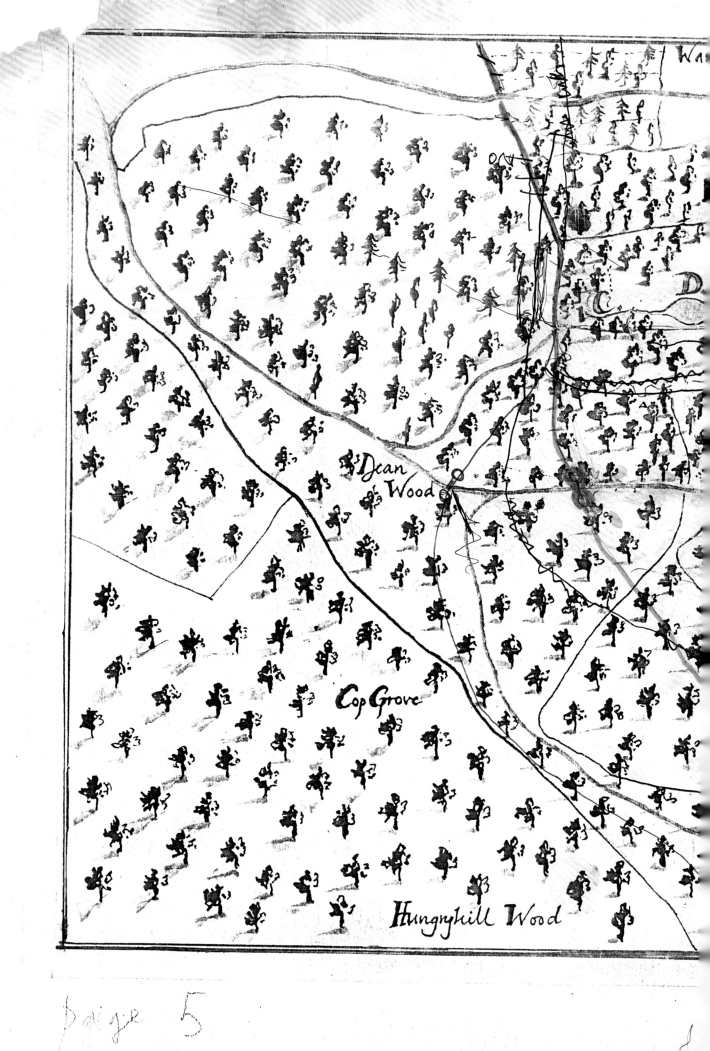

Dean Wood

Cop Grove

Hungryhill Wood

Wa

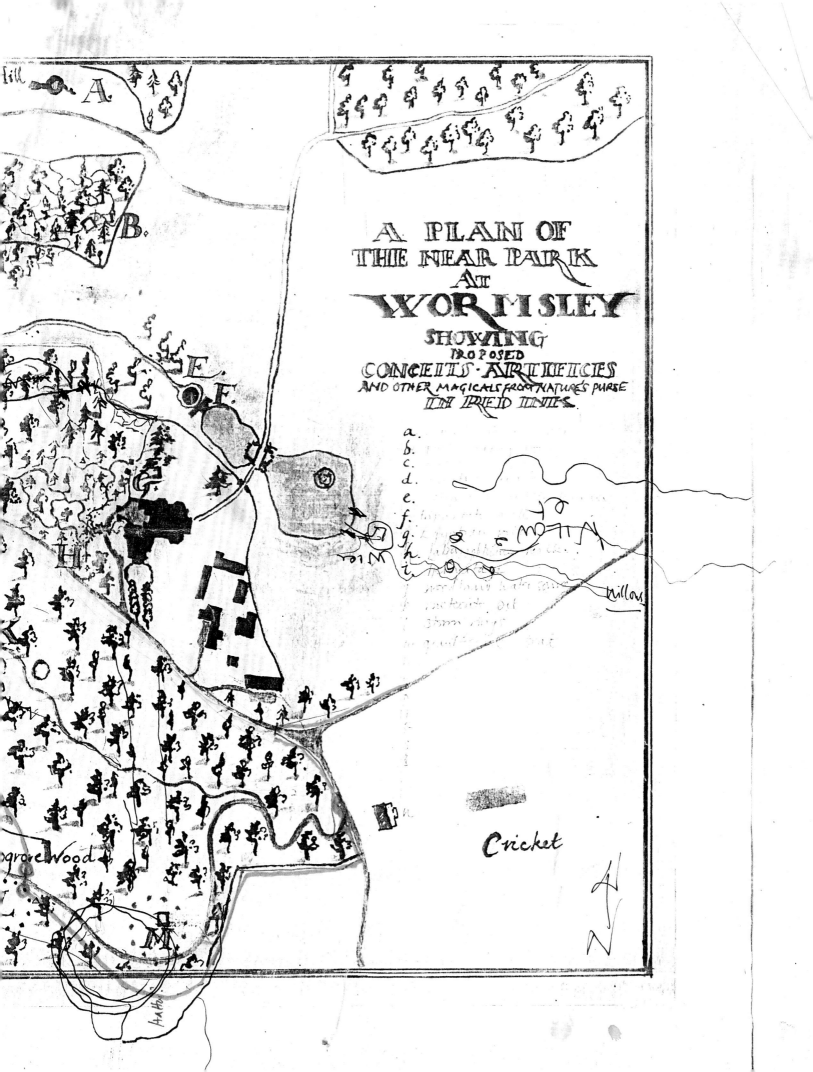

A PLAN OF
THE NEAR PARK
AT
WORMSLEY
SHOWING
PROPOSED
CONCEITS · ARTIFICES
AND OTHER MAGICALS FROM NATURE'S PURSE
IN FREED TIMES

a.
b.
c.
d.
e.
f.
g.
h.
i.

Cricket

Willow

SECTION NORTH-SOUTH

The tower came to nothing. Security swallowed up budgets and attention. Christopher counselled patience; it was always difficult to get decisions made about exciting things when there were so many horrors to contend with. Asked to help with the deer fencing, we drew up details for kissing gates, car gates, junctions with ha-has, cattle grids and horse gates, and we masterminded miles of high park railing to keep special deer in and rogue deer out. We then helped to re-configure the island on the lake, conceived by Christopher along with the ha-ha and an excellent Sarsen stone bridge. A Silbury Hill or New College Mount, this island had never quite worked or pleased anybody and, as it turned out, neither did our efforts. In the shortening, frost bitten days of November one year, we set up a bailey bridge and moved heavy plant across the water with which to scrape a large part of the mound away. We thickly planted holm oaks and hazels for Squirrel Nutkins to visit on their rafts. We scattered some Norman stone tombs from Ireland, found by Robert Kime, and put up a terrific Tudor fireplace with the intention of suggesting some long-gone chapel or hermit's cell, and also to encourage a bit of fire-building and sausage-roasting.

The grand plan of our book was never going to happen, but fate colluded to bring us in on something necessary and extraordinary. Wormsley is folded into the light-filled beech woods that are a feature of the Chilterns; high vaulted, in spring their leaves are underwater vivid and their feet bluebell flooded. We prepared to build a lightweight, twiggy, rustic, bridge over the drive which swooped round the back of the house, as Christopher wanted people to walk out from the house to all this beauty, but the cutting made it impossible to step out from the library by the little turret stair and walk up into the woodland. Fire engines, the vans of service engineers, security men, librarians, distinguished antiquarians, above all Paul and Victoria's barouche passed through this passage, carved as though through pack ice, to get to the back door. It was a hundred yards long and fifteen yards high in places. That winter was plagued by particularly damaging frosts and in spring chunks of clunch (soft limestone) the size of chest freezers were loosed from its cliff sides, landing on the tarmac below. We were summoned to the site, and everybody looked anxious. The twiggy bridge was clearly not going to happen; something more along civil engineering lines was called for. With sang froid Julian picked up a piece of the offending chalk and began to draw, like a Silk-Cut-smoking Galileo describing the planets, upon the tarmac. Everybody had twigged that what was needed was a reinforced tunnel, but his vision of a tunnel was a Piranesi tunnel, or the tunnel at Pozzuoli by the tomb of Virgil. It could be monumental, but to stop it being oppressive, it should be 'derelict', its barrel vault holed to the sky, jagged gapes letting light shaft down upon a tightly laid limestone floor below. Strands of ivy could tendril through the holes and, as Christopher added, ash saplings, nuts and holm oaks could cling to its mortar.

By the summer the tunnel had been engineered – very seriously, as at first it was thought it impossible, but the structural engineer David Osborne came up with something bomb-proof and durable. The ex-SAS security firm was worried that insurgents might gather in the grotto on top, but more cameras and cables could be laid to prevent this and little by little a plan was devised, planning permission granted, and a budget teased out of these complexities. The tunnel was to be made of water-washed limestone, sometimes called tufa. But 'tufa' is a mercurial word, often erroneously attributed to limestone of varied properties. Technically it is a porous rock composed of calcium carbonate and formed by precipitation from water, e.g. around mineral springs. This true tufa is extraordinarily light and, unnaturally strong for its density; it was used by medieval master masons in the critical parts of fan vaulting. It is almost impossible to get at present. But often the term is also used to described water-washed limestone, or 'holey stone', which generally comes from the top layers of a limestone quarry, and is heavy. The holes may be rattled out by little stones in a vortex of water. Worm eaten or 'vermiculated', it has been greatly prized for millennia. In China they call specimens 'Scholar Stones', and they were used in seventeenth-century gardens such as Suzhou. In England in the eighteenth century their use in grottos, as faux cromlechs or megalithic structures and as standing stones, was executed most effectively by the Joseph and Josiah Lane at Wardour and by Thomas Wright amongst others.

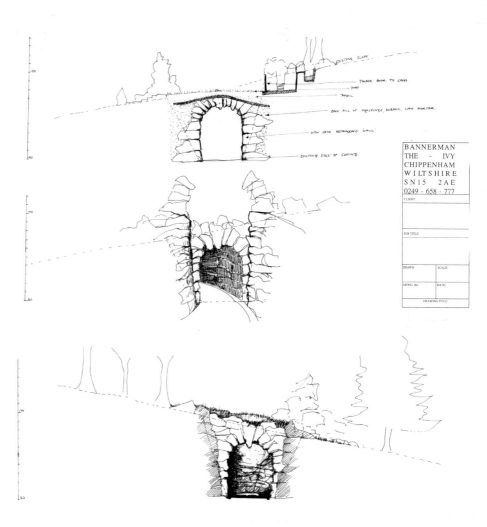

EXISTING SLOPE

TIMBER DOOR TO CRYPT

TURF

TOPSOIL

BACK FILL OF SCALPINGS, SUBSOIL, LIME MORTAR.

NEW LIME RETAINING WALL

EXISTING EDGE OF CUTTING.

BANNERMAN
THE - IVY
CHIPPENHAM
WILTSHIRE
SN15 2AE
0249 - 658 - 777

CLIENT

JOB TITLE

DRAWN   SCALE:

DRWG. No: DATE:

DRAWING TITLE:

Above: IB's 1990 charcoal sketch for
the entrance to the tunnel based on
Thomas Wright's mid-18th-century
Belvedere in Ireland (left); a Piranesi
engraving of ruined vaults, mid-18th
century (right).

Opposite, top: A model of a rustic
bridge over the back drive; made of
polystyrene, popcorn and yew roots,
1990.

Opposite, bottom left: The arch and
tunnel through to the Bay of Naples
from the Park of the Tomb of Virgil.

Opposite, bottom right: Pen and
ink sketches, elevations and
sections for the proposed tunnel at
Wormsley, 1990.

Wright, the Wizard of Durham, has somehow been a companion to us all along
this road. The front façade of the tunnel is very strongly influenced by his extraordinary
building at Belvedere in Ireland, which we had visited with the Harrises on a tour of grottos
and follies of Ireland. This trip had been instigated by the Knight of Glin, who asked us to
visit him at Glin Castle in 1988 and for whom we made a model of a little gothic Belvedere
to look out over the castle to the River Shannon. Finding materials, be it stumps or curious
stones or crystals, is always a problem, and a growing one. It is more difficult than ever to
obtain English curiosities such as ammonites – 'Dragonstones' before people knew what
fossils were – which we try to use in every job we do. Where Alexander Pope was able to fire
a musket at the stalactites in Wookey Hole and take them home with him, we are not even
permitted to pick up pebbles from the beach, for reasonably good reasons. Small quarries
are increasingly uneconomic and often bought up and then closed by monopolies, although
seemingly less so on the continent. To find the quantity of water-washed limestone to build
the tunnel required a miracle – quantifying how much we would need was a greater trial.
But we felt that to have built it in cut stone would have been next to pointless, and as prosaic
as building a fake Victorian railway tunnel. It would have been much simpler to make it
with flint but there was already rather a lot of that, and we ploughed on with water-washed
limestone from the continent.

Curiously the tunnel did gain an intimate connection to Victorian railways: the base
stones, which form a sort of skirting to the sides and the steps over the top, we made
from what it transpired were the very first sleepers on the first ever line from London to
Birmingham. Our digger man, Pete, who had worked also on Waddesdon, found these
square pads of a hard gritstone, which had been set on the diamond every few feet to hold
down the tracks, dumped exactly where they had been left when superseded by the new
wooden beam sleepers which joined the tracks to each other and hence were infinitely more
stable. Pete had been asked to get rid of them from the trackside near Aylesbury just as we
came along looking for materials. By some other miracle, a source of 'holey stone' – 'anti-
deluvian' stone as it was known in the eighteenth century – materialised as we drove up
the M5 near Bridgwater one day. We spotted from the motorway metal cages and pallets
of highly desirable giant lumps of this limestone in an industrial estate. Upon investigation
it turned out it was possible to purchase this stone, originating in Spain. Not only that,
there were great big natural keystones and voussoirs (curved stones for arches) with flat
backs which could be joined as if by the hand of nature into 'natural'-looking architecture.
This naturalness had been important in the movement epitomised by Thomas Wright and
William Kent who were entranced by ideas, like Rousseau, of a Golden Age when savage
men made beautiful things without artifice – almost as if 'dame nature', wrote Wright, had
made them herself. The stone was duly tested by the engineers for integral strength and
stability and at last, at considerable cost, 'artic' loads began to pour in from the continent. It

was almost impossible to predict how much stone would be needed. Having given a fixed price to design and build the tunnel, the real difficulty we encountered was building up the side of the open holes in the roof to the level of the landscaping and planting that was going over the top. Had we just built a tunnel it would have been relatively easy; it was building a ruined tunnel that nearly ruined us. Over a field of eight acres every stone was laid out and moved about like a jigsaw puzzle, each piece selected for its position in the arc of voussoirs either end, and other strategic architectural details. Then each stone was carried by forklift about half a mile and fed to the lorry with the hiab crane at the tunnel face which placed each on top of the last. Each stone had to be drilled more than once with a big drill, the resulting hole 'puffed' with a big puffer to remove the dust from said hole, and then filled with epoxy resin which glued in giant steel staples which could then be clamped into place and connected with the steel reinforcing and the whole thing buried nightly in a sludge of concrete. To build the reinforced concrete sub-structure, steel erectors would knit the steel cages behind the façade each day whilst Julian and his team placed the stones studded with staples artfully and then tied them in to the reinforcing after the stones acted as shuttering. At the end of each day, concrete would be pumped in and riddled to remove air pockets. By this means the sides rose all along the tunnel, until they had reached the springing point (the level where the vaulted roof was to begin). Then a vast scaffold was erected between the straight-sided walls the entire length of the barrel vault, and a former, made from plywood, was constructed to take the weight of the stone of the vault, and its complicated holes, until it too was all locked in with epoxy and steel rebar (reinforcing steel bars) backed with concrete. Everywhere the concrete had to be stopped from slipping through any holes and going where it was not wanted. The sides of the open 'chimneys' of the holes had to be built up in a different way, so that they looked natural, collapsed but rigidly safe.

The relief on our faces in the photograph taken the day the shuttering was first unpicked months later, when the whole thing stayed up, is tangible, and the feeling must have been very similar for medieval masons when building fan vaults, only they were more skilled and infinitely more knowledgeable and they didn't have any hydraulic lifting gear. After that there was only the road to make by hand, the ammonite archway at the top over the stone steps leading to the other side and the planting – ferns, ash saplings, ivy, primroses, cowslips, rambling roses, valerian and acanthus – to be done. The road has a camber, a swollen central belly of cross-laid limestone, and beautiful gullies flanking each side: the same stone only smaller and running lengthways. The stone was from the last surface workings at Langton Matravers near Corfe Castle, where Dickensian characters maintain their rights to quarry the top, hard, non-friable layer of Portland stone, which made the most durable, long, thin cobbles; our quarryman was head of the Parish Council. They chopped it to length with a guillotine, but it came up out of the ground in laminated slices like walling stone but frost-proof. It was laid for the same price as tarmacadam.

More than ten years later we built what Christopher called the 'Campo Santo'. By then Victoria and Paul were truly ensconced. After so much effort the deluge of builders had ebbed away, re-introduced red kites were wheeling over the Chilterns and down on Paul's cricket pitch leather was cracking on willow. Invited to the odd cricket match we were lucky enough to dine with former archbishops and several heads of the SAS. We added and altered the planting round the back of the house and the top of the tunnel, creating spring drifts of the smell of hot-cross buns from *Ribes odoratum*, *Viburnum × carlcephalum*, and summery mounds of scented lilac and philadelphus outside the library. Underneath these, the mossy ground and rocks were jewelled as a book of hours, with primroses, cowslips, snowdrops and fritillaries. Hellebores, ferns and white periwinkle lapped and lurked about in hollows, steps and 'cavey' places. Paul's son Mark Getty took friends to see the tunnel, and he expressed a love of the long tresses of ivy that were beginning to hang like drapes through the holes in the vault. These days they brush the stone pavement thirty foot below.

Christopher thought it might be time to make the foray into the bosom of the woodland, as envisaged in our original book. He moved a statue of Hecate, which he'd originally found in Rome, from a place near the house and asked us to dream up a confection. Hecate is a Greek goddess depicted in triple form. She was variously associated with crossroads,

Opposite, top left: Working on the tunnel (above); the completed roadway in Portland stone (below).

Opposite, top right: The tunnel entrance, cobbled road and flint library.

Opposite, bottom: The back entrance to the tunnel, retaining walls, digger and crane placing vault stones.

entrance-ways, dogs, light, the moon, magic, witchcraft, sorcery, and necromancy. Worshipped in Athenian households as a protective goddess and one who bestowed prosperity and daily blessings on the family, she also closely parallels the Roman goddess Trivia. She is usually depicted, as in this case, with three heads facing three ways, a clever choice for the beginning of the adventures in the woodland. We pushed back into the hillside opposite the library and built a recess with a basin of limestone into which water gurgled via three bearded male heads, eighteenth-century river god keystones with a curiously 'hippy' look to them. Either side, a pair of simple curved stone staircases curled round and took one up to where Hecate broods over the fountain. A strong presence, she presides above all this facing east to the castle and library, her dog's nose pointing to mysterious paths through the woodland. With Victoria's encouragement we produced some ideas for things to go to in the woodland, and ways to visit her collection of fowl and her pigs. It was around about the time of Paul's seventieth birthday, a lunch of steak and kidney pie and a medley of wonderful and eccentric friends. At a loss for a present we gave him seventy little oak seedlings in a box, which we had grown from acorns picked from the veteran oak at Hanham Court, a tree under which James II had dined on venison in an act of reconciliation with the owners following a misunderstanding during the Monmouth Rebellion. Most oddly, in the way of a John Aubrey *aperçu*, on the night that Diana Princess of Wales had crashed in a tunnel in Paris, this hollowed-out husk of an oak, blew over on to its side and finally died, though there was not a whisper of wind.

The design of the Campo Santo was a development of the Stumpery at Highgrove, and of an idea which we had originally suggested to Simon Sainsbury. We made what is our favourite model of it, in paper and ink. Our scheme was a hub in the woods, a rustic space-lab with exits leading out through the wild wood to places of interest. Henges, such as the wooden Seahenge uncovered on the beach near Hunstanton in 1999 when we were in Norfolk, Maeshowe on Orkney, Ħaġar Qim on Malta, and all the Richard Demarco 'Road to Meikle Seggie' land art and Neolithic trail coalesced in this work. Some understanding of this in Paul and Victoria also coalesced. Paul watched from the tall windows of the first-floor long landing as we toiled and moiled on the hill above the back of the house. He became gripped by the strange processes which Robert Hibberd and Julian used to put together a kind of wooden 'Lego' using a 'telehandler' – a machine that effectively gives you giant fingers – moving heaps of sweet chestnut stumps and the three-metre curved 'oven chips' made of oak, which formed the skeleton structure. It was by turns terrifying and electrifying. Working in massive pieces of oak is not child's play, and the steeply sloping site meant colossal excavation, masses of chalk bulking up four-fold, greasy in the rain, getting everywhere, then mass concrete ensuring the whole thing would not slide down the hill with a 'whoosh'. In the spring sunlight we lay on our bellies planting up the entire hillside to the west of the house with snowdrops and pheasant's eye and little native narcissi in tens of thousands. The paths and the stumps which marked the paths we delineated and punctuated with hart's tongue ferns, king ferns and queen ferns, *Polystichum munitum* and *Dryopteris × complexa* 'Stablerae'. The arched banks skirting the henge we spangled with ten thousand primrose plugs, and inside the holy of holies we fashioned beds of roots set about with hellebores and martagon lilies. We sat with Paul on the landing and looked out of the windows at it all, and he said that he loved it, and that he would love to continue further into the woods and round into the park with some more of the ridiculous fancies contained in the book. A week or so later we were working in the West Indies when we learnt of Paul's death from a creepy phone call from some journalist asking if we had anything to say about it.

Back at Wormsley Victoria asked us to decorate the grave, which they had agreed should be in the Campo Santo beneath the obelisk. On the day, everyone stood about among the roots and branches in the pale light and late spring chill, the family, friends, his greatest friend Christopher, John Mortimer in his wheelchair, the great and the good, whilst the 'mechanicals' shovelled chalk back into the ground, which Julian had lined out with moss threaded with rosemary and hellebores. He placed a packet of cigarettes and a cricket ball at one end. Ashes to ashes, dust to dust.

Opposite: Constructing the Campo Santo.

Top: The paper, pen and ink model of
the Campo Santo, IB 2002.

Above: JB under an old beech tree.

Right: Steps up to the tufa and
ammonite arch, with the Hecate
fountain beyond.

Opposite: A root screen and
inscription from Chaucer's *The
Knight's Tale*.

Overleaf: The finished Campo Santo
with roots and ferns.

Chelsea '94

Possibly the most nerve-wracking job of all was the first Chelsea Flower Show garden that we did with Clifton Nurseries for Lord Rothschild, building and planting a bit of the Waddesdon dairy rock garden. This was followed closely by our second Chelsea garden, designed for *The Daily Telegraph* in 1994. Max Hastings, the *Telegraph*'s editor, approached us in his jovial way at the end of the 1993 Flower Show when we were going home exhausted to face moving house in August, with two tiny boys and another on the way. Our new house, Hanham Court, appeared then as a kind of Gormenghast: medieval, monumental, grey, cold, filthy, and nothing worked. Five days after we moved in the third boy was born and a couple of days later Julian went to see Max at Canary Wharf having thought up an idea for the garden and found the key element, a veteran mulberry tree. The idea of inventing a town garden in an imagined cathedral city came instantly, an amalgamation of the new house – a tumble-down monastic settlement on the 'shed-land' eastern edge of Bristol – and Julian's teenage home, a small Georgian town house in Wells, Somerset, which has a long, thin, walled back garden with an ancient mulberry tree. All we needed then was a mature mulberry tree, massive topiary and some walls speckled with medieval fragments or made of real gothic ruins. Max perhaps did not see the essential difficulties and luckily he liked the idea. The vision was very 'Barchester' and drawn from real nineteenth-century natural historians, deans and canons, such as Canon Ellacombe, who wrote a gardening classic *In a Gloucestershire Garden*. Ellacombe presided over the tiny chapel of ease, as it then was, at Hanham Court, our new house, as it was within his parish, that of Bitton in Gloucestershire to the west of Bath on the Roman Via Julia. He had the most wonderful life: he was a cleric who wrote a gardening column for some fifty years and he catalogued all the wild flowers that he found within the parish boundaries. Educated clergymen of this period were some of the pioneers in natural science, sometimes creating delightful museums filled with collections of fossils and minerals, bones, stuffed birds, eggs, shells and jam jars of wild flowers, such as the one in Wells that bewitched the bored teenage Julian. Wells is Julian's loadstone of proper life from this Museum to the Swan Hotel and the worn-down Chapter House steps that he and Candida campaigned successfully to prevent from being 'restored'. All this he wanted to encapsulate in a Chelsea garden, his vision of a way of life still visibly connected with the world of Chaucer.

The flower show is also a part of something very specific to our culture and history; although increasingly tawdry it remains almost Chaucerian and it was fascinating to be part of this 'Showman's' show with all its foibles and itinerant dynamics, the pinnacle of the horticultural year for those that exhibit there, especially in the 'tent'. Being part of it was like being part of a greyhound meet or a circus: three spring weeks of mayhem, tears and tribulations, bitter rivalry and hearty camaraderie. In the early 1990s it was still fairly relaxed, not so much about celebrity and not as bureaucratic or safety conscious as it has had to become. We found a fifty-year-old mulberry tree in a field near Keynsham when driving back with the children from a Sunday with Julian's ancient parents in Wells where they lived. Ruskins, tree movers of Essex, with all the artfulness that that implies, were employed to excavate around the base about two metres out from the trunk and then pull a wire underneath, thereby cutting all the roots. After that a giant 'root ball' was created using chain link fence and hessian pulled through from one side to the other, wrapped round and tightened, enmeshing the fibrous roots and soil. This travelled up the M4 on a lorry, and with an immense amount of effort it was planted in our patch in the Royal Hospital grounds. Not a leaf was out. All the mulberries in London, even those right there in Chelsea Hospital, were in full leaf. Everyone thought ours was dead. It looked dead. On the advice of Sue Dickinson, the peerless head gardener at Eythrope, we built a greenhouse around it, using scaffolding and clear plastic, and sprayed it daily with a fine mist. Outside the greenhouse it was raining cats and dogs most of the time.

Opposite: Isabel planting pinks.

However, it was a bit warmer for the mulberry inside. Eventually the sun came out. In the humid baking heat, tempers shortened as the show's opening approached, but eventually the leaves lengthened and unfurled.

We had prepared all the stone elements in a yard in Bath during March and April during one of those early spring heat waves. Finding the bits of stone to make the garden had been another miracle. The tracery window was relatively easy to find among the many nineteenth-century inner-city churches that were being demolished and sent to Japan via the reclamation trade at the time, and the summer-house turned up in the trade. From Walcot Reclamation we bought a twelve-foot-tall stone 'crocket' finial for the garden, and someone there suggested that we call in on the Salisbury Cathedral stone yard. Salisbury is built of Chilmark stone, one of the softest most friable of the limestones that you could have the misfortune to use to build a cathedral. It melts, particularly under the acid rain of the 1970s, but even in Turner's day the spire was a vertical meadow of valerian plants all happily rooted in its stonework. The masons yard at Salisbury is full of sucked-up and spat-out sweeties of medieval carved fragments, and – the *Telegraph* having provided a large donation for the Restoration fund – with the help of the masons working on the cathedral, we managed to make a frieze and a balustrade course from the pieces that were to be replaced, which we incorporated with old brick to make the walls of the garden.

Three weeks from starting on our corner site, a patch of grass with a fenced-off horse chestnut tree in the middle of it, with our team of three Bath masons and a Buckinghamshire labourer, we completed it in time and were all pleased with the final concoction. The plants came from a nurseryman in Suffolk who was not particularly taken either with the design or the designers. The planting plan was an old-fashioned cottagey mix, with two huge pieces of yew topiary, a lawn, the wretched enclosure for the horse chestnut woven into the plan and beds against the walls on two sides with the Bath-stone summer-house in the elbow. The mood of the planting was drawn from mouth-watering, turn-of-the-century illustrations, by Helen Allingham and others,

Previous pages: A simple cut-out elevation of the stonework for the garden (above); The finished garden after a downpour (below).

Below: Behind the planted border, a 19th-century tracery window with an old brick wall and a Chilmark-stone diamond-pattern frieze from Salisbury Cathedral, all put up at Chelsea in three weeks.

glued by hand between the text pages, with tissue paper protectors. Although we failed to get the much-desired Madonna lilies, there were martagon lilies, and regale lilies brought on instead, and everything spilled over the gravel paths as much like a real garden as possible, with lupins, lavender, lychnis, delphiniums, pinks, shrub and rambling roses – mature specimens of the latter provided by the infinitely kind and helpful Robert Hunter Mattock, one of six generations of Oxfordshire rose growers and breeders. We added a lot of semi-weeds or wild plants to calm it down, which might then have counted against us in the arcane RHS marking system. Valerian growing in the ruins, Welsh poppies, daisies growing in the lawn about the mulberry tree were not then very 'Chelsea' – the gardens opposite being mostly composed of rocks and staggering rare specimen rhododendrons in full blazing flower. But the fun about Chelsea is the other people. The pressure makes it all a bit like a boot camp, and the masons, being naturally rebellious, developed a giggly game of taunting the guy who called himself 'Bronze leader' when communicating on the walkie-talkie to other janitors and 'security', such as it was. The inmates of Leyhill prison near Bristol, fellow garden-makers, could not have been more generous and charming, providing us with gorgeous, fabulously healthy prison-grown foxgloves and tobacco plants to fill gaps. Old hacks dispensed valuable advice. Fred Whitsey, *Telegraph* gardening correspondent, and Graham Rose, *Sunday Times* gardening correspondent, cheered us along daily – as they took to phoning in their copy from the summer-house where we somehow rigged up a telephone. After all the hard labour and triumphant finish came the nightmare of the Gala opening night, when the *Telegraph* top brass came to inspect. Julian warned Barbara Amiel, the journalist and wife of the proprietor, Conrad Black, not to walk on the grass, especially in those high heels, as we all knew that the perfect turf was in fact floating on a deep soup of muddy water. She paid no mind. This did not improve our chances of enjoying the dinner after, with the bigwigs and the Blacks, in a local trattoria. Just before midnight Robin Lane Fox disappeared to ring the RHS judging panel and returned triumphant with a gold medal for us all. How relieved that made us.

Top: Our corner site under construction.

Above: Planting the site.

Opposite: The scaffold and plastic tent erected to bring out the leaves of the mulberry tree.

Top: Laying out the jigsaw puzzle of
the Salisbury cathedral frieze in the
yard, Bath.

Above: The anxious first day at the
Royal Hospital ground.

Top: Cutting, grinding and laying out
in Bath.

Above: Moving the 4m-diameter root
ball and fully mature mulberry tree
from near Hanham Court.

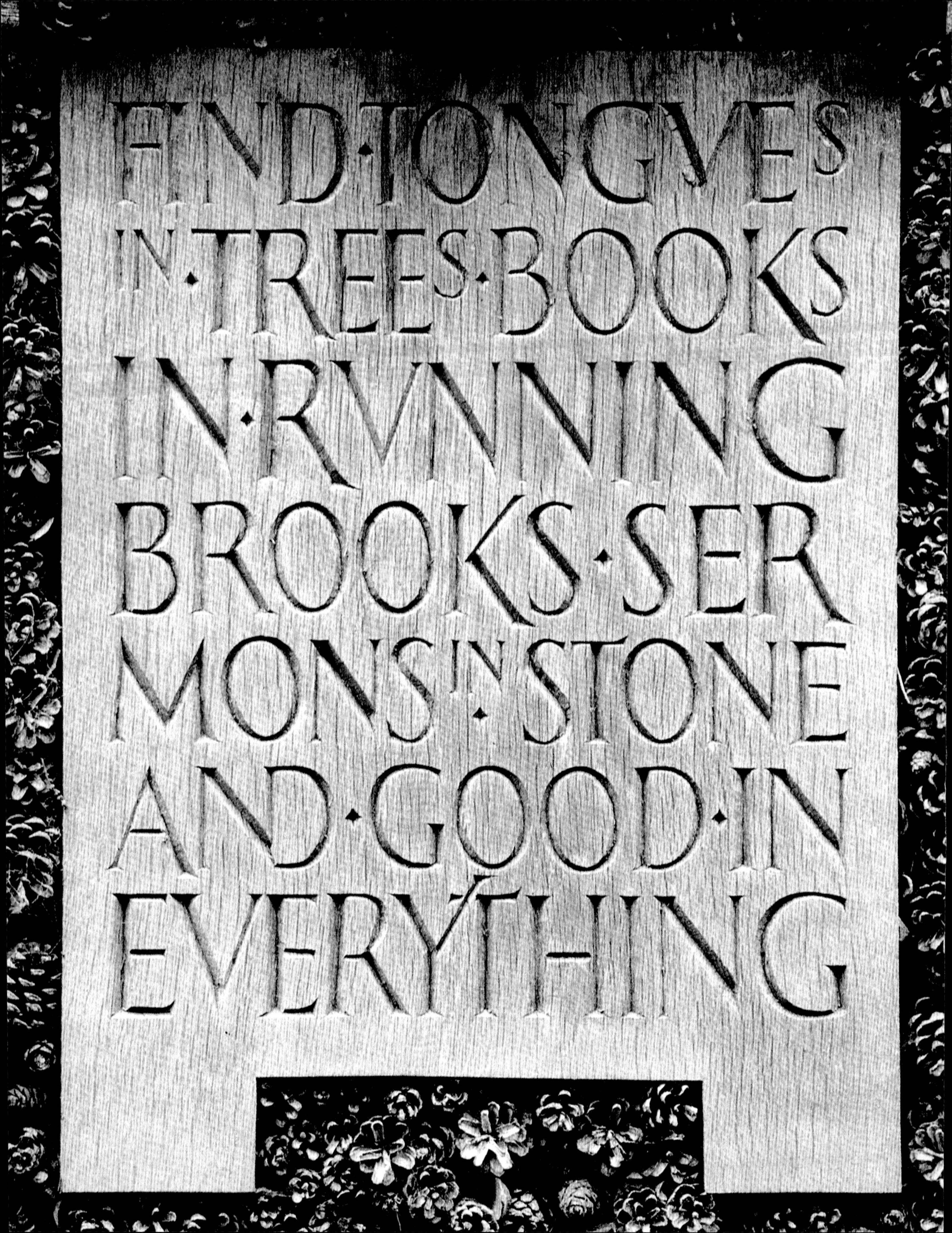

FIND·TONGVES
IN·TREES·BOOKS
IN·RVNNING
BROOKS·SER
MONS·IN·STONE
AND·GOOD·IN
EVERYTHING

Highgrove

When Julian and I left Scotland for good, I had finished my degree and we set about trying to restore the remaining portion of The Ivy, rescued from the jaws of bulldozers by Julian in 1981. Local architectural, poetical and rural rider and writer Candida Lycett Green came into our lives, having been the Boudicca of a campaign to save the house along with, among others, her father John Betjeman. Candida had long been one of the watchful eyes behind the 'Piloti' column which highlighted wanton destruction of buildings in *Private Eye* magazine, and was contributing to the Prince's new publication *Perspectives on Architecture* – treading a difficult line between the conservationists and contemporary architects. Candida saw us as part of a new generation: informed and educated advocates of contemporary art and design who were also passionate about history. She thought that the Prince of Wales might be interested in the project of restoration and resuscitation of The Ivy, marooned as it was amongst housing estates and tangled in highways and ring roads. What to do with mansions like ours in insalubrious settings was the kind of problem which exercised the Prince of Wales and she suggested bringing him to tea.

Later we took the Prince to Walcot Reclamation in Bath; he found the reclamation world fascinating and some time later he asked us to look at a corner of his garden and suggest some ideas possibly using reclaimed things. Amidst a dark tangle of cherry laurel we suggested that we place some limestone architectural fragments, probably from the front of some torn-down high-street bank, and plant them round with a collection of ferns. 'Capital Seats and Concrete Assets' we called them. Much is altered but they are still there. The whole garden at Highgrove is much altered and infinitely more professional these days, and kept with loving and incomparable care by Debs Goodenough. In the early 1990s the garden was relatively humble compared with what it is now and, although already famous, it was much less extensive.

Pleased with our little tribute-to-Ian-Hamilton-Finlay fernery, the Prince showed us a windy corner, between the woods and the parkland, where he and Rosemary Verey had made a woodland garden using rhododendrons. Our diagnosis was fairly brutal; plant some shelter to reduce the searing east wind; clear out some scrawny sycamores and hence encourage the decent lime and oak that were there to broaden and develop; use plants congenial to the locality – things like the martagon lilies which

Above: A temple of green oak.

Opposite: An inscription chosen by the Prince of Wales from *As You Like It*, letter cut by Belinda Eade, 1998.

were already naturalising deliciously about the place; and above all, we recommended, make some inner world or secret place to go to. We sketched up a plan, centred as requested around a fine oak tree and the David Wynne seated female form in agate, 'Goddess of the Woods', which was already there at its feet. Julian envisaged rustic arbours and the building up of a defensive bank of earth and tree roots, like an Iron-Age fort, in front of some depressing but necessary cherry laurels that were providing some shelter. The bank was to keep out the world and keep in the poetry. It would be planted with butcher's broom, ferns and hellebores. Three narrow paths, one a like a cave of roots, would give admittance and, within, two 'tempiettos' made from rustic poles. A sheet of A4 paper with a sketched plan and elevation, some description and a bit of a collage of hellebore flowers was our simple presentation. The planting too was to be simple, native and robust.

At this time we had become became obsessed with *Ruscus aculeatus*, butcher's broom, as we had found heaps of it – which we used for the banks at Waddesdon – on a site in Thame where they were building a new Waitrose, which pleased the Prince. Also for Waddesdon we had scoured the site where they were building new council chambers in Shepton Mallet, because it was in a garden that had belonged to a great galanthophile. Alas we were a week too late and the snowdrops had been scraped away by the diggers. Our passion for hellebores and snowdrops had been ignited when DV had introduced us to the ritual of early-spring pilgrimages to the shrine at Mathon near Malvern of Helen Ballard, great dame of horticulture, Queen of Hellebores. She would inspect her helleborine troops from a mobility scooter using a stick to lift their heads. Her two assistants were very kind to us; only a very few people made it to the garden in the depths of winter – there were fairly few that were that interested in those days – and Helen and her stalwarts enjoyed our company and appreciation enough to

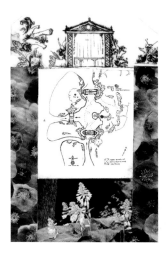

Above: The original sketch scheme for the Temple Grove, IB 1995

Below: A pen and ink sketch, IB 1995.

White Roots

Roots

Arch

Roots

White Roots

Green Oak

Green Oak

White Root 'Grille' or 'Trellis'

IB

Rustic Temple Arbour

Above: One of the green-oak temples under construction, summer 1996.

Below: A model of the Temple of Concord, Agrigento, Sicily. Mid-19th century, cork and moss on a wooden base.

Overleaf: The temple grove viewed from the treehouse, winter 1997.

eventually give us slithers of the 'specials'. We learnt a great deal from Mathon about north-facing borders, planting snowdrops and hellebores with peonies, especially species peonies which are generally earlier, and also the use of ferns. Ferns are a subtler but more binding addiction. We learnt much from Ursula and the Key family at Fibrex Nurseries near Stratford. They also grow another favourite, the scented pelargonium. They helped us with our first Chelsea garden, based on the Waddesdon rock work, and Ursula's father taught Julian how to pack a car to the roof with ferns without damaging the fronds.

A number of further drawings, developing the temples from rustic poles to our new experimental way of using green oak, were done and Barry Humphries, author and satirist, was there when we presented them to the Prince one teatime and admired the pen and ink drawings of our slightly more developed second presentation. One drawing shows the simplest of Doric temples in chunky bits of wood used like stone, decorated with whispers of stag oak for capitals and acroteria, surrounded by stumps. The idea really came from a cork model of the Temple of Concord, Agrigento, Sicily, which we had bought in the visitors' car park. Pretty basic though it is, this model is somehow imbued with a genius quality. As a souvenir, it is a hangover of the Grand Tour, which it was still possible to buy on our trip in 1995 and even ten years later when we sent Matthew Rice and Simon Thurley to buy more of them. The simplicity was what we took from it, thinking that we could use green oak in a similar monumental fashion to the cork, without detail or decoration. The model has a rounded almost abstracted quality and, we hoped, the building would have this too, unlike most pastiche buildings in gardens.

VIRTVTEM
VERBA
PVTANT
ET·LVCVM
LIGNA

Right: The gunnera fountain.

Opposite, top: An oak leaf, palm leaf and twig nest in mild steel, fabricated, beaten and gilded by us (left); the 'Columnbird', a pen and ink drawing by IB, 1998 (right).

Opposite, middle, from left: Unloading chestnut roots; a lorry tipping roots; the pathway through the stumps, made from discarded Cotswold roof tiles and ammonites, with spring ferns.

Opposite, bottom: An inscription from Horace 'They Think Virtue is Just a Word and the Sacred Grove just Sticks' (left); a carved oak bench, after a William Kent hall seat (right).

With this design and a limited budget to supply and erect a pair of arbours and to organise the planting (with the planting we were to have the help of David Magson, head gardener, and his two staff officers, Gilly Hayward and James Aldridge) we set off to make the best thing we could with what we had to hand. Our friend Guy Channer runs a building company and we worked using really chunky pieces of green oak, building something resembling the monumentality of stone but much cheaper, and possibly with more charm. We realised that by rendering parts of it with lime mortar painted with coloured lime wash, it would be something like building a half-timbered classical temple, or the Tudor-style Pitchford Tree House. It might also end up being not unlike all the mad things that we had been reading about thanks to Eileen Harris who had introduced us to a whole world of rustic buildings from the eighteenth and nineteenth century. These were not rustic in the commonly understood way of James Shirley Hibberd and his *Rustic Adornments for Homes of Taste* (1856), but classical and fantastical like the Bark Temple at Exton, the Badminton Hermit's Cell, Merlin's Cave at Richmond and William Chambers' account of the primitive origins of Classical temples and how the ancients first built these out of logs. On top of these influences was also that of Ian Hamilton Finlay; his garden at Little Sparta was part of our Scottish education, and very much a direct inspiration for these and other buildings we wanted to make. Guy Channer's joiners were brave enough to work with us along with Lee the Tree, our friendly tree-feller and electrician from Melksham. A dear friend since he electrified The Ivy in 1980s, Lee would spend his days off with his girlfriend protesting outside Greenham common. He came over to Hanham where we made the temples 'dry' and, with his chain saw, made the big important cuts, while Guy's joiners made the mortise-and-tenon joints. Once we had the jigsaw puzzle in pieces Lee would run the chain saw, 'bumpety bump', like a light sabre over the band-saw marked surfaces of the colossal pieces of oak, thereby taking away the industrial scars and making the surface of the oak look wind-worn. This process was entirely the brainchild of Julian who then had to wire-brush the oak to his ultimate required finish.

Throughout a blessedly hot summer we plodded over to Highgrove and laboured under the lugubrious watch of the 'Goddess of the Woods'. I overdid it one day and went into a spiral of migraine winding up in the 'neuro' unit of Frenchay Hospital, where I was soon right as rain and showered with hampers of goodies from the Royal

Below: A pen and Ink drawing, IB 1999, of an exedra proposed initially as a poet's 'Temple of Worthies' centred around a pyramid with a bronze plaque of Ted Hughes. This was made into a much simpler version, and altered, when Queen Elizabeth, The Queen Mother, died in 2002.

Household. Julian got to know 'the plod' as they plodded round on security duty, comparatively relaxed in those days, but for the waving of mirrors under the car and bonnet. They were mystified by what we were doing, but they were also amused; they made detours to see how it was going, began to encourage us, and, in the end, declared it was the best thing ever.

Everybody helped in some way. Tom the groom with his terrible arthritis-knobbed hands would come and share a roll-up and a chat. James Graham-Stewart, great countryman, friend and mentor in all things to do with the rare or remarkable furniture and things in which he deals, came to get bruised shunting spiky stumps around with Julian. David Magson described their bruises as being the colour of all Rosemary Verey's dresses – purple and blue. Stevie 'Wonder' from Bucks, our top trooper at Waddesdon, came and moved heaven and earth. He also met many of the great and the good, once asking the Duchess of Devonshire why on earth she lived in Derbyshire. The Prince himself would sneak out whenever possible and help, chat, despair of Julian's Coca-Cola drinking and send for tea and sandwiches to be shared by everyone among the roots. He also made us use the 'Stumpery', as he began to call it, to house a national collection of hostas, our least favourite plant, but in the process we learnt to love the subtler, wilder and more scented ones.

As the whole came together it developed a spiritual power and profound presence within the wood, which none of us could really have hoped for. On being shown round by her husband Robert, who was working much greater magic decorating the inside of the house, Helen Kime burst into tears, saying that it was extraordinarily moving, like finding the wooden shrines that once lined the Appian Way. The woodland became, with subsequent further additions including the very peculiar and wonderful gunnera fountain, spiritual, like its master. The Prince always wanted his garden to have meaning and spirituality, to be a record of things and tributes, hence the memorial to his very dearly beloved grandmother, Queen Elizabeth The Queen Mother. Building that was a particularly rare moment when, being in official mourning for two weeks, everybody had to wear black armbands and the Prince, freed entirely and for the first time in a long time from public duties, was able to come and labour in the woods all day. All these places are perhaps imbued then with the nurture, the attention to detail, the sweat, tears and the determination of everyone who made them.

Above: The green-oak pyramid and stumpery with three Italianate benches. The bronze plaque is of Ted Hughes.

Left: JB in the wood yard.

Opposite: JB building an archway from sweet chestnut roots reinforced with hidden steel.

Houghton Hall

The summer following the year we finished the temples I fell into conversation with David, Marquess of Cholmondeley, whilst walking round the garden at Highgrove before dinner, and he seemed to like them. A couple of months later we received a letter on crunchy Houghton Hall paper, kindly inviting us to visit him. North Norfolk is full of fun and friends, wonderful architecture, light, bright, dry, seabound with open skies. We have spent years trying to go and live there. David had been re-making the walled garden with his head gardener Paul for some time, alongside the great restoration works he was doing in the house. It was all going swimmingly but he felt a little unsure about how to progress in the garden.

Houghton Hall, built by Britain's *Premier Premier Ministre* as David's French friends so neatly describe Robert Walpole, is a legend to anyone interested in architecture, painting, furniture, politics, history, William Kent and all the things John Betjeman called 'plush and saloonery'. The thrill of walking across the vaulted undercroft in the quiet of the day or taking the Parisian *fin-de-siècle* lift installed by David's *grand-mère* to one of the panelled and poster-bedded bedrooms never diminishes. Everything about Houghton is big and bold, confident but understated, right down to the glazing bars.

Outside, everything is much as Sir Robert and his son Horace left it. It is thought that, having overspent on the house, the park was never finished – nothing changes. David has worked tirelessly with his agent Robert Miller to reclaim the park from unproductive industrial farming. When we first went up, there were white deer moseying up to the windows, 'natura naturans', as if in a Gobelins tapestry but there was maize growing in the outer park and I doubt if a tree had been planted that century. Now there are clumps of oaks and sweet chestnut avenues, Arcadian scenes of livestock grazing, a ha-ha has been built, 'boscos' (groves) planted and David has quietly inserted land art and sky spaces by Richard Long and James Turrell.

Houghton doesn't really have a garden in the sense that we understand it today; it has it's park up to the window sills and a walled garden, intended originally as a food factory to provision the great house all year round, and it was here that our job was to collaborate with David in making something rich and magical in planting terms for the visitors to see after all the architectural and decorative fireworks. Five acres of walled garden is big – so big it is no joke if you forget your trowel – and it is set to one side of the house behind the beautiful and monumental carrstone stable. How we may have helped was by looking at the thing as a whole and trying to be brave. Over the ten years we talked through with David a lot more besides the walled garden: the ha-ha, the park, avenues of lime trees and re-vivifying his parents' 'Golden wedding' border, which was fun because it is not that often that one can get clients to go for bright brassy yellows and en masse they look terrific. We helped with the private swimming pool garden to the north of the house and in the extraordinary Piranesi ruined space beside it, and came up with ideas for Cholmondeley Castle in Cheshire as well. We had a very easy understanding with David; it was an enormous pleasure to work with him on a proper estate so competently and happily run, developing the planting and building strange structures for the ends of vistas in the kitchen garden.

Propagation under glass, house plants, cut flowers, fruit, vegetables, hedges, gigantic borders, pleaching, rose pruning, twining of wisteria, chasing rabbits, talking to the public – there is a great deal going on, on a great estate where everyone is part of the team. The soil is deliciously friable, light and sandy, worked for hundreds of years by hundreds of gardeners. David has specialist interests of his own, like the orchid house, but together we all re-planted the giant borders in a wave of saturated colour using old-fashioned border plants, West Country lupins, strong-flavoured crocosmia and gorgeous rockets of *Eremurus stenophyllus* and *E.* × *isabellinus* 'Pinokkio' with the real magenta *Gladiolus communis* subsp. *byzantinus,* which we cannot seem to get any more, and we introduced buttresses of yew, thresholds and textures on the ground.

Opposite: The antler temple and borders.

83

The walled garden, clockwise from left: Lupins with *Onopordum nervosum* and *Crambe cordifolia*; irises at the foot of *Prunus* 'Tai-haku'; a rocket-shaped rustic rose tower in a colour-saturated border; irises with pots of *Agapanthus*; the colourful borders entirely edged with *Nepeta* 'Six Hills Giant', with the temple at the end; *Onopordum acanthium*, *Crambe cordifolia*, *Rheum palmatum*, *Kniphofia*, Oriental poppies and lupins.

Opposite: *Crambe cordifolia*, Oriental poppies and West Country lupins in the walled garden, with William Kent's stables visible beyond the hedge.

We developed the Lady Sybil Cholmondeley box garden and the meteorite fountain, bringing the basin up above the paths by two feet and planting box beneath the overhanging stone coping. Local nursery Howards provided much of the material, including fabulous *Iris pallida* subsp. *pallida* which we have continued to buy in bulk from them for Hanham Court, for here and for almost every garden we have ever done. Irises are an abiding passion for David; they are, somehow, an East Anglian thing – there is Cedic Morris's famous collection at Benton End – and they are happy in the dry. We have no delicate notions about their colours, liking them all and liking them all together. We designed a trellis of box beds under the hot south-facing wall for the bedding out of heliotrope 'Chatsworth'. Sue Dickinson let us have some cuttings from Lord Rothschild's Eythrope garden as stock plants for Houghton, from which new ones are propagated each year. They are planted with scented pelargoniums and teepees of the 'Houghton Blue' sweet pea. This looks very like the 'Cupani' sweet pea from Sicily, and it is curiously historically connected with Sir Robert Walpole via Dr Robert Uvedale whose plant collection he bought in the early eighteenth century.

We suggested a long oak pergola to be covered with wisteria for visitors in April and May and to the side of it a peony border mixed with regale lilies – a pairing we had seen at Vaux-le-Vicomte and vowed to reproduce. For the end of the year there are aster borders and cutting beds of annuals. David had a crush on the plum garden at the Villa Cetinale in Tuscany, and together we incorporated small standard plums into the formal squares of pleached limes with gravel and strips of turf, which we had drawn up when it was agreed that an earlier garden of hornbeams had not worked. Finally we replanted the big beds round the outer ring of the rose garden with mixed Sissinghurst-like planting: shrubs and shrub roses underplanted with delights, just the usual favourites, philadelphus, lilac, old-fashioned roses, washed about with pinks and aquilegias. David and Rose have brought life, light and hope to Houghton, twin sons and a new daughter called Iris, knitting a twenty-first-century sophistication and 'outward' thinking with the gentler, older ways of an estate which is rigorously run while remaining benign.

Above: The pleached lime garden
with long grass and plum trees.

Left: Yew hedges and the *Prunus*
'Tai-haku' walk.

Opposite, top: The Lady Sybil garden
fountain and raised water tank with
box swirls.

Opposite, bottom: The peony border
with *Wisteria floribunda* 'Cascade' on
the pergola (left) and beehive-clipped
standard holm oaks (right).

Top: An arbour of criss-cross oak
(left); *Cardiocrinum giganteum* (right).

Above: A Vicenza stone statue with
rose arches.

Right: Wave -form yew hedges in the
rose garden.

Opposite, above: A green-oak fruit cage.

Opposite, below: massed peonies
with lollipop holm oaks.

94

Wisteria floribunda 'Multijuga' (syn *W. f.* 'Macrobotrys') on the oak pergola.

A stone Janus head looks both ways
through the yew hadge.

Seend

Clarks have lived at Seend Manor for half a century, but different families of Clarks. Alan Clark, supremo of the maverick political diary, lived there in the 1970s and kept a corner of walled garden with a garage in it when he sold up. Alan was followed by Brigadier Clark who gardened with military enthusiasm and for whose birthday the oval beech hedge was planted within the walled garden proper. Stephen and Amanda Clark came in 1997. They live and work in Hong Kong, but Seend Manor has been their passionate project for nearly two decades, although they have not yet returned to live there as anticipated.

Nestled hard by the parish church, the Manor was built as a hunting box in the eighteenth century. It is a neat, confident Bath-stone house among half-a-dozen similar that form the village of Seend running along a ridge below Devizes. The house has two perfectly proportioned rooms of parade, a cube and a double cube effectively, with views across a miniature park falling to farmland to the south and rising beyond up to the horizon which is Salisbury Plain. Even more confident are the U-shaped stables further down the street, which must have once bustled with ostlers and farriers, who presumably needed to be fed from the walled gardens, long since in separate ownership. Sometime after they bought the Manor, Amanda and Stephen found the opportunity to buy the stables back and bravely did so, thereby reuniting this hamlet of walled gardens and handsome buildings with the main house.

Stephen, whom it turned out Julian had known in youth, is a superlative draughtsman and connoisseur of old master drawings. Amanda understands and collects Chinese antique furniture and ceramics and runs a worldwide interior design business. Together we were to collaborate in what Stephen first determined would be a David-Hicks-influenced, very formal design for gardening the principal walled garden. David Hicks' book *Garden Design*, published in 1982, remains a bible of simple, great, gutsy advice for making gardens. It is all the more arresting, and teaches you more, for being almost entirely in black and white. (Interior designers, like John Stefanidis, Nicky Haslam, David Mlinaric, Robert Kime and Christopher Gibbs, are often at their best I feel when making gardens.) The garden at Seend Manor was, at the time, in a semi-impenetrable state. It had been crammed with small trees and shrubs, some of which, in the way of miniature conifers, were no longer small or shrubby. We insisted on doing a digital survey of the garden and – Stephen has had the goodness to find this funny – then razed it. We started making the garden in 1997, the year of the hand-over of Hong Kong to China. Because Stephen and Amanda have spent their working lives away from England, they were both amused by the idea of bringing something of their travels back in the manner of the Nabobs of the British Empire – the brothers Cockerell and their house at Sezincote being the most supreme example of this. One brother commissioned his other architect brother to design him a house in the Indian style in Cotswold limestone, and they employed Humphry Repton to make them a garden in the manner of Thomas and William Daniell's aquatints of India, something this uncle and nephew team described as a 'devilish undertaking'. Our devilish undertaking was to encompass themes important to the Clarks – Italy, Africa, China and England – though not, one hopes, to create a 'theme park', for it was our job to interpret these ideas and knit them into a balanced, consistent design that also speaks of Wiltshire and the chalk plateau of Salisbury Plain rising above it.

Julian proposed a simple cross axis of pleached hornbeam backed by yew hedge. He was rightly insistent that these be planted in gravel. Gravel is one of our favourite mediums; it reflects light, is not expensive and can be either completely formal or made informal if you grow things in it. Moreover, if you plant trees in it they grow like rockets from lack of competition – unlike those in grass. (We learnt this at The Ivy where we planted the drive with *Tilia cordata* for pleaching.) With this planted cross axis he hoped to create a strong neutral backbone to the garden which would then be a series of surprises. There would be a fountain the centre and at the ends of the north-south axis, while the west end would

host a wooden arbour for sitting. We were inspired by H.V. Morton's *The Waters of Rome*, and over the years, with a little help from the reclamation boys, we have put together some quite respectable troughs and fountains. The central one is a tufa 'Spugna' enclosed in a raised basin rootled out from a yard somewhere, which oozes water – as well it might, for, strangely, whilst being on the top of a ridge the water table is very high here and we lost a lot of yews soon after planting, finding the trenches in which they had been planted had filled up mysteriously with water; the swimming pool has to have water pumped away from it sometimes to relieve the pressure on the structure. On the walls to each side of the garden are two fountains enveloped in geometric patterns of clipped ivy against the red brick: a drinking fountain and, at the opposite end, a concoction of a basin copied from the central one, a stone river god, new Bath stone and a rose-murex shell 'splashback' with pyramids gleaned from Morton's Rome. Absolutely taken from *The Waters of Rome* is the bacchanalian barrel fountain in the loggia, which is made of English roach stone from Portland Bill instead of Travertine.

'England' can be the starting point of a tour turning right upon entering the garden, and it was the starting point once the plan was agreed – geometric box beds, a thatched *cottage orné* in the corner, a Nancy-Lancaster-inspired rose trellis dome or gazebo in the middle, and similar Dutch-painting-inspired obelisks to carry Noisette roses all round. I particularly like to use Noisette roses because they are long flowering, tend to be exquisitely scented and have a great 'garlanded' quality, forming natural swags of flower. We used them hugely at Asthall for the same reasons, and also because they come in hues that suit the limestone – buffs and ochres almost, never in hot or saturated colours. Pots were made to Stephen's drawing by Jim Keeling, the trellis in the Far East, and the 'thatchery' by our men of oak from Wiltshire. North Wiltshire planning department in

Above: The rusticated western arbour with its oak 'Venetian' bench inscribed with Ovid's 'Tremete omnes vestrum qui appropinquat ad solium alaudae' – 'Tremble all you who approach the throne of the lark'. The planners refused our request to put the arbour up three steps as it would 'protrude' too far above the garden wall.

Above: A high view of 'England' showing the trellis obelisks and the Nancy-Lancaster inspired rose gazebo, with box-edged borders of old-fashioned roses, mixed herbaceous planting and Jim Keeling pots of lilies and pelargoniums. The only remaining tree from before, an old apple, is in the foreground.

their wisdom dictated that no building should be higher than the garden wall, which runs along a double-decker bus route, hence the western arbour is truncated and missing its three steps up which is sad, but the resulting structure is a greater delight to children for being so squat. The planting is cottage garden in style: the one old Bramley's cooking apple which was originally in the garden hosts a 'Rambling Rector' rose, and peonies, pinks, irises, clematis, scented pelargoniums and lilies abound. Roses were chosen for old-fashioned loveliness and scent, plus a few whose names would amuse Stephen and which he enjoyed placing: *Rosa* Cardinal Hume, *R.* 'Blairii Number Two' and the spicy Moss rose Chapeau de Napoléon (*R.* × *centifolia* 'Cristata') cluster in obeisance around the thatchery along with all things 'Clarkei'.

Crossing into 'Africa' the formality steps up a notch. Obelisks and sphinxes were ordered by Stephen from Haddonstone, and cluttered with giant gunnera by Julian. Our initial scheme showed the yew hedges with battered monumental clipped doorways, Egyptian style à la Biddulph Grange, which have yet to really solidify. The square tank of water, which we felt needed to be in this quarter, corollary of the long thin bathing tank of water in 'Italy', was to be minimalist and Arabic if not sub-Saharan. The Chusan palms have been a great addition; it pleases the Clarks that they come from Central China, and their leaves rattle in an outlandish and atmospheric way. The formal square here is nicknamed 'Tripoli', southern Italy crossing into Carthage with a touch of Babar the elephant. One can see the pagoda in 'China' from here, peeping out over the top of the hornbeams on stilts. The outer section is more *The Adventures of Tintin* than Babar with mud huts based on ones in Mali, and tall, shifting, singing grasses. This whimsical side-show leads to a dark and cool grotto right in the furthest corner of the garden. In this corner the presence of roads and houses beyond led us to plant a narrow holm-oak grove, underplanted with ferns and tree

ferns and dotted with menhirs of holey stone, (water-washed limestone) which logically forms the way out of the grotto although it was made before it.

The third quarter is 'China' encircled by the pre-existing beech hedge, whose top has been cut in waves. This was the Clark's pet project, and for it they brought over from China an antique pagoda in a container, along with attendant stone dogs and dragons. Planted with tree peonies and acers, this is another world, and very charming. We helped with the 'cracked ice' design for the floor using English pebbles in a Chinese fashion. The peripheries provide a home for camellias in pots and a massive peony bed for picking.

The fourth quarter is nearest to the house and is for dining and bathing. It was always going to be 'Italy', although it is really just a formal and delicious garden. By a stroke of immense good fortune we found, in a reclamation yard, a Bath-stone front to a loggia which had been removed from a house in Bristol, almost certainly built in the 1840s at a moment when the West Country was swept up in the 'Fiesole' fashion for architecture. Thus, with the help of friendly stonemasons, we drew up a brick and stone back to it, to accommodate eating out plus a kitchen and bathroom. The pool is narrow, stone lined with steps right across the loggia end; always Hong-Kong-hot when in use. The paving is stone banding with pebble infill. At the far end, should it get too hot in the loggia, there is dining under a vine-clad oak pergola. Cylindrical clipped ilexes stand above box and pots of agapanthus. Stephen finds it amusing that the Italian nurseries from which they came are bemused that *l'inglese* keep them thus clipped like a can of tomatoes, as originally this 'hair-cut' was intended solely to protect the trees during trans-continental transportation. Lollipops or cans on sticks suit the jollity of the garden. It has slightly the mood of a curative spa for the 'taking of waters'; the roach-stone barrel fountain might, as in Charlie Chaplin's film *The Cure* which Julian remembers seeing in the Stanhope cinema in 1957, one day accidentally flow with gin.

Above, left: The tufa 'Spugna' fountain in the centre of the cross axis.

Above, right: A grit stone river god from a reclamation company, on a new stone plinth with lead water spouts designed by Stephen Clark, and a reredos of rose-murex spikey shells and Bath-stone scrolls based on a fountain in H.V. Morton's *The Waters of Rome*.

Right and overleaf: Geometric shadows on the gravel from the pleached hornbeams.

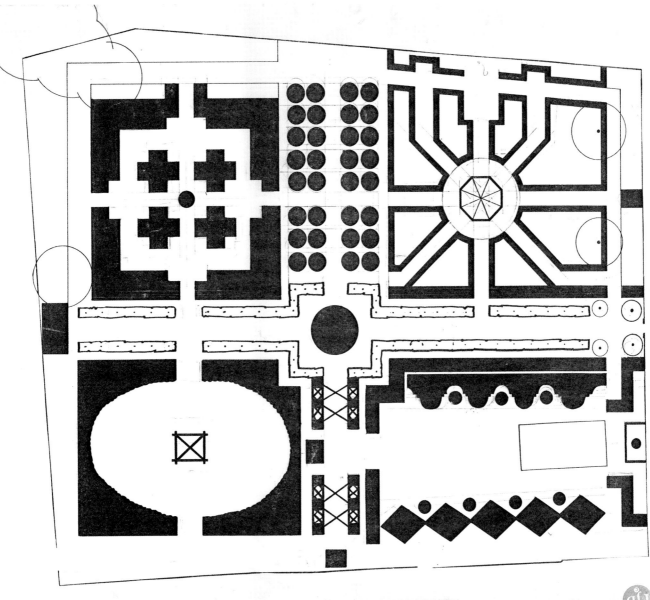

Above: An early indicative block plan of the four quarters of the walled garden in 1997.

Right: A trellis arbour border, with roses and geraniums.

Opposite, clockwise from top left: A trelliswork Dutch obelisk, with 'Blush Noisette' roses; the *cottage orné* or thatchery in the right-hand corner of 'England'; *Rosa* 'Complicata' in front of the gazebo clothed in *R.* 'Cécile Brünner'; a rusty steel support with *R. × odorata* Sanguinea Group; Bill Painter, keeper of the garden.

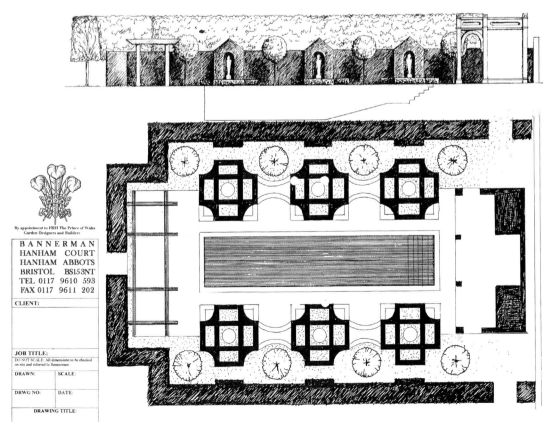

Above: The reclaimed Bath-stone Italianate loggia, at the end of the long narrow stone pool in 'Italy'.

Right: The plan of 'Italy' 1999.

Opposite, above: Cylinder-clipped holm oaks, box beds and agapanthus in 'Italy'.

Opposite, below left: Agapanthus in front of the loggia with the roach-stone barrel fountain from *The Waters of Rome* in the background.

Opposite, below right: The vine-covered pergola for dining.

Overleaf: 'Africa' viewed through the palms (left); clipped ivy (top right) to one side of the river god fountain (bottom right); the obelisk and gunnera fountain (bottom left).

By appointment to HRH The Prince of Wales
Garden Designers and Builders

BANNERMAN
HANHAM COURT
HANHAM ABBOTS
BRISTOL BS153NT
TEL 0117 9610 593
FAX 0117 9611 202

CLIENT:

JOB TITLE:
DO NOT SCALE: All dimensions to be checked on site and referred to Bannerman

DRAWN: SCALE:

DRWG NO: DATE:

DRAWING TITLE:

MUD HUTS

GRANARIES

Mud domes, no reinforcement sometimes thatched over

granaries

's room

unmarried sons' courtyard

stable

enclosure of family head and wives

Above and right: Collages and drawings of huts for 'Africa'.

Opposite: Bananas and Chusan palms with a thatched hut just visible in 'Africa'.

Overleaf: a corner of the grotto in 2015, with rocks and ferns.

Asthall Manor

It was January, dim and tempestuous, and the Windrush was in flood approaching Asthall along the river from Swinbrook. Our excitement at the prospect of a possible new job was further electrified by the strangeness of thunder and lightning in the middle of winter. On top of this, the house we were to visit had been the home of the celebrated Mitford sisters, who included writers Nancy and Jessica, Diana, wife of the leader of the British Union of Fascists, Oswald Mosley, and Debo, Duchess of Devonshire. Asthall was the house where the 'Hons' – pre-war characters from the novels of Nancy and real sisters in the memoirs of Jessica, had had their 'cupboard'. Jessica wrote of the second 'Hons' Cupboard' at Swinbrook that it was 'where Debo and I spent much of our time, and still has the same distinctive, stuffy smell and enchanting promise of complete privacy from the Grown-ups.' The first 'Hons' Cupboard', familiar to readers of Nancy Mitford, had been at Asthall – where the family spent only a few years, but miraculously time had almost stood still since they had left. Mr Hardcastle, from whose estate Rosie Pearson bought the house, changed almost nothing and lived in increasingly antediluvian isolation like a character in a novel.

Rosie Pearson was, at that wintry moment, sensibly in Jamaica, where she had been living for some time with her husband Palma Taylor and had opened a school, until, drawn back home with her two young daughters, she lighted on this at the time slightly mournful looking neglected house near Burford. Built about 1600, it faces the parish church to the east and water meadows to the north; to the south the front drive had been blocked up by Mr Hardcastle and the back parts to the west had been absurdly extended by the Mitfords' 'farve', Lord Redesdale, during the time that the family lived there in the twenties. Inside, almost untouched since then, there was still an upstairs schoolroom which had rook-black linoleum on the floor, marked with ink and dragged chairs. In the attics, the enormous linen cupboard, holy of holies for Mitford fans, is still full of family laundry. Rosie has cleverly curated this shrine along with a bi-annual sculpture show with her now partner stone carver Anthony Turner and adapted it for twenty-first century life. The dark telephone kiosk off the hall with Bakelite telephone, the pantries and sculleries, lots of brown and dusky blue paint all survive, and Rosie made the builders keep the piano-key 'clickety-clack' tiles in the bathrooms while updating the plumbing. By demolishing the servant-world buildings she created a west-facing courtyard, central in the 'U' of the house, for living outside. Rosie and her children inhabit the house properly, with dogs and people, painters and yoga teachers, blowing through in a thoroughly in bohemian way.

Rosie wanted roses. She wanted 'cosiness' and 'embowerment' within the remit of her ecological principles. She wanted Charleston not David Hicks. Miraculously she found Mark Edwards to look after the garden and they live in a mutual turmoil of differing views, but the result is that the garden, as we tell him every year, is poetry: almost anarchic but just under control in a way that illuminates the beauty. The climbing roses, all over the house from top to bottom, he painstakingly, painfully, ties and cuts during short winter days so that in summer they look as though nobody has cared for them in a long while, an exceptionally difficult thing to achieve. Together we went mad on roses, clothing the rather brutal long loggia or cloister, which connects the main house with the glorious Arts-and-Crafts ballroom, in Noisettes, favourites of mine for their long flowering, 'appley' scent and Cotswold-stone colouring. The house is draped and muffled in roses such as 'Gardenia', 'Albertine', 'Madame Grégoire Staechelin', 'Desprez à Fleur Jaune', 'The Garland', 'Noisette Carnée' – even though it balls – 'Climbing Pompon de Paris' and 'Paul's Himalayan Musk'. The beds are filled with traditional favourites peonies, phlox, geraniums, astrantias, sage and Jerusalem sage and, in this lovely limey gravelled world, there arc cushions and pillows of pinks everywhere – the highly clove-smelling 'Mrs Sinkins' creeps out on to the gravel. There is a lot of gravel-creeping and self-seeding, destroying the rigid formality of the plan and letting things loosen up. There is more philadelphus and lilac than it is possible to imagine, and *Crambe cordifolia* always, with Rugosa roses, with artichokes and with *Rosa* 'Complicata'. Mulleins people the paths, things like angelica wander, and the overall feeling is cottagey and wayward.

Opposite: *Prunus* 'Tai-haku' through wedges of yew hedges.

115

To set the house on its 'tapis' we proposed first and foremost the reinstatement of the drive and of the vestigial gravel paths all around it, so as to throw light outwards and upwards into the leaded windows of the sitting rooms inside, but these should be skirted with borders and box-edged abundance. Rosie, rightly we all now agree, refused to hedge in the house from the entrance drive, as we would have had it, so as to hide the cars coming and going. But her leaning was always for an open and loose feel, with structure but no rigid formality; frequently she felt our plan was too 'prescriptive' as she described it, but she learnt that if you imposed a structure you could then let it go and somehow that works better than something without any structure at all. Mark, whilst gardening without chemicals or much labour, is master of the seedling-invaded gravel and not afraid to have plants flopping over his box hedges, which are untainted by blight. Everywhere is abundance, be it love-in-a-mist or the pelargoniums in pots. Angelica self-seeds in the courtyard, with *Verbena bonariensis* and naughty marijuana-smelling cleome. Together we worked our way round the different 'rooms', trying to diminish the impact of pool and tennis court, cosseting the existing naturalised *Tulipa sylvestris* under magnificent beech trees, and mowing as little as possible.

The courtyard that Rosie made by taking out yet more pantries and boot rooms looks out awkwardly onto steep east-facing banks. To begin with these felt as though they loured over the house, rising as high as the first floor windows. We puzzled how to deal with this. Rosie had settled on an enormous bay window in the kitchen to make it part of the garden. Almost obliterated in summer by *Rosa* 'Albertine', it looks out directly into the banks and it seemed that the only thing to do was to cultivate these 45-degree slopes, making simple saltire box parterres, one each for daughters Annie and Dora, in which to grow marigolds and sweet Williams, tulips, alliums, forget-me-nots, salads, herbs, and vegetables – to try something different every year. Together with Mark, his son Liam sometimes and with Anthony who as a sculptor has an innate and practical understanding of three dimensions and form, Rosie has experimented with the yew boundaries that we planted to edge these parterres, and carved curvaceous shapes – waves, very female forms – out of solid yew. The form of the grass terrace above with grouped *Prunus* 'Tai-haku' was inspired by Russell Page's 'green rooms', Keith Steadman's green garden and Dartington Hall. Above this, another dreary bank presented the opportunity to do something which may have been in my head since childhood. I had watched my father's weekly battle with a Flymo on a long string, which he swung across the steep undulating banks behind our house at Hendred throughout each summer of my childhood. Planting the sloping risers solidly with yew, which you then could clip to shape from the top, would be easier to do and much easier on the eye. The solid blocks of

Previous pages: The view of the church and the Manor at Asthall from the Windrush Valley.

Above: 'Noisette Carnée' roses on the laundry roof (left) and growing into Rosie's bedroom window (right).

Opposite: Roses all over the east front.

yew we cut into triangles, providing narrow passageways through to secret destinations. We planted the tiny yew trees in torrential rain, drowning them in mulch, but Rosie was patient and un-fazed and today the reward is a solid geometry, somewhat mysterious, where light plays on the surfaces, and the resulting spaces are cool and inviting.

The peripheries of this were stuffed with scent and spicy shrubs: lilac, philadelphus, elaeagnus, *Ribes odoratum*, *Viburnum carlesii*, and *Rubus* 'Benenden'. *Rubus* 'Benenden' is an example of a favourite 'non' plant of ours. A 'non' plant is a sort of inverted snobbery worthy of Nancy Mitford, and in her terms it is very 'U' as it is something so ordinary you will not find it in a garden centre. It is a term we use to describe the essential down-playing plants which make the kind of 'forgotten' gardening that we aim for. These are things like hazel, hawthorn, *Rubus* 'Benenden', butcher's broom, honesty, guelder rose. Trying to make it look as if gardening is not happening particularly is a very tricky deception, full of contradiction since it is actually tuned up and put on steroids. We want more than is natural while hoping that our bit will join on to the natural landscape beyond. To the mix at Asthall we juggled troughs, pots, benches, a gypsy caravan, gurgles of water, and chatty corners with seats and tables. Round the house and in the courtyards are limestone troughs, with tulips and spring planting, and regale lilies and scented pelargoniums in summer. In the outer areas we cut paths through, but kept the elder, nettles and brambles and added rambling roses to the insect safari park. Cow parsley, meadowsweet and nesting birds abound.

This approach has been developed by Mark and Rosie, who plan to grow more snakeshead fritillaries in the perfect water-meadow alluvial silt and have got the wild flower thing really going now, which is not easily done. The leat pond is watched over by a thatched shelter, with a fireplace, which we concocted, wherein the family coracles are kept. The garden is organic and the compost magnificent. We had a lot of debates, the three of us, sometimes quite heated, about where to put the pool, and the necessity for a dreaded tennis court (although, at all events, it does get used a lot) and now Rosie and Mark mask it by growing massed sweet peas up the netting. These debates about what to remove and what to keep are always subjective, and we were all right about something. Even the swimming pool which Rosie has further 'naturalised' is both beautiful and has a purpose. The plant and changing room is discreet, a cross between Jamaica and an English Scout Hut. The water meadows and pollarded willows of this stretch of the Windrush valley are exceptionally beautiful, with cattle lowing and swallows and swifts zooming after insect life. For all the difficulties of decision-making that reared up, there seem to be few regrets. The vegetable garden over the road is working and now provides for its own pop-up café in the summer. The whole *raison d'être* of the garden is the bi-annual exhibition of sculpture, which Rosie dreamt up with Anthony. It has proved a giant success, and has added to the gaiety of the nation.

Above: Annie's garden in clipped box.

Opposite: Yew hedges on the banks above Annie's garden, clipped into tunnels and slices of cheese. The tree is *Prunus* 'Tai-haku', the great white cherry, also shown overleaf in a set of six.

Overleaf, following pages: Our plan for the garden.

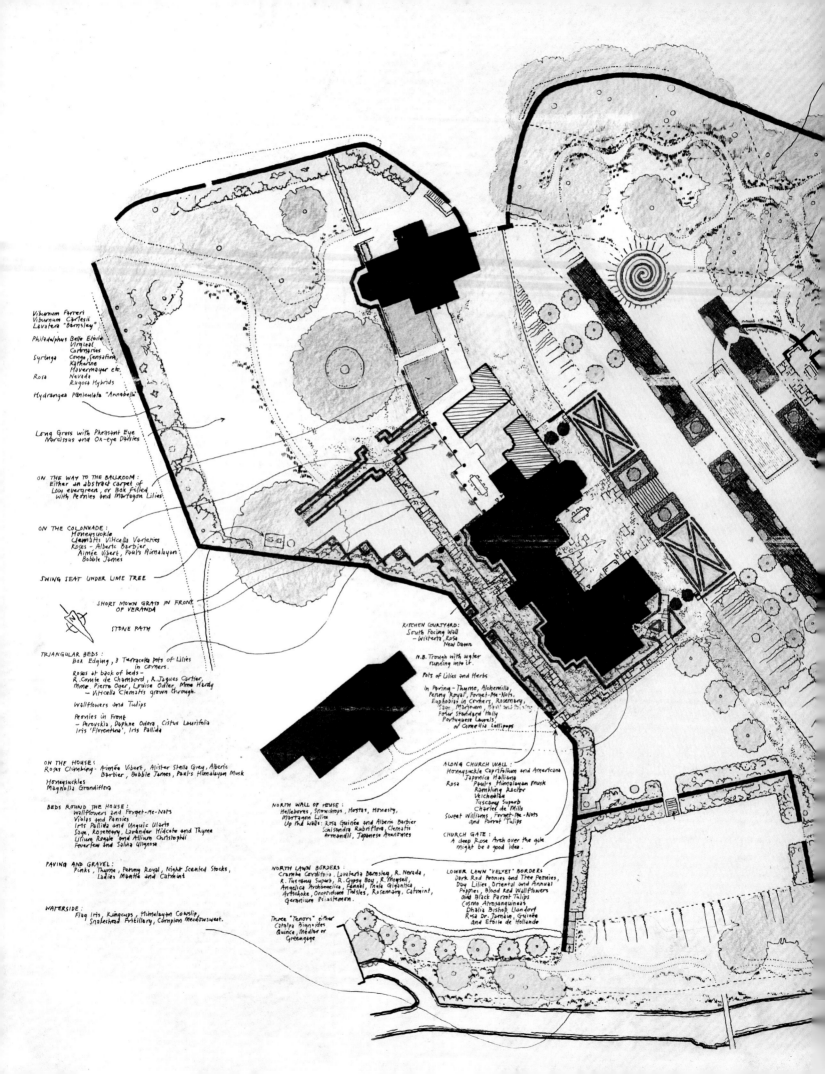

Viburnum Farreri
Viburnum Carlesii
Lavatera "Barnsley"

Philadelphus Belle Etoile
Virginal
Coronarius
Syringa Congo, Sensation, Katherine Havermayer etc.
Rosa Nevada
Rugosa Hybrids

Hydrangea Paniculata "Annabelle"

Long Grass with Pheasant Eye Narcissus and Ox-eye Daisies

ON THE WAY TO THE BALLROOM:
Either an abstract carpet of Low evergreen, or Box Filled with Peonies and Martagon Lilies.

ON THE COLONNADE:
Honeysuckle
Clematis Viticella Varieties
Roses - Alberic Barbier
Aimée Vibert, Paul's Himalayan
Bobbie James

SWING SEAT UNDER LIME TREE

SHORT MOWN GRASS IN FRONT OF VERANDA

STONE PATH

TRIANGULAR BEDS:
Box Edging, 3 Terracotta pots of Lilies in corners.
Roses at back of beds -
R. Comte de Chambord, R. Jaques Cartier,
Mme. Pierre Oger, Louise Odier, Mme Hardy
- Viticella Clematis grown through.

Wallflowers and Tulips

Peonies in Front
- Perovskia, Daphne Odora, Cistus Laurifolia
Iris 'Florentina', Iris Pallida

ON THE HOUSE:
Roses Climbing- Aimée Vibert, Alister Stella Grey, Alberic Barbier, Bobbie James, Paul's Himalayan Musk

Honeysuckles
Magnolia Grandiflora

BEDS ROUND THE HOUSE:
Wallflowers and Forget-Me-Nots
Violas and Pansies
Iris Pallida and Unguic Ularis
Sage, Rosemary, Lavender Hidcote and Thyme
Lilium Regale and Allium Christophii
Feverfew and Salvia Uligrosa

PAVING AND GRAVEL:
Pinks, Thyme, Penny Royal, Night Scented Stocks, Ladies Mantle and Catmint

WATERSIDE:
Flag Iris, Kingcups, Himalayan Cowslip, Snakeshead Fritillary, Campion Meadowsweet.

KITCHEN COURTYARD:
South Facing Wall - Wisteria, Rosa New Dawn

N.B. Trough with water running into it.

Pots of Lilies and Herbs

In Paving - Thyme, Alchemilla, Penny Royal, Forget-Me-Nots, Euphorbias in corners, Rosemary, Sage, Marjoram, Basil and Parsley
Four Standard Holly
Portuguese Laurels
or Camellia Lollipops

NORTH WALL OF HOUSE:
Hellebores, Snowdrops, Hostas, Honesty, Martagon Lilies
Up the Walls: Rosa Guinée and Alberic Barbier
Schisandra Rubriflora, Clematis Armandii, Japanese Anemones

NORTH LAWN BORDERS:
Crambe Cordifora, Lavateria Barnsley, R. Nevada,
R. Tuscany Superb, R. Gypsy Boy, R. Moyseii,
Angelica Archangelica, Fennel, Inula Gigantica
Artichoke, Onopordum Thistles, Rosemary, Catmint,
Geranium Psilostemon.

Three "Tenors" either Catalpa Bignoides Quince, Medlar or Greengage

ALONG CHURCH WALL:
Honeysuckle Caprifolium and Americana
Japonica Halliana
Rosa Paul's Himalayan Musk
Rambling Rector
Veichenblau
Tuscany Superb
Charles de Mills
Sweet Williams, Forget-Me-Nots and Parrot Tulips

CHURCH GATE:
A deep Rose Arch over the gate might be a good idea.

LOWER LAWN "VELVET" BORDERS:
Dark Red Peonies and Tree Peonies,
Day Lilies, Oriental and Annual
Poppies, Blood Red Wallflowers
and Black Parrot Tulips
Cosmo Atrosanguineus
Dhalia Bishop Llandorf
Rosa Dr. Jamain, Guinée
and Etoila de Hollande

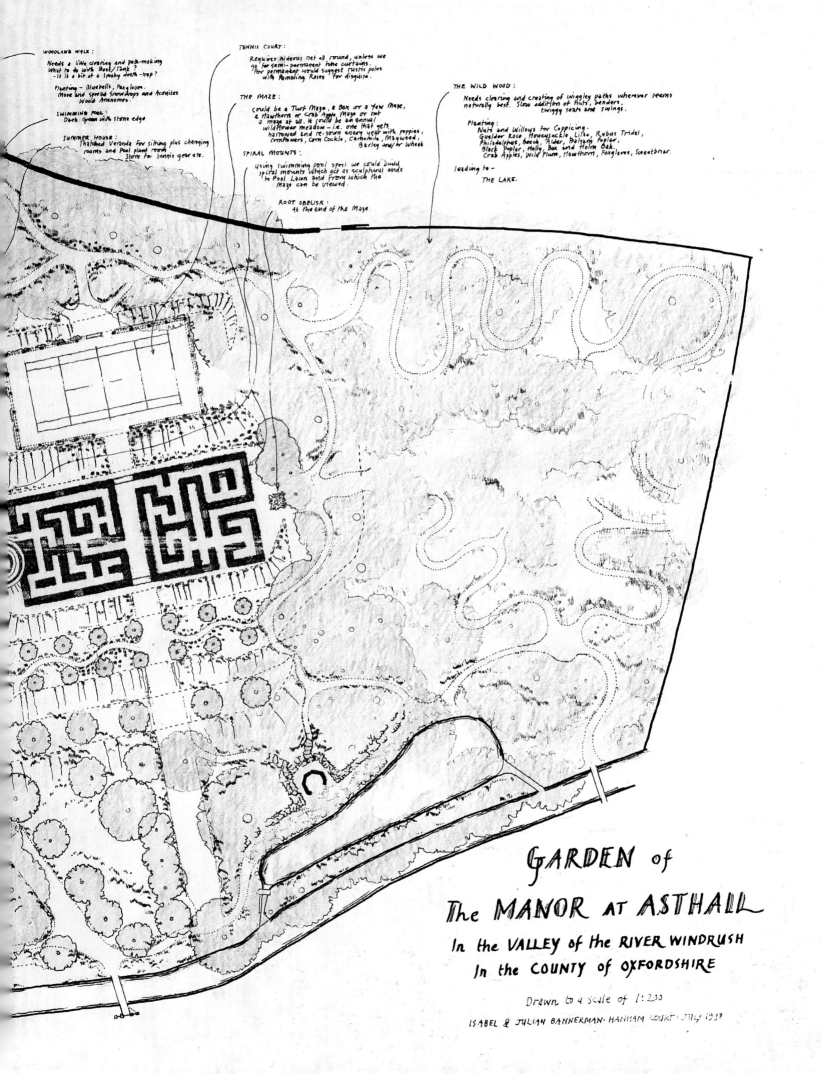

WOODLAND WALK:
Needs a little clearing and path-making
What to do with Boat/Tank?
- Is it a bit of a spooky death-trap?
Planting - Bluebells, Foxgloves.
Move and spread Snowdrops and Aconites
Wood Anemones.

SWIMMING POOL:
Dark Green with stone edge

SUMMER HOUSE:
Thatched Veranda for sitting plus changing
rooms and Pool plant room
Store for tennis gear etc.

TENNIS COURT:
Requires hideous net all round, unless we
go for semi-permanent tube curtains.
For permanent would suggest rustic poles
with Rambling Roses for disguise.

THE MAZE:
Could be a Turf Maze, a Box or a Yew Maze,
a Hawthorn or Crab Apple Maze or not
a maze at all. It could be an annual
wildflower meadow - i.e. one that gets
harrowed and re-sown every year with poppies,
cornflowers, Corn Cockle, Corn mint, Mayweed,
Barley and/or Wheat

SPIRAL MOUNTS:
Using swimming pool spoil we could build
spiral mounts which act as sculptural ends
to Pool Lawn and from which the
Maze can be viewed.

ROOT OBELISK:
At the end of the Maze.

THE WILD WOOD:
Needs clearing and creating of wiggley paths wherever seems
naturally best. Slow addition of huts, benders,
twiggy seats and swings.

Planting:
Nuts and Willows for Coppicing.
Guelder Rose, Honeysuckle, Lilac, Rubus Tridel,
Philadelphus, Beech, Alder, Balsam Poplar,
Black Poplar, Holly, Box and Holm Oak.
Crab Apples, Wild Plum, Hawthorn, Foxgloves, Sweetbrier.

leading to-
THE LAKE.

GARDEN of
The MANOR at ASTHALL
In the VALLEY of the RIVER WINDRUSH
In the COUNTY of OXFORDSHIRE

Drawn to a scale of 1:200

ISABEL & JULIAN BANNERMAN · HANHAM COURT · JULY 1998

Top: *Cercis siliquastrum* and cow parsley behind the swimming-pool pavilion.

Above and right: *Rosa* 'Hillieri'; the meadow; a bench with forget-me-nots.

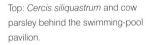

Opposite, clockwise from top left: Yew waves with *Prunus* 'Tai-haku'; *Rosa* 'Blairii Number Two'; the back courtyard with ping-pong table; the view down the east front from the drive; *Rosa* 'Roseraie de l'Haÿ' with the Manor and church behind; yew waves and Dora's garden.

Clockwise from above: *Echium vulgare* and *Leucanthemum vulgare*; aquilegia and *Rosa spinosissima* 'Mary, Queen of Scots'; *Lupinus* 'Masterpiece' with *Cenolophium denudatum*; *Isatis tinctoria* with *Daucus carota*.

Opposite, clockwise from top left: Mixed *Cyclamen coum* with *Galanthus* 'S. Arnott'; *Lychnis coronaria* and *Salvia nemorosa* 'Ostfriesland'; *Allium stipitatum* 'White Giant' and *Rosa* 'Duchesse de Buccleugh'; *R.* 'Paul's Himalayan Musk' on the stone arch; astrantias, verbascums, *Geranium* 'Ann Folkard' and peonies.

Above, clockwise from top: The thatched hermitage, ox-eye daisies in front of a landform; meadow flowers in front of the tin-roofed pool pavilion; cattle in the Windrush Valley.

Opposite, top: The swimming pool and pool pavilion.

Opposite, bottom: From the rose garden, looking north across the wild meadow and the Windrush Valley.

Above: *Rosa* 'Cécile Brünner' on the porch.

Right: JB in front of *Rosa* 'Cécile Brünner' on the veranda surrounded by verbascums, alchemilla and daisies.

Opposite: *Paeonia lactiflora* 'Sarah Bernhardt' amidst *Crambe cordifolia*.

Euridge Manor Farm

John Robinson's story is a remarkable one. He was brought up by his widowed mother on a tenanted farm in Worcestershire; beautiful and smart, he got into agricultural college and somehow to Istanbul in the summer doing the 'overland' thing with friends in a van. They stopped and filled the van with Afghan coats, turned round and took them to Carnaby Street. He moved on and into jeans, making 'Loons' in Wales and befriending Lord Kagan of Gannex fame, intimate of Harold Wilson, who happened to have some sort of monopoly on the importation of denim from the US. His passion though was always farming and, with his first fortune, he bought a farm in Surrey. He made his second fortune in the west, founding Jigsaw in Bristol, having moved with his mother to a new farm, Euridge, 'ridge with yews', near Bath. It was 'a two overcoat farm', always a few degrees colder than anywhere around, a farmstead high above a distant church, besieged by swallows in summer; it looks like the cover of a 1940s Batsford book about the English countryside. We first met at supper with some antiques dealers who kindly thought we would get on and that there was a chance we might get to help John with his garden. Driving home that night Julian said he was, as usual, bewitched by the girlfriend, Belle, in her fluffy white jumper, but quite unusually enchanted by the farmer from Worcestershire. 'Who was the farmer?' I queried. 'The organic farmer, John Robinson, he was the gentlest, most intelligent, interesting and proper person I have met in ages.' 'Oh yes, absolutely,' I said 'and I love buying clothes from Jigsaw too.' John once told me how he loves girls: 'Because' he, said head slightly cocked to one side like a Robin redbreast, 'they just can't help always wanting to buy something new.' John has since become a very dear friend.

When we met, the farm had expanded and contracted, the clothing business was growing exponentially, and he soon found himself acquiring five children. He had no intention of moving, but the house was not big enough, though it was unlisted and so could be expanded. We spent the best part of a very happy decade working together on his *grands projets*: the farm, two shops and a Palladian palace in the West Indies. He was the best of clients: coming from retail he was businesslike and visual, knew his own mind, but respected the talents others brought to bear in all aspects of the development. Building Euridge was probably the happiest thing we have ever done. It involved many children, dogs, stonemasons, chippies, hippies, builders and project managers, drinking, dancing, fancy-dress, head-scratching, problem-solving, invention, discovery, surprises, shocks, contention and even inspection – from the Prince of Wales, who developed a healthy fascination with the proceedings.

John said that he loved the 'ruined pool' we had just made at Hanham Court and asked us to make a total plan of what we thought he should do at the farm. The land sloped up directly behind the house and he had started digging back into the hill to extend the house and make bedrooms for the multiplying childern, but, coming up against his old neglected swimming pool he was unsure what to do next. In August 2001 we made a model showing the complete 'Monastic settlement' idea. In this we totally re-modelled the steeply sloping hillside, showing a level garden in the centre of a courtyard made by the existing house and new buildings built against what would be the resulting cliff face to the north. By sweeping away the old falling-to-bits 'Diana Dors' swimming pool and underpinning the house, we planned to dig down metres and metres, cutting a level and sheltered garden right back into the hillside. These would be big works, but John was not daunted. He said 'Let's do it', cracked open a bottle and called in a team to help us work out how to build a stone cloister. The cloister was to get you into a high classical 'saloon' in which would be a long stone pool for swimming. Above the cloister, pool and plant room, higher than the first-floor level of the farm house, we suggested making a terrace roof garden overlooking the quad garden and a stone- and lime-rendered orangery for plants, with two bedrooms for guests and a kitchen for parties tucked behind. Later we went on to fiddle about with the house,

Opposite: Viewed from the boathouse, the new façade of the bedroom with the loggia below and the new retaining wall, tripartite cave and water tank in Bath stone and water-washed limestone.

changing the kitchen and John's office and designing a new wing, a drawing room and loggia below, and principal apartments above. All this was done in new Bath stone, most of it quarried from the garden itself. But first we went sifting through salvage yards for fragments and windows and doors from redundant churches all over Britain with which to make the faux monastic buildings. The building work was almost entirely done with direct labour: together we found journeymen lead workers, electricians, plumbers and pool makers, joiners, labourers and stonemasons and shell-workers galore. Some almost lived on the site, with their three-legged dogs and vans and girlfriends, and some have never left.

The architectural shenanigans were similarly convoluted, so that visually the story might be read as a monastic medieval settlement, added to in the sixteenth century, aggrandised in the eighteenth century, reduced to farmstead in the nineteenth century and then re-worked in the twenty-first. Directly behind the kitchen, a quarry was excavated first, going way below the finished level that you see today, producing a hard, good-quality Bath stone, before being back-filled to form new paths, beds and lawn. The 'hortus conclusus' fits into the elbow of the house on the back of the kitchen and drawing-room, surrounded by vestigial remains of an abbey cloister. It was in a way the natural extension of the Chelsea garden we had done nearly a decade before, only writ large. For the family it provided a hot sheltered square of lawn, paved areas for eating near the house and another in front of the pool, box-edged beds overflowing with roses, pinks and, John's special love, peonies. As a boy he had grown sweet peas to sell at market, but he claimed not to possess a sense of smell or much understanding beyond vegetable growing, which he loves. A stone staircase leads out of the flowery bower to what is a roof garden and which – for practical as much as stylistic reasons, because most of it has barely a foot of soil – is more 'Italianate'. Designed as a parterre of box with fountains, *Magnolia grandiflora* spreads green magic

Above: The new gatehouse in reclaimed and random Bath stone with rambling roses, yew topiary and a Regency iron bench.

Right: The new cloister and its reclaimed windows and stone, with topiary, climbing honeysuckle, wisteria, roses and tree peonies.

Above: The cloister, built in 2002, leading to the bath house. It has a reclaimed Cotswold stone floor, an oak ceiling, Euridge stone corbels and quoins, with candlesticks, benches and three-legged chairs designed by Nigel Coates for Jigsaw.

Opposite: Topiary in the cloister garden, viewed from the new cloister window in 2015.

across the lime-washed elevation of the orangery, which has tubs of oranges out in summer, inside in winter. Like at Houghton, box is planted under the coping of the raised pools of water and there are corners to sit in amongst cistus and scented pelargoniums in huge terracotta pots. There are battlements upon which to lean and look down on the intricate garden below and to look up at the huge landscape beyond.

Returning to his garden from London on a summer's evening John lights the braziers and watches the swallows' bedtime antics over the formal pool to the south of the house. This wildly dramatic tank of water flanked by colossal stone staircases came in the third phase, not even dreamt of when the first model was made. In 2003 he asked us to sort out the south side and we suggested doing away with the slightly tepid water garden which vaguely meandered down a grassy hillside in front of the new drawing room with it's 'Elizabethan' loggia and belvedere upstairs. Because Euridge is really all about the view, the tank, which collects water from the house for use on the farm, is tucked into the hillside. The design draws on Portuguese and of course Italian models, but most perhaps on the crazy lost Tudor gardens of Roy Strong's book *The Renaissance Garden in England*, the drawings and engravings over which we had pored for years; the tri-partite grotto harks back to the Enstone Marvels of 1628. The curious boathouse was a device to deal with the fact that the garden comes to an abrupt end in a massive laurel hedge. Which was where John drew the line. The laurel hedge was to stay and beyond that we were not to go. But we continued to expand eastwards, making walled kitchen gardens, terraces for boules, re-jigging the entrance and the 'Vulture Trees' – weeping beeches planted by John when he moved in in the early 1980s. These trees have always made Julian weep and gnash his teeth because he feels they are like Harry Potter's dementors: they menace and stoop over like vultures. John has kept one just for a giggle.

Above: The bath house and new orangery with the Hybrid Musk *Rosa* 'Felicia' in the foreground.

Left: The view from the French doors of the bath house and orangery

Opposite, top: A view of the bath house and cloister.

Opposite, bottom left: The parterre and topiary in the cloister garden in 2002 with purple honesty and red-oxide benches.

Opposite, bottom right: A cloister window and *Daphne odora* 'Aureomarginata', a favourite, to cover the bare ankles of the rose 'Climbing Etoile de Hollande'.

Overleaf: The ruined wall soon after building in the winter of 2003.

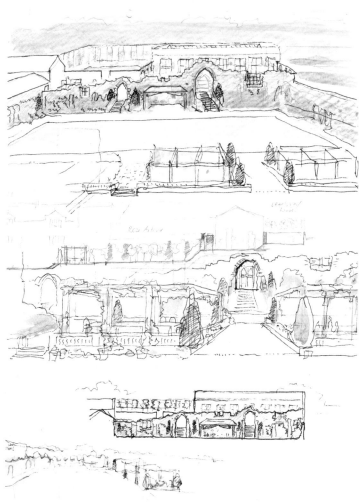

Top: The setting of Euridge, so redolent of an illustration from a post-war Batsford book, with its Dutch barn, farm gates and Colerne Church in the distance.

Right: An aerial view from the west before work started in 1999; and (below) from the south in 2008.

Opposite, top, from left: A crane placing a standard Portugal laurel on the top terrace, 2002; the loggia pillars covered in 'Noisette Carnée' climbing roses; laying the lawn, 2002.

Opposite, middle: The back of the boathouse with mixed aquilegias (left); original plans and sketches, 2000 (right).

Opposite, bottom: The oak duck house based on the bedroom and loggia façade, 2004; JB inside the cloister; Martin Gane making the grotto, 2004.

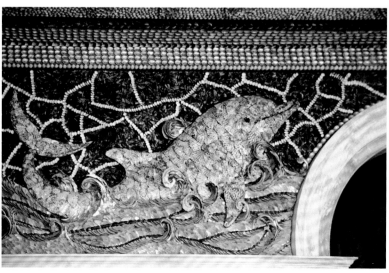

Above: The bath house grotto based somewhat on the Woburn Abbey grotto of the 1630s. The dolphins and octopuses in oyster, mussel, cockle, abalone and paua shells were constructed on plywood at Hanham Court in the winter of 2002.

Left: A dolphin and waves.

Opposite: Through the looking glass – a reflection of the view across the pool to the open French windows onto the lawn and topiary.

Above: *Deutzia scabra* 'Plena' with a ruin behind.

Left: The yew and box parterre in the cloister garden.

Opposite: *Rosa* 'Albéric Barbier', *R.* 'Paul's Himalayan Musk' and *R.* 'Rambling Rector' on the east face of the ruined wall.

Overleaf: Climbing roses 'Félicité Perpétue' and 'New Dawn' with wisteria on the walls of the cloister and orangery building, with irises and pinks at their feet. Erigeron daisies carpet the paving, and to the left is the pink shrub rose, *Rosa* 'Felicia' underneath a medlar tree.

Above: Inside the orangery, a limestone trough fountain with a pedimented reredos made from rose murex shells. The floor, quoins and carved ovals above the door are of reclaimed Portland stone.

Left: The thatched oak boat house with a bell tower, wisteria pergolas and 'cow' obelisk fountains in the water tank. Colerne village and church are behind.

Opposite: A spiral mound – the Tump – made from all the left-over excavated stone.

Overleaf: The orangery terrace with a gothic tracery wall fountain and orange pots. The 'Vulture' weeping beech tree is behind.

Sienna

While we were working on Euridge in about 2003, John Robinson bought the plot next door to his house on Mustique. At first he asked us to build an 'annex', a wooden Caribbean gingerbread house in the manner of the first Oliver Messel houses on the island, a study of which we had made when staying with John on holiday there. Somehow the plans for Sienna grew and transmogrified into something more akin to a villa in the Veneto influenced heavily by the Villa Vizcaya, Miami. Built to comply with the island's strict planning restrictions it is a series of single-storey pavilions around a 'piano nobile' sitting room and cloister.

The house was set as far as possible along the contours of the steeply sloping site yet still required a lot of terracing and steps and retaining walls, which makes opportunities for architectural divertimenti and provides varied spaces to work with. On the east side of the island, where a reputed ton of sea salt per annum is dumped by the constant trade winds and washed by the rain back into the sea, it is hard to get any but the toughest things to grow. We learnt everything we could from John and his friend and mucker from his early rag trade days, Steve James, horticulturist, and his wife Susie with whom he now did the flowers for Jigsaw and ran a nursery growing plants for the general public and for the remarkable Derry Watkins' 'Special Plants'. Steve was the man who tie-dyed the first T-shirts and sold all of them one Saturday morning in the King's Road. He is a fantastic, funny, bombastic Captain Haddock of a man, preferring the plastic-bottled wine he brought over from the continent on regular fag runs to anything fancy. He was a greater nicotine addict than Julian, and his attitude to horticulture, like his northern attitude to most things, was a mixture of tenderness and doom. We used to tour the gardens of the island for inspiration and on one occasion reduced the highly wrought American lady owner of a highly wrought garden to ashes by fulminating over her woolly aphid infestation. He gave it her straight: 'There is no bloody option but to burn every plant in this garden and start again.' Trying to advise John at his other house we learnt from both of their jolly pessimism about the climate, the care and the combatant pests and diseases. We learnt to keep expectations low and planting simple. Not so very different from our usual approach. But we did have epic romantic notions about the new house and its garden. We used the topography of the site to make a long drive which we determined not to

Above: A bedroom cottage with JB.

Opposite: The house from the shore through the coconut palms at Macaroni Beach.

Above: A bedroom cottage and main portico beyond. Sweet lime is used like box.

Opposite, top, from left: The rainbow shower tree, *Cassia* × *nealiae* in blossom and Mexican stone quoins; a palm tree fanlight on the front door – a tribute to Oliver Messel; a royal palm in the garden below the piano nobile arcade.

Opposite, middle, from left: An open Mexican limestone serliana; palms and rainbow shower tree; a fretwork door in the entrance court leading to the kitchens with *Bauhinia* × *blakeana*.

Opposite, bottom, from left: The arcade seen through frangipani branches; the fountain and reclaimed statues opposite the front door; gate pillars with 91 cast concrete cannon balls.

'garden'. Everywhere we all made monumental efforts to destroy as little as possible of the native scrub, to save plants like the spider lilies that abound by digging them up and moving them and planning everything round the best existing trees. We decided to enclose the entrance yard, where everyone parks, in high walls, partly retaining, to hold up the hill. We based this entrance on Seton Castle, a castellated house in East Lothian designed by Robert Adam in 1789. There are wall fountains on two sides opposite the entrance and the front door, which opens into a high stone hall stepping down into an arcaded courtyard with a dancing crown fountain around which the main house is wrapped. The far side of the cloister is a wider vault and acts as dining room leading into the salon, which is a double cube opening on to the portico overlooking the pool at the basement level directly below and Macaroni Beach below that.

The garden is a series of rooms and terraces outside the bedroom pavilions and around the pool. The soil is rich and the right things grow fast: frangipani, sweet lime which we used like box and clipped, palms, seagrape and pandanus. Made to withstand earthquakes, with a huge underworld of tanks for collecting rain water, the amount of footings, infrastructure and construction intervention created problems when it came to planting as it always does. Pots, troughs and planting pockets were desperately needed to green up certain areas and we are still working on that. Architectural details, quoins, door and window cases, pillars and arcading are Mexican limestone full of fossils and the rest is concrete and block covered with lime render.

Sienna needs time to settle, to gain that Jean Rhysian 'lost' quality, but already the royal palms rattle over your head in the ceaseless freshening trade winds from Africa.

Clockwise from above: The pool in front of the rusticated under-storey of the portico; the view down the arcade; the portico and far bedroom pavilion viewed from the long terrace above the loggia; a giant column and noughts and crosses floor in Derbyshire gritstone, Ancaster limestone and Ashburton marble in the central courtyard; palm shadows on the outdoor shower.

Opposite: The loggia for eating by the pool which we felt like painting in Neapolitan colours.

Top: A bench and royal palm with frangipani below the arcade.

Above: The entrance court based on Seton Castle, East Lothian.

Right: Four giant columns on the drive, reclaimed from the front of a former bank.

Opposite: Construction took in excess of eight and a half years. The loggia before painting (top left); the dining room and salon with chandelier behind (top right); the path to a lookout point (right middle); The log-table and terrace on top of the loggia (bottom left); a bedroom cottage (bottom middle); JB surveying all (bottom right).

Woolbeding

It is hard to remember precisely a first project meeting with Simon Sainsbury and Stewart Grimshaw. But I remember the excitement, anticipation and curiosity in the run-up to whenever it finally happened. It had been in the offing a long time. We had met at the Chelsea flower show probably a decade before, and whilst we were working at Wormsley, Christopher Gibbs had often mentioned these very dear friends and the garden in Sussex that they had created with the legendary American landscape architect, Lanning Roper. Simon had vaguely mentioned to Julian he had a woodland- cum-water garden but that it felt unresolved and might be something for us to take a look at one day. He was particularly anxious about two bridges, made in brown wood, which Christopher Gibbs had felt were all wrong. We heard no more until about 2006, and could not have predicted what a positive and fruitful mission it would turn out to be.

The first meeting was, like many more to come, immensely civilised and civilising. We learnt a lot from Simon, from his measured and intelligent approach to things, from his connoisseurship, from the paintings and things in the house, and from Stewart we continue to learn about plants, plantsmanship and perfectionism. We toured the garden entranced: the formal and productive parts, the double border, lawns tumbling to the River Rother and, close by it, enormous sprawling oriental plane trees, whose limbs, coated in 'combat' khaki bark, snaked through a haze of blue *Campanula trachelium,* the nettle-leaved bellflower. It must have been summertime.

Our real mission was to take the 'Long Walk' to the south of the ha-ha and find the woodland garden, a slightly lugubrious large copse of some specimen trees and a stretch of motionless water. It was a long morning and thankfully we rounded up our thoughts over a delicious lunch in the cosiest dining room in England, sitting under Dora Carrington's 'Tidmarsh Mill', white West Highland terriers about our feet. Over many such pleasurable Monday lunches as things progressed, conversation would not linger much on the garden, as Simon always averred, 'there is only so much one can talk about pumps'. But on that first day both Simon and Stewart were clear about what they required and, an even greater joy to us, they clearly wanted to get on with it.

It was agreed that what the garden needed was a circular route, punctuated with diversions and vistas; a better bridge than the sticky chocolate brown things that they had chosen in haste and regretted at leisure; more drama; more reason to trek the thousand metres across the park to get there. The topography, trees and views out were good. There was a remarkable, tall *Taxodium distichum*, not necessarily to our taste, but powerful; it had something which Simon's perspicacity pinned down – it was straight from a Caspar David Friedrich landscape. There was open water, but it was dusty, listless, and lacking. There were dark shrubberies, but they had no mystery. There was also a painted wooden Gothic pavilion, ingeniously brought with them from a previous garden at Petworth and designed by their dear friend and architect Philip Jebb, already mentioned, the kindest and cleverest of men always happy to help us out with architectural conundrums. But this building was slightly stranded on its grassy knoll. There was not enough incident in this melange to draw one in and draw one on round to the next thing. What there was, was comprehensible in a moment, lacked mystery, and needed 'lifting'. Lightness of touch is an intangible quality, something we all always seek to achieve and can never be sure of finding. It was clear there were the makings of something very good given the confidence of the clients, the sensible budget and, as it turned out, an excellent contractor.

The first thing was to compose a story, to open it with a flourish and continue to enchant the visitor. It is a walk of perhaps a kilometre from the ha-ha at the edge of the principal garden, to the south of the slightly French-looking early-eighteenth-century house, to the copse. One approaches across open parkland which drops down to the bending river on one side and swells up beyond to a wooded brow. At length a lone

blue Atlas cedar stands in the park just before the railed-in copse; Simon and Stewart had planted a blue one by mistake twenty years before and could not bring themselves to start again when they realised their error. Now it is twice the tree and surprisingly handsome; it adds to the character of a nineteenth-century pleasure ground. Stewart had been supplementing the trees with scented shrubs, ferns, fabulous osmunda, and marginal plants, great stands of gunnera, lysichiton and rodgersia.

For the entrance we lighted upon the idea of a raggedy ruin, a whisper of Northanger Abbey, fragments in the grass, a gothic portal and a tracery window. This device made one's arrival concrete, marking the transition from simple open pasture to contrived arboretum with its considered planting and architectural and sculptural episodes. Step through the lost building and expect some adventure to unfold.

Julian has a mantra about water in a garden: it must make sense. All of us know how water works – it needs logically to come from somewhere and go somewhere, otherwise we subconsciously sense something wrong, and this will create a lingering doubt.

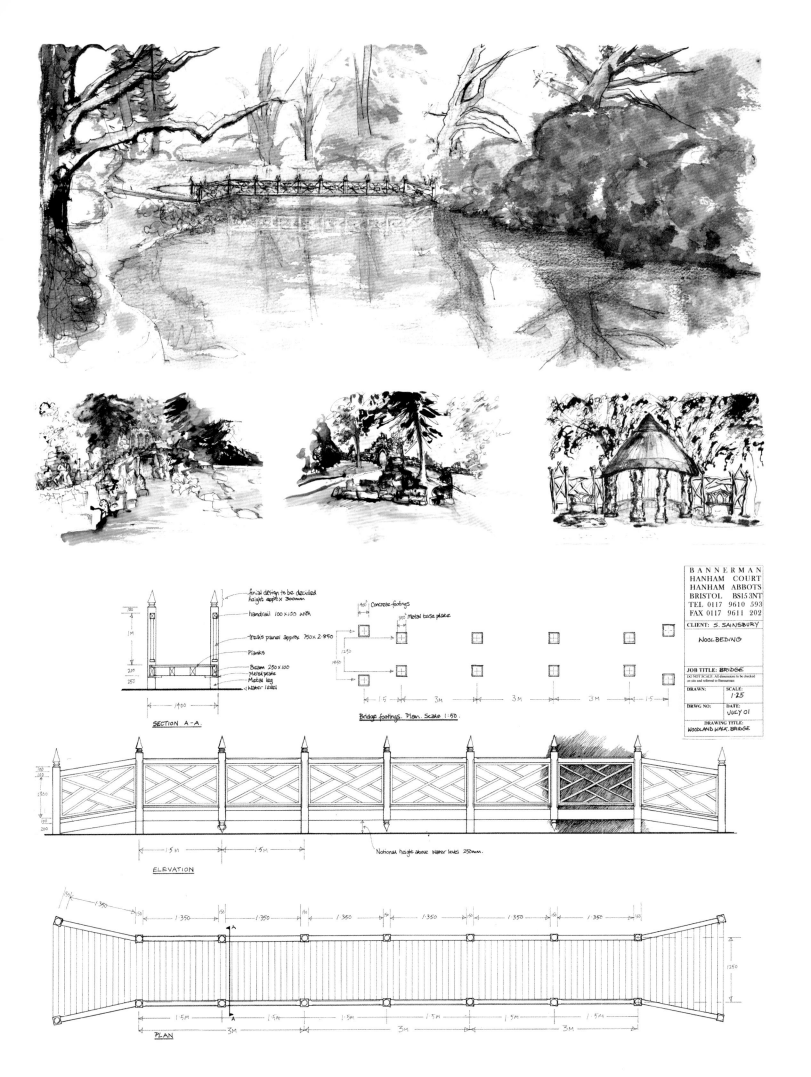

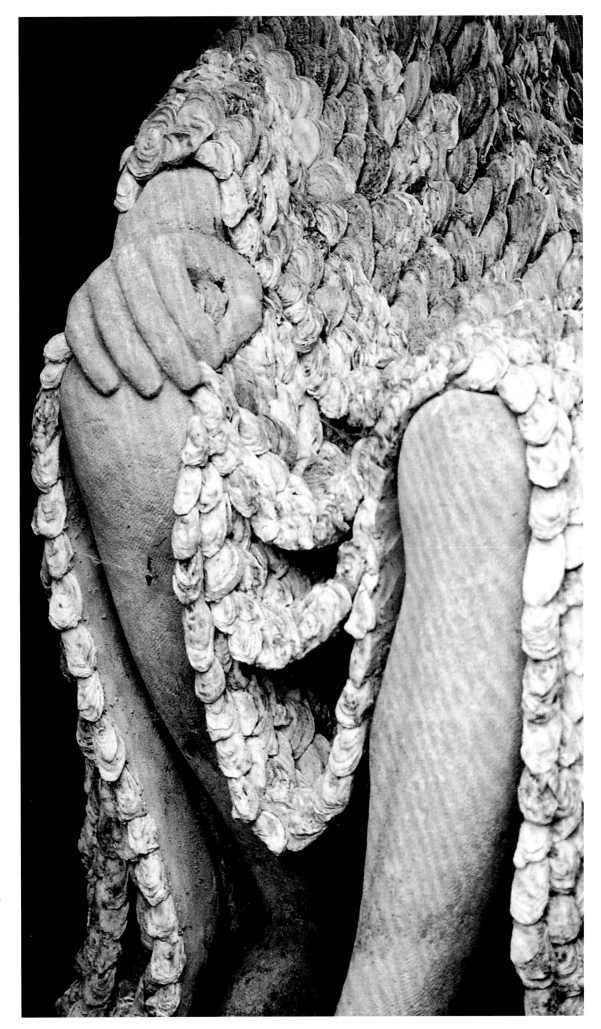

Right: A detail of the Rother god's cloak made from cement covered with oyster shells – Tom got them from Whitstable. He carved the head, legs and hand from stone.

Opposite, top: A sketch for the Chinese bridge, pen and ink, IB 2001.

Opposite, middle, from left: Sketches of the Gothic pavilion, the ruined abbey entrance and the rustic hut, IB 2001.

Opposite, bottom: Specifications for the Chinese Bridge, HP July 2001.

Also, on a purely practical level, water needs to be kept moving. Without movement, stagnant corners are created. But, for us, the actual starting point was the pavilion, which Simon wished to keep where it was.

We quickly conceived a plan which extended the water right up under the pavilion, by excavating and thus creating a four-metre cliff in front of it – a vertical in this predominantly horizontal landscape – shored up with beefy chunks of Sussex sandstone from which we could fashion a ferny rockscape and a cascade. Possibly our labours and researches in James Pulham's work at Waddesdon haunted us here, also the cascade at Bowood, Wiltshire, an example of the less formal grotto and rock work of the eighteenth century. Natural wonders like the High Force waterfall in Teesdale were a part of Julian's childhood. We made a model to explain the cutting away of terra firma which raised a few eyebrows. Providing the pavilion with a proper plinth meant that we could now develop an eventful ascent to it. There would be views across the enlarged lake from a new bridge, which we quickly determined should be long low and elegantly Chinese – something like Painshill – and views back all the way to the ruin. The Chinese bridge had figured in our imaginations since forever, and seemed to chime instantly with everyone as the solution, as did the suggestion that it be painted a good yellow – the colour of the spathes of the skunk cabbages already planted by Stewart close by. This bridge was intended almost to hover on the surface of the water and the meticulously engineered pumps had to ensure that the gallons of the River Rother remain tempered in their flowing through and back to the river, always ensuring no stagnant corners.

The 'story' follows a circular route in either direction. The generous high path takes one along a bank with grass and bulbs falling to the water below. Quickly enclosed by the dense thicket edge which is all nuts, viburnum and holly, one comes suddenly with

Above, left: The Rother god in his cave; water issues from a pot under his arm, the 'source' of the river here. His crown is of carved river reeds. The cave is made from huge chunks of Fittleworth stone from a nearby quarry.

Above, right: The painted Gothic pavilion designed by Pip Jebb for Simon and Stewart's house at Petworth. We created the cascade close up under it, to give it a plinth and to add drama.

childish surprise and delight upon a knobbly elm-pillared and thatched hermitage. It is hard to remember in what order things got built, but the plan was conceived and agreed almost in its entirety and then handed to W&A Baxter, of Petworth to execute. The inestimable Sandy Baxter, who might have risen from the pages of P.G. Wodehouse, a sandy-haired, smiling Scot, dedicated to detail and planning almost to his own detriment, together with his remarkable team of tradesmen formed a company or troop in the trenches with Julian as their commanding officer. They riddled out the Weetabix-chunks of Sussex ragstone – needed to make the cliff – from the Fittleworth quarry down the road, and arranged their transport by low loader to the field by the river. Meanwhile machines munched out bucketfuls of Sussex clay, doubling the size of the water, cutting right up under the pavilion. Sandy dug the footings and built the hidden steel structure for the 'ruin' and together Julian and Sandy masterminded the putting of stone on stone to make a convincing ancient monument. The hermitage was crafted in Wiltshire, our private cache provided the elm trunks, collected ten years or more before from Colin Passmore at Llanthony Priory Court Farm. But it was Sandy who got his men to lay the paddle stone floor, to chop and split hazel wands to clad the internal walls and to hew and joint the branches of the fallen tulip tree (fallen in the storm of 1987) to make the bench with stag-oak legs. Stag oak is a name for the worn-away lifeless oak branches which we collect from veteran trees. The wood is hard and twisted like antlers, and we used our stash and Sandy's ingenuity to piece together the 'Rivendell' rustic handrail which leads down from the hermitage to the bridge.

Having sailed over the bridge, the path winds along the southern bank through outcrops of ragstone and royal ferns and begins to climb gently to the cave of the Rother god. He is the fictional father of this noble river which winds its way through Sussex,

Above: The view back across the park to the river, through the Gothic ruined archway.

past the Parish Church at Trotton three miles away, from whence the squire set out for Agincourt and slumbers still in armoured effigy. The Rother god in his cave surveys the water and tolerates the ruin. He was a fun creation which we dreamt up with mason and sculptor Tom Verity, making reference to such rival river gods as that at Parham not far away, Stourhead, Goldney's Grotto in Bristol and perhaps with a nod to Giambologna's great Appennino at Pratolino, now part of Villa Demidoff, a colossus or mountain god part real tufa and part carved stone and render. Simon was sceptical, 'We have no Giambologna' he opined dryly. But, we argued, if we were to fashion him more of an Anglo-Saxon worthy, a Wessex monarch, with a cloak of oyster shells, massive ankles, feet and head carved by Tom and crowned with river reeds he might have some dignity. Simon capitulated and the inestimable Sandy found a colossus of stone with which to roof his dryads cave.

In front of Pip Jebb's octagonal pavilion water gurgles and chortles through rocky channels at hand height, only to thunder down over the cliff into the pool. The Fittleworth stone, being friable and sandy, has proved the perfect host for mosses and lichens and, even where it is not splashed, it develops a hirsute pubescence of wondrous texture and luminescent hue. The pleasure in the whole ensemble, sitting in the pavilion, the cascade roaring outside and the sunlight glancing off mosses and ferns, the yellow bridge yonder and the high gothic window was mentioned by Neil MacGregor in his eulogy at Simon's funeral. Finally the overgrown path of Dante pulls one on and into the tangled nether world of a laurel grove. The flint-lined rill quickly snakes away from the path into a dark territory of coiling trunks. Stumps and ammonites edge the path, and a stygian gloom pervades the dead leaves underfoot, leading one on – but where? At the farthest edge of the wood Simon and Stewart had made a circular glade, almost a drum, of shiny holly and laurel leaves, home to some rather lost stone statues of the four seasons. Here, Julian felt, were the makings of an inner sanctum, a wellspring for the water, a sacred grove. He chose to construct at its heart a tufa monolith from which would ooze the waters of the Rother, as pumped by Sandy's engineering, set in a circular rill boiling with springs, as the river Test boils up at Mottisfont or the wells of Wells bubble up by the Bishop's Palace. Similar strange blancmanges of tufa sit in tanks of water at the Villa d'Este at Tivoli, spurting and oozing. This monolith is a strange and powerful beast, slumbering, closed-winged but latent; presiding powerfully, it is intended to be the mysterious heart of the whole endeavour.

Above, left: The thatched rustic hut made from the last of the knobbly elm trunks we brought from Llanthony in 1988. On the outside the building is clad with elm waney board.

Above and opposite: Inside, the hut was decorated by Sandy's men using hazel wands and fir cones.

Overleaf: The spring source for the waters of the lake. Concentric circles made from flint hold the water, which both oozes out of the tufa fountain and bubbles from the bottom of the pools like springs, setting off on its journey through the dark woods in a flint rill to the cascade.

Mary's Garden was a very different endeavour, but none the less pleasing or rewarding. With Simon's death everything changed and Stewart battled with a new role, new brooms, public opening and, if it were possible, heightened standards. We were touched to be asked to think of a way of making an 'anteroom' for visitors who were to be bussed in from Midhurst and hence might have to hang around a bit at the beginning and end of their visit. All the usual visitor things were to be in the barns, and outside was a sloping yard which needed to interest them and, we all agreed, being self-contained, could be entirely different to the rest of the garden, a blank canvas for Stewart's understanding and virtuosity with plants. Sunny and surrounded largely by walls and buildings, the enclosure was completed with a further wall, hornbeam hedges and hedges on stilts. Within the rectangular space gravel, and water pouring into reflecting tanks, were intended to produce a small garden room that was dynamic and playful. Our visual proposal to Stewart shows a great picture of Sylvia Crowe standing in a modernist garden about 1955 by what I can only describe as a pair of concrete coffee tables filled with water – but in the end something a bit more West Sussex and a bit more 'farmyard' was opted for. As the site sloped to the north, gravity could be employed to move the water across the garden at right angles to the direct route the visitors would take to the entrance building. The flinty fine gravel is light-reflecting, as are the tanks of water and the rills between, and these draw a formal line through the composition which we aimed to weave with Stewart's botanical waves of perennial planting in dusky, tawny hues, all

Above and opposite: *Mary's Garden*. This space is an anteroom where National Trust visitors to Woolbeding wait upon arrival and departure. Set in a former farmyard, there are tanks of water flowing one to another. Domes of yew are surrounded by planting and gravel. Shown top left is one of the French limestone troughs which Stewart planted with old olives.

fronded and feathery. Eryngiums, echinaceas, eschscholzia, cleome, sisyrinchium, stipa, dierama, eremurus – what we termed a succession of tall 'wandy' plants – with nerines, alliums, nectaroscordum, and *Tulipa sprengeri* in the gravel. The way was to be marked and the whole bolted down by solid thigh-high domes of clipped yew at the edge of the gravel path and the biting lime-green mounds of *Euphorbia characias* subsp. *wulfenii*. The simplicity of this planting and the consequent danger of 'off' moments were to be buoyed up with huge pots filled with orange tulips and orange African Queen Group lilies followed by orange *Brugmansia vulcanicola* in high summer. We found a pair of vast curvaceous limestone vats and Stewart found two old knotted olive trees which, with the walls, the sun and the planting, push the mood in a 'generally Californian direction' – at least this is how I imagine Simon might have wryly described it.

Simon's underlying sense that time was running out had given everything a special urgency in the long walk. It is very rare indeed to work for someone who 'gets it' so completely, who is so focused and effective in their thinking, so vigorous and so rigorous. But, at the same time, together Simon and Stewart were adventurous and humorous, generous and kind. Great clients will produce great work and they also surround themselves with great workers, like Sandy Baxter, Lanning Roper, Philip Jebb and all the others we have encountered there. Stewart has carried it all forward with supreme grace and talent, inspiration and perspiration and it has been an unparalleled pleasure throughout.

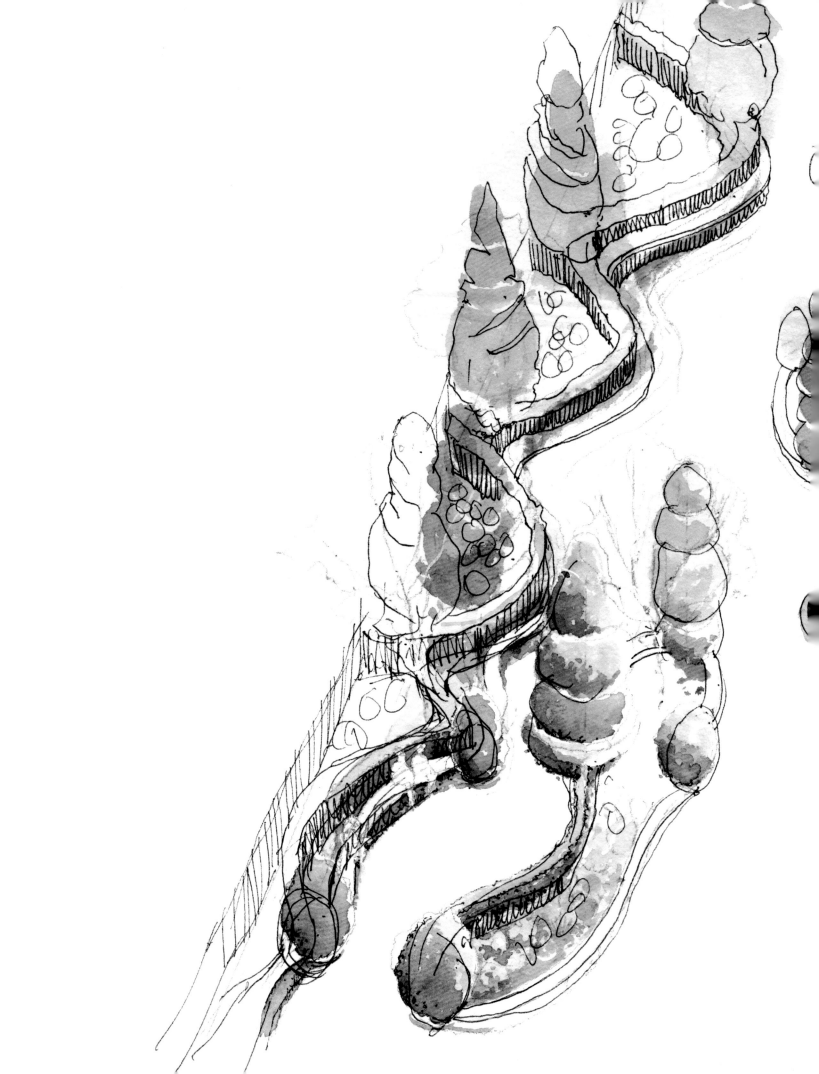

Queen Elizabeth II Garden

It all began with an invitation to enter a competition. Entering competitions is not something we have ever been able to afford to do, and are rarely asked. Such submissions require a level of work and expense and such a high standard of presentation that they are better suited to large practices. But this was a special case. We had all watched on September 11th; watched it happen, knowing things would never be the same again, and the ideas came fully formed and asking to be put forward. We plunged in, almost failed to get it across the Atlantic on time owing to the vagaries of DHL and were only saved by Jackie Jones from Jigsaw who knew how to courier documents last-minute to the US by taking us to a no-mans-land between motorways backstage at Heathrow. The portfolio arrived and we won the competition. The design was for a garden, a triangle called Hanover Square, a few blocks from Ground Zero, given by the City of New York Parks Department to a British 9/11 Memorial Trust to make a garden in honour of the 67 British-born who died in the World Trade Center. This was the simple reason for the garden, and remains so. Everything quickly became very complicated, but we, and all the unbelievably dedicated and well-meaning people involved, were working on it on account of the victims and especially their families.

The triangle is a dark canyon among the high rises, though luckily along the bottom south side there is a five-storey late-nineteenth-century brownstone house; this was an Astor house that is now run as a rather old-fashioned club. The 'square' was paved with concrete, and a dozen gleditsia trees (which had to stay) grew there among rows and rows of heavy benches, which filled up in the middle of the day with office workers eating their sandwiches. It was undoubtedly a challenge, but hugely enjoyable. The brief was for a full-blown English country garden, all singing, all dancing, with flowers and shrubs but it had to have as much seating as was already there (220 running feet). We considered the conditions, extreme climate, limited light, biting winds, stultifying humidity, gods knows what beneath the ground (that nightmare turned out to be much worse than the anticipated worst) and in all likelihood untrained labour to look after it. Even before the garden was made there were endless demands upon the space to have events and lots of people do things in it. Our plan was therefore quite simple, intended to be calm, contemplative, abstract in form. We wanted above all a green enclosure, just that bit removed from the hurly-burly. Our design did not really use flowers at all; it used clipped curvilinear forms and the important thing was the texture of these with the texture of stone. Green forms with stone forms. We wanted *Cyclamen hederifolium,* flowering in September, to be almost the only colour in the planting. In the rest the colour was to be found – for the ten years or so that it would take the yew to grow into our amorphous shapes – in the armatures, formed in these shapes as a guide for clipping, which were to be powder-coated red. This was all in our submission, but only some of it got through the production process.

In plan we took the triangle and drew the rough shape of the United Kingdom round it like a ribbon, imagining a light-coloured stone cut into a dark-coloured paving of huge pieces, two yards by a yard across, of Caithness granite, which often still pave the old streets of New York. These had been brought over in the late nineteenth century, as ballast on the clippers which were taking goods back across the Atlantic to Britain. It was Julian's idea to inscribe the pale ribbon of Moray sandstone, also from the north of Scotland, with county names – Norfolk, Suffolk, Shropshire, Staffordshire, and so on – as reference points for memories of people and places for the victim's families. Moreover many of these names exist also for places in the United States. This simple idea was complicated by the Foreign Office who insisted on including British Dependencies. Simon Verity relieved some of the tedium of carving every single one of these by, for example, placing such curiosities as the 'Sandwich Islands' just outside a delicatessen. Simon Verity is the enormously talented sculptor, master stone carver and letter cutter.

Opposite: A watercolour illustrating the shape and rhythm of the evergreen planting.

181

This page: The view north up the triangular Hanover Square. The gleditsia trees were there already. The curving benches are Portland roach, the ribbon of counties Moray sandstone, and the rest of the floor is Caithness granite. Yews for topiary were planted but without armatures.

Opposite: An artist's impression of the topiary and beds planted with *Cyclamen hederifolium* (top); tall buildings looking south, the ribbon of counties and stone benches (with bobbles to stop skateboarders), Simon Verity waiting for the Queen to arrive, 7th July 2010, 40°C (middle); a model of the garden (bottom).

We had worked with him at Leeds Castle among a brotherhood of journeymen and women grotto makers, after which he was invited to finish carving the front of St John the Divine on Manhattan. When we started the project, there he was, living in Harlem, the most talented man for the job, ready and willing to create magic with letters in stone.

Simon helped with everything to do with stone, the backbone of the design, and he alone carved every single letter in the garden, almost losing his mind in the process. The plaque announcing the opening of the Henry Cole wing of the V&A Museum had been made by Simon in a similarly bold nineteenth-century 'Showman'-style typeface similar to that which we all chose for the 'ribbon' of Britain round the garden. Many and various a British stone was used: large flints and pebbles, slate, granite, sandstone and roach, a creamy fossil-filled limestone from the Portland seam, of which Simon had long been master. He had used it at Leeds Castle to great effect, making an ashlar wall of it and then carving back into it a giant mask that oozes water – like the one at he Villa Vizcaya Miami. In 'Hangover' Square, as we couldn't resist calling it, we used it for the sinuous high backed benches, all two-hundred-plus feet with which we wrapped the mounds and waves of clipped greenery behind, and with which we drew the wavy outline of the open spaces. The benches were to be cantilevered on steel, underneath which we drew and specified a solid green line of box hedging as at Houghton or Euridge, so they would seem to float, a white line amongst living greenery. Very sadly we were too far removed from the execution of this idea, despite copious drawings and explanations, and the steel was set in an ocean of concrete leaving no room for any plant to flourish.

The planting in the curving beds enclosing the garden were to be 'the eternals' of British downland: holly, ivy, rolling clipped box, out of which were to rise weird and wonderful whipped-ice-cream topiary shapes of yew, formed round bright red-painted steel armatures. These were absolutely central to our design, for we realised from the start that to get full-sized 'Painswick-Churchyard'-style bubbly yews grown and clipped into shape would take a decade. We therefore thought of the armatures; these would be like freehand-drawn cages of bright red-painted steel made to the three-dimensional shapes we required. They would create vertical but abundant shapes in the

Above and opposite: Each individual shape for the topiary rendered in three dimensions and three stages of growth, showing the flame-red steel armatures that were proposed. The shapes were to be wonderful, un-traditional, amorphous. We felt the idea of the armatures was central to the whole concept. The 'Art Committee' thought they would be too strong and compete with the proposed sculpture.

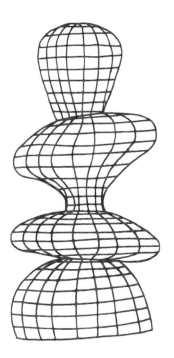  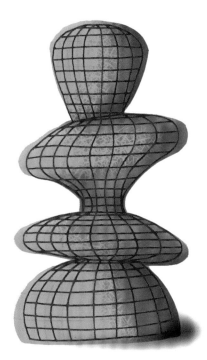

garden instantly and also provide a guide for the gardeners to clip to. The shapes were amorphous but like any sculpture were very thought through. The point about these towering yew shapes was that they could be both sombre, even forbidding, yet at the same time light-hearted and eccentric – harking back to Alice in Wonderland. Perhaps there were too many concepts for all the many people involved to compute; some got it, some didn't, and as a result the crucial armatures fell by the wayside.

For flower we suggested something bordering on a white garden, with light acid-green *Philadelphus coronarius* 'Aureus', as it has the ability to not only flower but enjoy being in the shade. We chose similarly acid-green *Euphorbia characias* subsp. *wulfenii*; anciently cultivated and shade-loving cottage plants *Lunaria annua* and *Hesperis matronalis*; white periwinkle; white *Rosa* 'Blanche Double de Coubert'. The existing gleditisia came into their own among all this, their lime green frondy leaves, interesting bark and ragged branches adding something, and we suggested they be hung with strings of light bulbs to give a festive feel. In the beginning there were to be no signboards or memorials, only a classic London iron railing with 67 finials beautifully topped with daffodils, thistles, flax and English roses carved by Simon and cast in a foundry in England. It was to be totally understated and everyone hoped timeless. Because of the many cooks this got overlaid with a superfluity of national symbols and the subtlety and practicality of the planting, the use of 'non' plants and understatement was never really understood. This was not how the garden was conceived; the distinction between hard and soft landscaping is a purely practical thing and has no bearing on the complete design in which the two are inalienable parts of the whole endeavour. But in all gardens the planting changes itself however hard you try to stop it; it is the structure which remains constant. The total ensemble was intended to be simple, plain, bold, shapely, comfortable but arresting, thought-provoking – green forms, stone shapes and planes, dappled light, real and lasting materials, an outdoor room of solid tranquillity for people to use in the midst of the city. It was built above all else for the 67 who went to work in the World Trade Center that day and never returned, for their mothers, fathers, brothers and sisters, daughters and sons, lovers and loved ones who never saw them again.

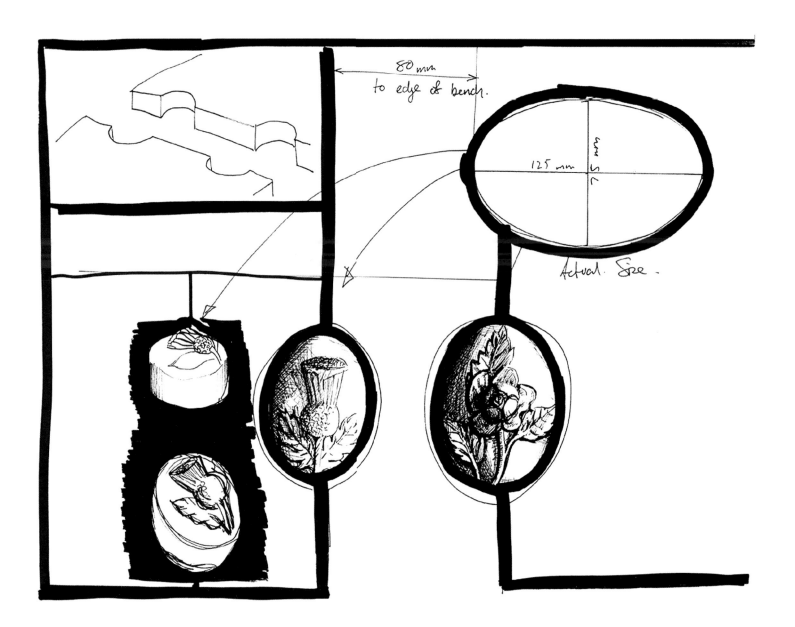

80 mm
to edge of bench.

125 mm

Actual Size.

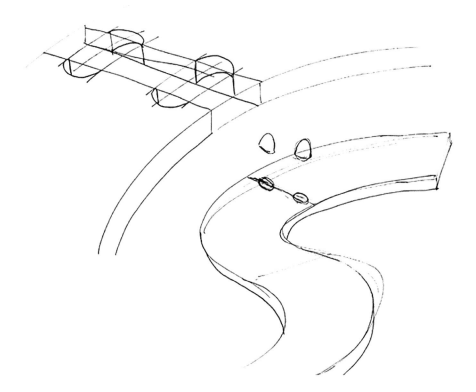

This page: Working drawings for the carved pebble joints, an anti-skating device.

Opposite: Three working drawings showing the development of the curvilinear forms.

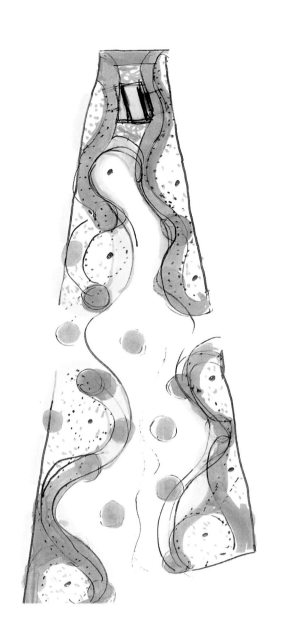

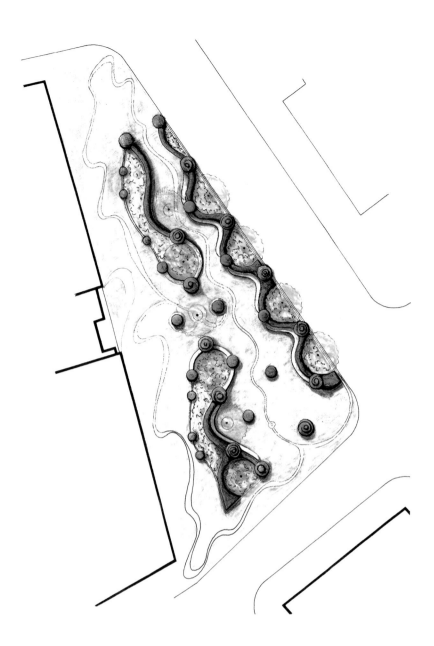

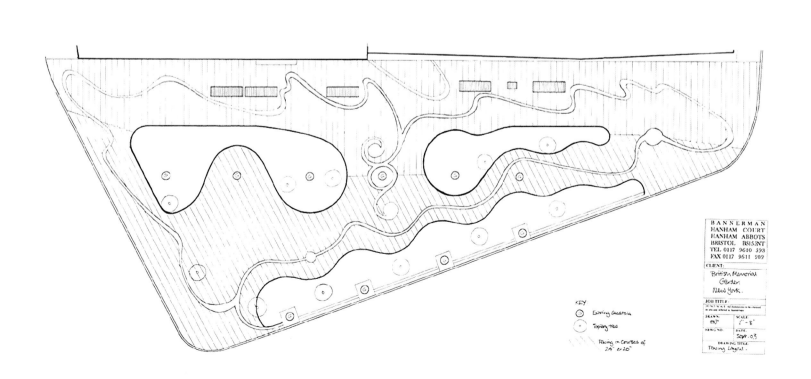

BANNERMAN
HANHAM COURT
HANHAM ABBOTS
BRISTOL BS15 3NT
TEL 0117 9610 593
FAX 0117 9611 209

CLIENT:
British Memorial
Garden
New York.

JOB TITLE:

DRAWN   SCALE
PJB   1" = 8'
DRWG NO: DATE:
               Sept. 03
DRAWING TITLE
Paving Layout.

KEY

○ Existing Location

⊙ Topiary tree

Paving in Courses of
24" to 20"

Wychwood

On the edge of what one thinks of as the High Cotswolds, between the towns of Burford and Charlbury, Wychwood Manor sits slightly north of the remains of the Wych wood, which John Piper describes in his 1953 *Shell Guide* '... now a fragment of a forest, deep and curious, that was once as large and important as the New Forest' in 'some of the best of the Oxfordshire landscape; open upland country under grass and corn ... with ochre stone walls ... and isolated clumps of sombre trees.' It is 'open' and 'upland', hugely arable with good hedgerow trees but the general feel is not lush like the Windrush and shelter is important. Alex and Fiona Wilmot-Sitwell took some persuading therefore that the house needed to be set free from its hugger-mugger poorly planted suburban bonds and required us all to be as bold about the garden as they were already being about the house, a faux-Jacobean gabled confection built in the 1920s by a blind cement magnate who seems to have insisted that it be pointed with thick black mortar like a child's drawing. The Wilmot-Sitwells had spent a long time looking for a suitable house in the perfect location and the first thing they did was chip away at the pointing. They were neck deep in portakabins and scaffolding when they called us in, having seen our work at Houghton Hall in Norfolk and been prompted by our compatriot from Waddesdon Manor days, Milly Soames. They felt that we could provide the bold structure and full, generous planting that they had admired at Houghton, and hoped we could help them in connecting the garden to the surrounding countryside through the dark, enclosing woods and shrubs that grew around the house. When we met them, we all agreed instantly that beautiful views were, sadly, excluded. The landscape, the trees, the spires, and the broad sweeps of farmland that lay all around, were frustratingly hidden, the house closely hedged in by mixed plantations. But, while the garden had been very well tended by the previous owners and, especially, by their gardener, Shirley Emery, whom the Wilmot-Sitwells were lucky enough to inherit, the feel of the place was closed in to the point of claustrophobia. It wasn't hard for us to persuade them that the mission was to see beyond the creepers and the shelterbelts, but they were nervous about the blasting they might be exposed to by opening up the broader landscape and the pastoral vistas. Alex particularly was alarmed at the prospect of removing trees but was eventually persuaded by the opportunity to embark on a massive programme of sapling planting, and by the idea of hiring a tree spade, with which we moved the best of the twenty-year-old trees from the mixed plantations into the outer fields to create a parkland.

Glamorisation and extension of the house brought with it all the horrors which leave a garden pulverised. To come up with a design, we found the chief problem was that close to the east and west ends of the house there were mixed plantations of native trees, established under a grant scheme of the 1980s, but entirely neglected since. Over planted and then left un-thinned and uncared for, these woodland belts right near the house had been a pretty misguided operation, but it is always heart-breaking to take trees down, and the ones left were often lopsided and leaderless. One solution was to keep the best trees, move the second best out into the field to create parkland clumps and to fell the rubbish and short-term planting such as wild cherry and conifer. To the south the remnants of a formal Arts-and-Crafts garden dropped away in stages, but even here a crop of self-seeded ash and sycamore straddled the skyline, hiding a sodden and derelict tennis court. The plan we came up with meant moving the tennis court to the east alongside a new kitchen garden and was quite radical. It required considerable persuasion to prove that clearing the saplings and starting again with the tennis court would reveal a dipping meadow, a Samuel Palmer-esque pear orchard, and a small new lake which was quickly nestled in the very bottom of this meadow, Toti Gifford diverting the stream with his diggers.

The garden needed to connect to the landscape on all sides, but such unpicking had to be done stealthily to calm Alex's understandable anxieties about the destruction, and with a clear aim in mind. Shelter and protection, once removed, take a long time to re-establish. The plan envisioned a layered, lush formal flower garden in the middle near the house.

Opposite: A view of Wychwood Manor, looking north from the Charlbury road.

Overleaf: The south front, extended and altered in 2001. The Manor was originally built in the 1920s.

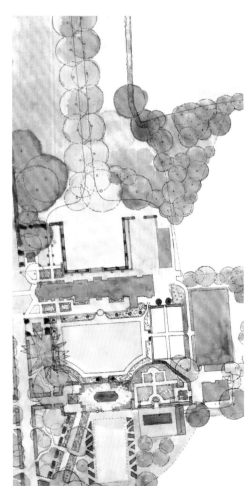

After this we would create radiating 'rides' through the 1980s plantations on the west side by keeping the best trees of the plantation and moving everything else out. The resulting 'goose-foot' shape of triangles is a most satisfying transformation; its strong green lines hedged about with hornbeam, and its avenues, focused on existing trees and a church spire, radiate from the bay window in the new drawing room. Inside each triangle of the thinned plantation left behind, the addition of lilac, philadelphus and species roses in long grass spangled with spring bulbs is not laborious to keep up, and helps to make the transition from tight, highly wrought garden to broad open parkland. The park was made from a twelve-acre field and separated by a new ha-ha and iron park railing. The outlying copses were conjured from clumps of twenty-five-year-old oak, lime, ash and pine, moved by tree spade from the plantation and buttressed by masses of whips and saplings.

At the heart of the garden, contemporary with the house, was a large dry-stone walled enclosure, bordered with beds encircling a level sward. The curving wall to the right under the cedar was there already and the new design mirrored it with a new curving wall opposite, which provided a backdrop to the swimming pool, to the left. The introduction of a wide hoggin path round the central lawn here, was needed to add light and texture to the garden, and would allow for the lavish flower bowers to stretch out of their beds and sprawl luxuriously over the gravel. Coupled with floweriness we all agreed there must be scent and structure. Every doorway, window or cross path needed dotting and crossing with plants like *Daphne odora* 'Aureomarginata', sarcococca or philadelphus, to trail scent round the garden. Sentinel within the deep borders, a dozen three-and-a half-metre-high yew domes, a metre in diameter, were planted, to people the garden year-round. Grizzled on frosty days and fuzzy-coated when in new growth, they provide weightiness to the whole composition, a sober note against the exuberance of the floristry. Near the house Fiona's yen for glorious, generous planting – honesty and sweet rocket, irises and lupins, followed by poppies, delphiniums and shrub roses – was an opportunity for tour-de-force deep herbaceous borders. All this was only achievable thanks partly to the richly manured limestone soil and to the brilliant cossetting and devotion of Shirley, once she had overcome her consternation at the necessary initial phase of destruction which reduced her at one horrible moment to copious tears. A handsome young cedar of Lebanon presides on one side of a raised lawn, which again had to be freed from a thicket of sycamore, with the sunken garden and lily pond lying below. Here we added a rill at the base of the Arts-and-Crafts-style gazebo made from oak pillars with a Cotswold stone roof, pitched steeply and splaying out at the bottom as requested by Alex like those at Hidcote. This building presides over the peony walk, two broad borders about eighteen metres long, groaning with well-staked peonies, followed by lilies and *Verbena bonariensis* in high summer, and Lent lilies and ferns at the start of the year. The geometry worked out satisfyingly well; in this case the path runs southerly and downhill, out to a sturdy oak as a 'point de vue' by the stream. It is flanked by the goose-foot triangles with their tangle of rambling roses in the trees on one side, and a level football pitch edged with yew cones on the other. The football pitch was always on the wish list, but stylistically it provided the perfect breathing space, a green paragraph break before the walled swimming-pool garden, the kitchen garden and the tennis court all to the east of the main lawn.

The terrace on the south front of the house was raised and extended by the builders and paved with monumental slabs of old Cotswold paving that we found locally. The planting is aromatic, a 'maquis' of French lavender, rosemary, orange rock roses and magenta lychnis, which somehow survive the perishing high Cotswold winters. Rambling roses 'Adélaïde d'Orléans' and 'Albertine' tussle with wisteria on the gabled elevation, but the new 'Georgian' drawing room is harnessed by the solid green of *Magnolia grandiflora* and violet roses 'Veilchenblau' and 'Rose-Marie Viaud' between the windows. A sense of architectural enclosure was provided by yew 'wing walls' coming off the house, and into to these were placed green-oak doorways – spiky topped in a nod to the Jacobean.

The swimming pool required the complete remodelling of a corner of the garden because we were determined to keep it within the 'hortus conclusus' and not flung out somewhere like an afterthought as pools can be, dislocated and as a result slightly un-relaxed. Well within the walls it is a hot, appealing place to spend time, eat outside, drink, and chat

Previous pages: Five views of the hornbeam allées, with wooded 'boscos' behind them – formed from the existing plantation – and punctuated with green-oak pillars; shown bottom right are the flat-topped yew cones edging the football pitch.

Opposite, first row: Robert Hibberd with son Roger by the roof of the gazebo under construction in the yard (left); the yew sentinels just planted in front of the newly constructed terrace (right).

Opposite, second row: Before they were cleared, the saplings blocked the view to the south (left); the gazebo (middle); the tree spade moving trees out of the plantation to make parkland (right).

Opposite, third row: a watercolour plan of the garden (left); head gardener Shirley Emery (right).

Opposite, fourth row: the house under scaffolding, from the south (middle); Julian and Robert decorating the pool house with fallow deer antlers from Petworth Park (right).

on the four days a year when this is truly possible. The grey-blue water resulting from a polished concrete lining sits in a buff York stone terrace, set comfortably in the arc of the high dry-stone wall to the north, but you can see the 'policies outwith', as the Scots describe them, through an opening in the outer garden wall. Here later-flowering planting, hotter in colour for the hotter days of the holidays, surrounds the pool. We place pots filled with agapanthus right around the coping and elsewhere jolly July annuals and biennials, California poppies, calendula, sweet peas and shocking-pink salvias make it feel sunny even on a dull day. From here, a door leads to the kitchen garden, which we built up from the formerly sycamore-darkened back drive to the old coach house. This building had long since been converted into a surprisingly handsome and practical greenhouse, along with a compost corner and potting shed, centre of garden operations, so to have a semi-walled garden here for vegetables and cut flowers made sense.

New projects bring new pleasures in the continuing development of any garden. After the removal of the conifers and elder on the outer fence line of the front drive with its vaulting lime avenue, the grassy glades thus opened up each side were planted with Alex's longed-for planting with a Far-Eastern bent, witch hazels, magnolias, gunnera, acers and rhododendrons, a connection with gardens of his childhood and a life of travail and far-flung travel. Piers and finials have been added to gates, and the parkland and boundary planting grows and gets improved and modified annually. The business of freeing up this garden to read out into the big upland landscape, while providing a reasoned structure for a romantic garden within, has had to be undertaken with patience, unpicking slowly bit by bit, but the inner garden is sheltered and settled now, embowered in the broad sweep of the high wold and, seen from the Charlbury road, it looks like a 1930s railway poster of the perfect country seat. John Piper peppers his description of the Wych wood with the story of an argument between a horseman and a local: 'What is the name of this wood?' asks the horseman. 'Wychwood.' replies the local. 'This wood here.' 'Wychwood.' 'You've got a head like a block of wood.' 'One of us has, but I am not sure Wych.'

Top, from left: *Rosa* 'Albéric Barbier' with *Hydrangea paniculata* 'Limelight'; lupins and irises; eremurus and rosa mundi (*Rosa gallica* 'Versicolor'); poppies and irises.

Above: 'Manhattan' (New York Series) Oriental poppies (left); steps with rose 'De Resht' (right).

Opposite: *Lupinus* 'Noble Maiden' and *Iris* 'Braithwaite' glowing in front of a towering yew.

Opposite, top: *Rosa* 'Madame Alfred Carrière' on the pillar and, beyond the swimming pool, *Cistus* × *hybridus* (left); the peony border with the gazebo behind (right).

Opposite, bottom: a hornbeam allée centred on a much-pruned noble oak tree (left); an oak balustrade (right).

Above: An oak 'Jacobean' doorway similar to the one IB first thought up for Hanham Court; the flagstone terrace is covered with rock roses, stachys and cistus.

Right: Sentinel yews in the main borders below the terrace south front, planted in 2008.

Overleaf: The opened-up view revealing falling land, magical pear trees and a distant wooded rise. This was a breakthrough. We levelled the grass beyond the garden to provide a football pitch for the three Wilmot-Sitwell boys and flanked it with cones of yew.

Arundel Castle

'The Collector Earl's Garden', as we dubbed it, is not a recreation of a garden. It is more one imagined by us using all available historical data and concocted with a large pinch of interpretation, assorted additions and artifices, in an attempt to bring to life the garden belonging to Thomas Howard, 14th Earl of Arundel, and his wife Alathea at Arundel House. This London house of the Fitz Alans stood next to Somerset House, then a royal residence, between The Strand and the Thames, at the epicentre of the Jacobean world. Ancient baths, supposedly Roman, still exist on this site; before the Reformation it had been the town residence of the Bishop of Bath and Wells, then given to the Duke of Somerset, and sold to Henry Fitz Alan, 12th Earl of Arundel, in 1549. Thomas Howard is now remembered for being, among other things, an aesthete, patron of Rubens, Van Dyck and Inigo Jones, and possibly one of the most important collectors in the history of English art. Which is where the gardening story, one that had long gripped us and meant so much to his descendent, the current Duke of Norfolk, begins.

The site of the new garden was nearly half of the walled kitchen garden at Arundel Castle in Sussex, sloping southward, towered over by the nineteenth-century Catholic Cathedral across the road, in which by strange coincidence I had been christened. This part of the garden had long been a visitor's car park. The Norfolks had seen and been taken with the Temple Grove at Highgrove: Eddie liked the Temple and Georgie liked the wild roots and 'otherness' of it. They wanted something quite extraordinary to happen at Arundel, and they asked us to think boldly. We met late in the evening on December 1st 2006 at the Castle, where we were most kindly put up and royally treated throughout our working time there, and started to present our ideas around ten o'clock. At midnight we toasted the dawning of Eddie's 50th birthday and a grand new garden project.

In 1979 Roy Strong had published his seminal book *The Renaissance Garden in England,* which for the first time brought to bear a minute and brilliant understanding of all the arts, pulling together a coherent story that brings gardening in the sixteenth and seventeenth centuries into the foreground of the history of art and architecture.

Opposite: The Dancing Crown, a gilded metal crown that rises by the pressure of water.

Above: A pen and ink rendering of Oberon's Palace, flanked by the Lumley obelisks on its rocky outcrop, with pines and palms.

Overleaf: Urn fountains, a cascade, pillar screen, beech pergolas left and right, with alliums in the foreground.

The floor plan shows:

THE HOUSE

TERRACE

○ ○ ○ ○   ○ ○ ○ ○

Summer House (top left)
Summer House (top right)

walk with cloister beneath (left side)
walk with cloister beneath (right side)

4 Statues   4 Statues

FORMAL PARTERRES

Fountain   Fountain
○   ○

Summer House (bottom left)
Summer House (bottom right)

GROTTO

WALKS WITH TREES

Above, left: A detail from Mytens'
portrait of Alathea Talbot c.1618,
showing the hornbeam pergola,
the fountain and the doorway, used
as models for the Collector Earl's
Garden and inside Oberon's Palace.

Above, right: A detail from a portrait
of Thomas Howard, showing the
'Marbles', antique statuary bought
on the trip to Rome; the doorway
and railings were used as a model
for the Collector Earl's Garden.

Left: The oak portal (far left); a plan of
the garden at Somerset House (1620s)
which was next to and contemporary
with Arundel House (left).

Above: Oberon's Palace with the
Fittleworth stone grotto below. The
railings were taken from the portrait
of Thomas Howard opposite.

These fantastical and formal gardens, almost all of which have vanished, were a colossal expression of current thinking. Familiar to all of us through Shakespeare and Elizabethan lyric poets, painters and miniaturists, the early seventeenth century was a time of contradictions, an awkward, intense coming of age. The childish, superstitious medieval world was not yet dead, but grown-up science and reason were emerging with force in the wake of the religious revolution, which had spread from Europe. Everything was affected – religion, politics, society, the sciences, the arts, the court, and gardens. London was expanding and changing and in the swirl were the Metaphysical poets, Ben Jonson, philosophers and scientists like Hobbes, Hooke and Boyle, writers such as Aubrey and Evelyn, Van Dyck and other painters – and Inigo Jones.

The story we pursued was thrilling. For years we had poured over Strong's book and, equally, John Harris's collected drawings of Inigo Jones, enjoying John and Eileen's generosity of knowledge and friendship since first meeting them at Leeds Castle. It felt like destiny to find ourselves designing a garden which was a tribute to Jones because of his close connection with the Arundels. In the spring of 1613 Jones accompanied Thomas and Alathea Howard on a tour of Italy following their attendance at the wedding of James I's daughter, Elizabeth, to the Elector Palatine. Although it was the second time Jones had been to Italy, travelling in Europe had been made extremely difficult by the wars and revolutions of religion, particularly for English Catholic aristocrats, so the party's sense of adventure must have been high. They were all clearly of a single mind in their fascination with the Antique; whilst Jones returned with a copy of Palladio's *Quattro Libri* the aristocrats returned with the Ancient Greek sculptures and inscriptions that became known as the 'Arundel Marbles'.

Returning to London, fuelled with new ideas and passions, Thomas and Alathea determined to build a garden and a gallery at Arundel House in which to put their treasures. Although the house and garden are long gone – the collection went to form a foundation of Oxford's Ashmolean Museum – it has been described by garden historians as the first 'Museum' or 'Theatre' garden in England. However very little is known of it, except from details in the corners of the Daniel Mytens portraits of its owners and fragments of description. The plan of the similar garden that was at Somerset House is known, however, and this provided the two-terraced model for the former car park at Arundel. The upper terrace is a series of three courts bounded by a great oak pergola, something the like of which can be seen in the background of Alathea's portrait. The two outer courts are plain gravel with four catalpa trees and, also taken almost entirely from the picture, is a fountain, which we interpreted using the Talbot talbot, or hound, (Alathea was born a Talbot) and other armorial motifs – with help from John Martin Robinson from the College of Arms, keeper of the muniment room at Arundel at that time and a great supporter and friend of ours. The central court is a canal of water – in the seventeenth century it would have been the allegorical source of the River Arun – emanating from a tufa mountain in a building whose tympanum is supported by grotesque wild men, which we took from a seventeenth-century drawing by Francesco Fanelli, and made in green oak. This is flanked by water-spouting urns, based on some at Bomarzo. The Eastern Court has a simple pedimented pavilion, the Park Temple, which we invented and made in oak, whose capitals and acroteria are made from antlers, from local Sussex deer parks Knepp and Petworth, which have become miraculously gilded at the tips with natural lichen over the past eight years. The inside, in a later phase, we decorated with moss and cork and pinecones.

The lower section of the garden was to be a large open lawn laid out below a fantastical miniature castle, Oberon's Palace, the design of which was taken entirely from a set design by Jones for a court masque by Ben Jonson, commissioned by Henry, Prince of Wales, and entitled 'Oberon, the Fairy Prince'. This theatre-set 'palace' clearly bears close resemblance to the Little Castle at Bolsover, which is a curious mix of medieval and classically derived detail, built around 1621 by William Cavendish. We went to Bolsover to see it, looking for help in making a three-dimensional oak building from a pen and ink drawing. We chose to mount the building on a podium, a pile of Sussex ragstone rocks.

Opposite, top left: Inigo Jones's drawing for the stage set of 'Oberon, the Fairy Prince'.

Opposite, top right: A trestle bearing a rusticated column for Oberon's Palace being worked.

Opposite, middle left: The huge arch in a single piece of oak for Oberon's Palace, found by Robert Hibberd from the Woburn Estate wood yard.

Opposite, middle right: Routing the vermiculation on the oak piers.

Opposite, bottom Left: Rustication in oak.

Opposite, bottom Right: Sandy Baxter with bucket and braces, with Steve holding the Earl's coronets for the dancing crown, 2008.

Overleaf: Shadows on the newly erected pergola, 2008.

These came from the same quarry as those we had found with Sandy Baxter for Woolbeding. Our son Bertie calls it 'the Hollywood rocks', but they serve as a plinth and provide a vertical lift, competing with the mass of the Cathedral across the road, and from the door of the Palace there is a great view looking down over the garden. The inside is decorated with cork and shells, and we chose to recreate something that had fascinated us for twenty-five years. The climax of the theatrical experience of the garden is a sixteenth-century water trick, The Dancing Crown, which we first saw at Hellbrunn, Palace of the Archbishop of Salzburg, reputedly the first classical garden north of the Alps, all of whose water jokes and tricks are still working today. Only the other day I had to explain to someone that there is no steel rod holding up the crown, it is quite literally held up by the pressure of water. It makes people smile involuntarily. In similar vein to the mountain at Hellbrunn, which looks to be made of fired ceramic or majolica, we made the fountain a mini-mountain out of real stalactites which we are always collecting, upon which sits a gilded Earl's coronet. The coronet rises, spins and floats magically at any height you wish depending how high you turn up the pressure of the jet of water – but it also falls off.

The 'Inigo' gate, with three balls on top, is just discernible in a portrait of Thomas Howard and is known to have been designed and built by Jones from contemporary description. We used a similar gate drawn by Jones and described as 'Gateway at Newhill Essex'. It is a monumental rusticated portal, made from chunks of oak some of which are the size and more than the weight of a Smart car. It leads into the organically run kitchen garden. Opposite this, against the west-facing wall to St Nicholas churchyard, we placed the Italian doorway, suggesting that one might pass through to another place. It is based upon a drawing by Robert Smythson, architect of Longleat, of a doorway built by Jones at Arundel House, although it is not known quite where it was or how it worked.

Above: The pergola, June 2015, now almost entirely covered with hornbeam.

Opposite: Looking down the pergola with 'Bomarzo' urns, topped with gilded bronze agaves.

Sandy Baxter and his team returned to mastermind the building and ground works. The men of oak were wheeled in from Wiltshire after nine months, making everything and setting it all up dry in the yards back there. The stonemasons from Bristol came with fountains and plaques, and a lot of local landscapers and contractors worked with us, and of course the regular garden team under the leadership of ex-roadie Gerry. In the autumn the buildings began to be erected on site, which meant working through the dark days of January and February towards our goal of opening in May. We were lucky because we lodged in luxury at the Castle, log fires in our bedrooms at the end of a day wading through mud and working by arc light from late afternoon to stick on shells and stalagmites. Spring came hot and bright and time was running out. In the Easter holidays our children came to help, with their ineffable keeper, Martin Gane, who can do anything. James Graham-Stewart came, the Norfolk children came, Sandy's father came out of retirement, and lots of other people came to gawp. Out of the tarmac had risen this fantastical thing. It seemed only a matter of hours before the opening that Sandy rolled out the turf on the main lawn.

On the morning of the opening Eddie and Georgie suggested that we all get in the car and go to see something they wanted us to take a look at. At a farm on the hill behind the cricket ground was a shepherd's hut, one we had found derelict in a corner of the estate yard and cheekily asked if anyone wanted it or might we buy it. It belonged to the Estate was the rebuff. But here it was, all painted up and mended by Baxter's men and they said that it was a 'thank you' for working so hard and making such an amazing thing. The real kindness, we said, was giving us the commission and the opportunity to live out a most compelling and long-standing historical fantasy.

Above: The Park Temple, with fallow-deer antlers for capitals and pediment.

Right: Martin Gane fixing a fallow-deer antler acroterion.

Above: The Italian Doorway, after Inigo Jones.

Far right: A pen and ink drawing of the Inigo Jones doorway.

Right: The pediment of the Park Temple, now 'gilded' with lichen.

Opposite: The Park Temple.

Opposite: The green-oak obelisk with its sunray gilded finial; it was modelled after the Lumley obelisk at Nonsuch, the 16th-century palace once owned by the 12th Earl of Arundel. Behind is Oberon's Palace and, to the left, Arundel Cathedral.

Above: The 'Inigo' gate with three balls on top, the design based on a drawing and from the portrait of Thomas Howard.

Right: Looking through the portal's monumental doorway, made of only seven pieces of oak, towards Oberon's Palace.

Right: A talbot hound issuing water from the fountain carved in Italian limestone.

Opposite, top, from left: 'Sea monkeys', from an Inigo Jones drawing; Alathea's fountain, with carved dolphins, dogs and lions; a detail of the Italian doorway.

Opposite, middle, from left: A gilded bronze agave; a sketch for a gunnera fountain – not built; the Earl's coronet on three dolphins.

Opposite, bottom, from left: Another detail of the Italian Doorway; gadrooning carved in Italian stone for the weir; a wild-man caryatid for the River Arun Temple.

Overleaf: Oak urn fountains based on those at Bomarzo, Italy, with gilded bronze agaves on top.

Following pages: Looking south towards Oberon's Palace through the urn fountains.

5 Hertford Street

Robin and Lucy Birley brought designer Rifat Özbek to the preview party for our sale at Christie's South Kensington in April 2010. They were looking for esoteric things for the club they were going to open in Mayfair on the site of the old 'Tiddy Dols'[sic]. They mentioned that they had been thinking of calling us to see if we could help with the club's central courtyard garden. In the sale we had a collection of early medieval corbels; we suggested these might be the kernel of a way of decorating a dim internal outdoor space – where it was evident it would be difficult to grow very floriferous plants – after the manner of the Soane Museum. They bought the corbels and we joined the design team.

Tiddy Dols (or Dolls) Eating House was apparently one of a sort of chain of such establishments in the eighteenth century. One existed in the Marshalsea debtors' prison, home of Dickens' Little Dorrit; this one, in Shepherd Market, closed in 1998, was the last to survive. Tiddy Doll was an itinerant baker and maker of gingerbread who dressed like a dandy and was well known around Georgian London. The caricaturist and print-maker James Gillray once depicted Napoleon and Talleyrand's re-arrangement of Europe and its crowned heads as 'Tiddy-Doll, the great French Gingerbread-Baker, drawing out a new Batch of Kings', showing just how famous the baker was. It was apt that Robin Birley should be creating a new place of dalliance and indulgence, following the example of his father Mark, who also had a genius for such establishments, creating Annabel's night club in 1963. The building for Robin's club was a complete block of varied-aged buildings, which had been stuccoed and painted white in the early nineteenth century, part of the Shepherd Market development, originally laid out 1735. The builder, designer and promoter (London was ever full of wide boys) was Edward Shepherd, who built and designed on the Grosvenor and Cavendish Estates. The proportions are intimate, domestic and charming but the buildings were in a terrible state. A portion, used forever as a house of ill repute, had even structurally collapsed one night, ejecting scantily clad ministers of the crown. Julian's father spent time off during the war at the RAF club nearby, but would drink in the pub opposite, where the names of all the pilots are reputedly still graffitied on the ceiling, currently hidden behind anaglypta wallpaper. Julian encourages Robin in fantasies of expanding over there and putting it all back to wartime décor and ribaldry.

In the basement, Rifat Özbek a stately pleasure dome decreed with caverns measureless to man in the Ottoman fancy. Ground and first floor were quite polite by comparison, as civilised and urbane as Jane Rainey, her team, and then later Tom Bell could make them. Delightful places for luncheon or any other time. In the centre of all this, opposite the front door but leading on to the dining room and the cigar shop and looked down on from the bars and rooms upstairs, was the central courtyard garden, a light well the size of a London drawing room.

The design meetings were almost always a treat; there were lots of laughs, and dogs, and Robin did his best to have them in easy places where we could all smoke, rather than airless offices. That summer we presented our boards which showed pictures of the Soane Museum, 'master plaster caster' Peter Hone's extraordinary cast-filled flat, Petworth and Chatsworth – nothing if not ambitious. To begin with Julian wanted to cover the walls in gold and green mosaic such as we had just seen and been completely astounded by in the Friday Mosque at Damascus. This proved wildly beyond anyone's capabilities; it is after all one of the wonders of the world, and is thought to have been made by Byzantine workmen for the Umayyad caliphs in *c.* 715 AD. We got mosaic, but on the floor. We wanted the floor to be that classic brasserie mosaic and trailed round archeological museums in Rome and Naples while visiting the best mosaic makers and factories in Italy. Mosaic, it was agreed by all the team, would be ideal on account of its old-fashioned grand café associations, and also we felt on account of the light it would throw up into the space; it should be made of small pieces and the colours should be predominantly pale stone with a good flame terracotta, stitched up with black. The resulting space has,

Opposite: Julian in the smoking garden in front of the shell fountain.

one hopes, the sophistication of a world-class dining place, giving one a lift in the dark of the small hours or on a sunny morning, even on a wet London afternoon. But it was not obvious from the start that this could be achieved. In the beginning it was dismal, in its bombed-out dereliction. We were worried by the lack of light for many reasons, but most of all for growing plants, but we could not have known that this would be less of a problem than the sheer numbers of people who throng the courtyard late at night, sitting in and on the planters and fountains. Having researched round Italy looking for someone to make our dream floor, it was with inevitable irony that we actually found someone who could get the mosaic that we wanted down the New Kings Road opposite my mother's old antique shop, although it was actually made by Italians.

We were trying above all to create a room. Robin thought it a brilliant notion when I suggested that we steal a flue from the dining room and make a grand fireplace in the courtyard. We chose to take as our model a fireplace from Easton Neston, possibly by Hawksmoor, which we had always admired. Likewise Robin was thrilled with the idea for a large oak club fender, which I designed and had made in chunky oak so that it would work outdoors. The walls we chose to lime render and ochre lime wash up to a cornice just below the first floor; the cornice came in handy as a conduit for a gas pipe. The lime-wash finish was to act as a good foil for the pieces of stone carvings, and amplify the sense that one was in a 'room'. The walls above are the original London stock brick and also look fantastic cluttered, as they now are, with architectural, mostly faux-antique fragments, creeping higher up the building every year. The courtyard garden is very pushed for space, and we had to think about every inch of room, and how to use it, fight for it and arrange it like a spaceship or complicated kitchen. And it had to be versatile as well as beautiful. At the opposite end from the fireplace is a fountain, a mini grotto, with stalactites and shell decoration. Ferns grow happily round it. The base is carved with a pair of Assyrian lions toying with a lobster and other shellfish. Lions feature

Above, left: The fountain, like a mini-grotto, with Assyrian lions playing with assorted shellfish.

Above, right: Robin's dog, Arnie.

Opposite, top left: 14th-century angel corbels on the wall above the plant theatre flanked by lion-headed sarcophagi, with the mosaic floor.

Opposite, top right: Assorted architectural fragments and noses.

Opposite, below: More fragments, and the Roman birdcage temple made to hide the RSJ.

on the scaled-down sarcophagi, made from Italian stone. To save space they are absurdly narrow, only just big enough to make it possible to plant plants in them. Diamond-trained ivy grows on trellis up the wall, a well-used trick, with seasonal flowering plants at the bottom. It has to look great from the moment one arrives as it is directly opposite the very anonymous front door to the club. There are glazed doors into the courtyard and through them you see, beyond, a stone, classically influenced 'plant theatre', like a small auricula theatre. This was intended to offer the opportunity to show very extraordinary plants, such as striped Dutch seventeenth-century tulips, florists' pinks and Malmaison carnations that Oscar Wilde might have pinched for his button hole, and other plants or cut flowers that would be arresting and a delight – perhaps the wild flowers of England. It was mirrored behind for added impact. (Julian fought for his idea that it would be fabulous to have a flower stall right at the entrance to the nightclub on the corner of Trebeck Street where you could buy amazing flowers at any hour of the day or night; the planners put paid to that without even giving it serious thought.) None of this would have been possible without our friends the stone-masons from Bristol, who, having carved everything in the west, have come up endlessly to London to fix them.

Robin is a man of meticulous attention – to detail, and to his beloved dogs. There is no butter pat which has not been sifted, edited, rejected or elected, in a manner that reminds us of another perfectionist, Jacob Rothschild. Our attention to detail is insane too, and when Robin was in despair about the RSJ beam which mysteriously appeared across the whole courtyard – deemed necessary to carry the rain canopy, the heaters and our prodigious hanging baskets of mossy ferns – we dreamt up the 'Roman birdcage', a wooden temple seven metres long, exquisitely made in Wiltshire, to make it the best-clad RSJ in Christendom. The result of such profound engagement with a project is that it works on every level. Lucy too is a sleuth for vulgarity; her faultless eye for beauty and chic meant that however wild and crazy the leitmotif of 'Loulou's', the basement nightclub at 5 Hertford Street, there is never a wrong note. Bruce Cavell is Robin's ineffable architect, and had worked with Philip Jebb who was Mark Birley's architect at Annabel's. Philip's daughter, Magdalen Jebb, designed and made the uniforms for staff who are universally charming and all 'princes among men'. Julian, like Groucho Marx, would never wish to be a member of any club that would have him, but he does enjoy being numbered among his incredible staff by Claude the maître d'. All good design is in the end about collaboration and once again we struck lucky. It is the best place for a smoke and a cappuccino in London: even the blue and white ashtrays on pedestals, suggested by Julian, are perfection.

TIDDY-DOLL the great French Gingerbread-Baker, drawing out a new Batch of Kings.

Hanham Court

For eighteen years Hanham Court was the heart of our life. Bertie Bannerman was born five days after we moved in at the end of August 1993. Rex can remember nothing else, though Ismay has a vague feeling for Chippenham and the The Ivy. The rituals of childhood were all rooted in the garden: the dogs, the pet burials, the shin-scraping and den-making, although their father was rather competitive and territorial on that front, and the biggest ritual of all, the Christmas tree, decoration thereof in late December and burning thereof in early January. Heavily pregnant and having sold our house suddenly and much to our surprise while doing our first Chelsea, I was not at all sure about Hanham Court. Nor was my mother, who came to it for the first time right through the eastern backside of Bristol, which is where it was, and declared the curious purple grey local sandstone 'the most depressing thing' she had ever seen. It was unwieldy, rambling, leaking, nothing worked and the garden was dismally full of large dog turds and leylandii. Julian saw it quite differently as medieval, with its own church, every era of architecture from Norman up to Arts and Crafts (a great 1900 kitchen wing screaming to be put right). But it was so hemmed in with ghastly planting that he really seemed to have had x-ray vision. Through the claustrophobic conifers and, his bête noir, huge copper beeches, he saw undulating combes and rising limestone grassland, potential orchards, a 'hortus conclusus' behind the tithe barn, water running through the dell, a fortified formal garden around the house, a myriad of different moods to be teased out and so much room for experiment. He was particularly enchanted that, like the Bishop's Palace in Wells, the whole ensemble – and this was something I did get because it goes back again to *Alice in Wonderland* – is entered through a low wicket gate within huge Tudor wooden gates. Stepping through this you always felt enticed, energised, that you were entering into your own fortified kingdom, a place of magic. Very slowly, painfully, but together, we dragged and cajoled Hanham forcing it to be the place it had been and would be, a place most 'lived in' – the most 'lived in house' that she had ever been in, declared designer Ilse Crawford – and the most loved.

Hanham Court terrified me, and for several, if not ten years. I saw nothing but work, work, work. We lived in a flat on the first floor for a year; thank god the incredible Linda Haultain from New Zealand genuinely kept me sane and made the children blissfully happy with baking and making. To begin with the attics were floorless and plasterless because of a post-war beetle infestation and the roof had been leaking for god knows how long. But in fact we were cosy, had night-storage heaters and put down underlay instead of the greasy shagpile carpet until we could buy the seagrass matting to go on top. Christopher Gibbs came to see us after a while and we delighted in showing him all the leylandii cut down to reveal the church alongside the house and the opening up of the lawn. 'Well done, dear things,' he congratulated us, 'but what about the leylandii inside the house?'

We tackled inside and outside in tandem although the garden did not begin to look like much until we had the idea of building a swimming pool and hiding it in a walled enclosure made of 'ruins' in 1999. We built it that summer with seven Australians living in the house, as cheaply as is humanly possible, omitting to obtain planning permission. Somebody squealed on us and one bright day the following March when we were planting it up the enforcement officer appeared and told us to down tools. The conservation officer turned up a week or so later and was not amused that we had dug out a swimming pool amidst the remains of medieval monastic ruins; he was then even less amused that he had been duped by our confection of chapel windows and bits from a church in Devizes into thinking they were real monastic ruins. As to archaeology, the truth was that, at Hanham almost everywhere, the bedrock was inches from the surface and hence there had never been a burial, nor was there any archaeology to disturb. We were granted retrospective permission.

235

Wall-building and bed-making were the two interlinked and endless tasks. With a 'pecker', or by hand with a bar and mattock, one could excavate the stone and put back earth to make beds, or you had to sift out the stones from the poor minerally earth where you could find any. Only by bringing in earth to back fill the dug-out borders and adding compost year after year did we finally get a growing medium rich enough for the greedy roses we craved. However, the beds were fantastically well drained because the whole thing was raised up on medieval retaining walls which were part of the fortifications and defences of the early settlement. At the end of the lawn was a *Nothofagus*, the southern or bastard beech, which had some age but was stunted by the rock upon which it grew, forming a miniature old tree, bonsaied, which never got any larger in our time of watering and cosseting the beds of flowers we attempted to grow around it. The earth that there was was minerally and poor, except in the delphinium border by the church which was deep sticky clay, and in which we miserably buried Ivy,

Above: A view of the house and the 'bastion' within which lay the formal garden, from the south. The bastion wall was almost certainly early medieval, and the 13th-century church is to the right of the house with the tower just visible behind and the Hanham hills beyond. The corner tower in the elbow of the house is Tudor and would originally have had an ogee lead roof rather like the Tower of London.

To the left of the tower two Tudor gables created an attic storey in the early medieval hall house which formed the major part of the abbot's lodgings. The orchard is hidden behind the hawthorn hedge on the right-hand side, and the meadow below the bastion walls is ablaze with ox-eye daisies at the end of June. Rambling roses pour over every wall and over the house.

the first of our dogs. We had to build up the garden retaining walls in places, completely remaking the one along the dell side and joining this – by means of a 'Jacobean' green-oak gate of my devising – with the former ha-ha until it was walled all the way round. In order to make the garden badger- and deer-proof we also moved back the 'Golden Gate', as we called it, to its original place, since the previous owners had moved all the extraordinary eighteenth-century ironwork, cutting it up and making merry with it as decoration for little arbours and things. Interestingly it was also a mole-proof garden (we found out that moles will walk in through an open gate but will not burrow through wall foundations). From it one could look out onto undulating meadow and the 'downland' feel of the swooping and falling land. It was this wider landscape that Julian taught us all to love, ten acres more of which we eventually managed to buy from our neighbours who owned the pub on the river at the bottom.

We planted *Magnolia grandiflora* on the south-facing gable end outside what was

to be our bedroom, but it had a hard time. Only now that we have left has it reached the first floor window. But the house was blessed with much neglected wisteria all over the main façades, which look fairly young in the Second World War photographs of the house, and when the scaffolding went up to do the roof, we took the wisterias almost right down to the floor, wired the building and tied and trained them up like productive vines rather than the tangle of spaghetti they had been. To the wisteria we added – an obvious trick but it works – the very vigorous Banksian rose, which now has a stem that looks a hundred years old and intends to gobble up the entire house. *Rosa* 'Félicité Perpétue' grows up the corner of our bedroom and *R*. 'Rambling Rector' up the buttress which supported the little church tower bolted on to the east end of the house. The imagined garden slowly became reality; the orchard of old varieties on big root stock began to look like a Samuel Palmer; the yard below the great barn grew vegetables; a greenhouse gleaned on the reclamation network went up in a slightly odd place but it worked. It came from Haya Harareet, love interest for Charlton Heston in the film *Ben Hur* and widow of Jack Clayton, the director of *Room at the Top,* who had retired to Marlow and pigeon-fancying. She lived in a modernist house built in the walled garden of some lost mansion, and the pigeon lofts were old Foster and Pearson glasshouses, without glazing, but netted. These were the Rolls Royce of glasshouses at the turn of the last century, and may be seen still in working order in the famous Edward James

Above: Wisteria flowering around the Venetian window, part of the Georgian alterations to the eastern Jacobean wing, possibly the work of John Wood the elder who was a parishioner in neighbouring Bitton.

garden at West Dean. The key factor, apart from the fabulous cast-iron fitments, was that they were made from Archangel pine, and, having matured very slowly above the Arctic Circle, this pine, now unobtainable, is richly resinous and therefore never rots. The greenhouses came apart like Meccano and, with a bit of joining and splicing, and glazing, went back together again, along with their iron staging and wonderful, efficient opening mechanisms. On ours, the whole ridge of the roof lifted like clockwork and, as ventilation is the absolute key to growing under glass, even we managed seeds and cuttings and tomatoes and geraniums and all sorts in there. It did mean that, despite putting up one or two for clients, the barn was filled with an incomprehensible puzzle of greenhouse bits and cast-iron bits throughout our time at Hanham and when we left we had an awful time working out what to do with it all.

In our second year of opening the garden to the public we expanded the kitchen garden into the west field above the greenhouse because we felt the need for more vegetables, cutting flowers and late things like dahlias to amuse visitors. This was a lot of work and created a lot more work and hence was dubbed by me 'A Veg too Far' a play on the title of the film about General Montgomery's 'Operation Market Garden', the battle for Arnhem in September 1944. But it was a great pleasure to tend it in the evening light and look back at the warm crumbly west side of the house, with its glinting leaded lights and tottering chimneys. The men of oak made fabulous fruit cages with steel

cross braces somehow reminiscent of the early post-modern light-industrial buildings in Swindon, designed by the Foster and Rogers partnership before they split in 1967. Meadows and orchard were spangled with white narcissi and later there were banks of camassias. The snowdrops that Julian collected thrived in the beds and under the walnut tree beyond the Golden Gate. One of the great strangenesses about the Hanham Court garden is that the gable end of the west range plunges four storeys down to the dell; this is probably thirty feet lower than the front door and the 'bowling green' or – as Julian liked to describe it, 'aircraft carrier' – of a lawn, which stretches out southwards from the house. The juxtaposition therefore between wild woodland at the bottom of this drop and formal garden at high level is oddly abrupt, and yet it works rather fabulously. The Arts-and-Crafts kitchens hang out to the west half a storey lower than the ground floor of the rest of the house, which is mildly annoying, but it means that they are suspended on an elaborate Italianate loggia. This was only ever used for hanging out washing from the day it was built until the day we thought of using it for the visitors to take tea under cover yet outdoors – a purpose for which it might have been tailor made. Eventually in the dell hand-reared rambling roses finally clambered into the trees, something one may only manage once in a lifetime and, along with the great hearth in the hall, the biggest thing we miss about Hanham.

Editing the pictures for this book has reduced me to a tearful heap. Nostalgia is a weakness I remember being aware of from an early age, I can recall feeling prematurely

Above: The house and the tower from the south in winter.

Right: *Euphorbia characias* subsp. *wulfenii*, yew cylinders, yew balls, box balls, and eryngium flattened by the frost.

242

Right: The Golden Gate from the walnut tree, looking back towards the Tudor gables of the house. All the gates, which were in pieces elsewhere in the garden, were restored and put back in their original positions. They may be the work of the famous 18th-century iron workers of Bristol, the Edney Brothers. We had the pillars made in Bath stone, the design based on a found fragment .

Opposite: Wisteria on the Georgian front seen through a pot of 'China Pink' tulips and wallflowers.

nostalgic about leaving our house in the country before such a thing was even mooted by the grown-ups. The lost domain, as in all good stories, need never have been lost and sometimes it is hard to understand what possessed us, after all that work, and in spite of all the children's radical attachment, to move from Hanham Court. Bacci the Patterdale, whose kingdom it really was, is in almost every picture, tensing on the whiff of quarry, on a mission, ready to kill a fallow deer or a fox, but never a badger – he always came off worst with badgers. He would hear the click of the wicket gate, be there in an instant to greet you, stopping with you to smell the wisteria or the wintersweet by the front door, shadow you in to the kitchen for a bit and then settle down on the warm stone in front of the great fire in the hall.

Above: Clipped yews, *Euphorbia characias* subsp. *wulfenii*, box balls, *Iris pallida* subsp. *pallida* and *Erysimum* 'Bowles's Mauve' in the gravel garden

Left: Delphiniums and angelica (left); *Lilium regale* and *Argyranthemum* Madeira Cherry Red (right).

Below: *Argyranthemum* Madeira Cherry Red and *Iris pallida* subsp. *pallida (left)*; a border with irises, *Paeonia lactiflora* 'Jan van Leeuwen', a sweet-pea teepee, *Allium hollandicum* 'Purple Sensation' and *Lupinus* 'My Castle' (right).

Opposite, top left: A 17th-century statue of Neptune, an original vestige of Hanham Court's early formal garden, swathed in *Rosa* 'Bobbie James'.

Opposite, top right: A Gothic archway built by us in 1999 with *Rosa* 'New Dawn' and *Lilium regale*.

Opposite, bottom left: Part of the ruined wall around the swimming pool with *Eremurus himalaicus*, alliums and *Matthiola incana*.

Opposite, bottom right: Two views of the formal beds bursting with shrub roses and standard *Rosa* 'Félicité Perpétue'.

Top, from left: A 'Manhattan' (New York Series) Oriental poppy; *Rosa* 'Président de Sèze'; ammonites and tulips 'Abu Hassan' and 'Ballerina'.

Middle: *Euphorbia characias* subsp. *wulfenii*, *Erysimum* 'Bowles's Mauve' and yew balls (left); an oak balustrade and *Tulipa* 'Jan Reus' Right).

Bottom: *Rosa* 'Roseraie de l'Haÿ' and bi-coloured West Country lupins (left); lupins with *Salvia nemorosa* (right).

Top: Blue iris with fennel (left);
euphorbia and clipped box (right).

Middle, from left: The Oriental
poppy 'Beauty of Livermere'; *Iris*
'Mahogany' and *Lavandula* 'Hazel';
show auriculas.

Bottom: The view through to the
meadow with valerian, West Country
lupins and *Rosa* 'Madame Isaac
Péreire' in the foreground (left);
alliums and lupins (right).

Above: The auricula theatre, at this time showing ordinary pansies.

Opposite: The corner tower with *Rosa* 'Gloire de Dijon'.

Top: The pool on a summer's morning showing the newly built Gothic ruined enclosure, pots and standard roses.

Left: The pool in winter.

Above: Pots of *Lilium* African Queen Group by the pool in high summer.

Opposite: The enclosing Gothic ruined wall and fennel in the foreground.

Eryngium bourgatii, box balls and *Iris pallida* subsp. *pallida*.

An oak tree with a tree fern and
Hamamelis mollis in the dell.

Above: The walnut tree seat at different times of the year, with snowdrops, with snow, with fritillaries and with Bacci.

Opposite, top: The walnut tree lit up behind the Golden Gate with yews and *Malus* × *robusta* 'Red Sentinel'.

Opposite, below, from left: *Prunus mume* 'Beni-chidori' on the gate pier; *Eremurus robustus*; *Paeonia rockii*.

Opposite, clockwise from top left: *Camassia leichtlinii* subsp. *leichtlinii* and *C.l.* subsp. *suksdorfii* Caerulea Group in the orchard meadow with the scout tent; *Rosa* 'Rambling Rector' and *Robinia pseudoacacia* in front of the two towers; flowers in the meadow overlooking the house; the tent and meadow in summer; Classic annual flower mix from Pictorial Meadows surrounding the tent; spring blossom in the orchard.

Above: An oak obelisk, with lilacs 'Prince Wolkonsky' and 'Madame Lemoine'.

Right: *Rosa* 'Président de Sèze' and *Philadelphus* 'Snowbelle'.

Far right: *Crambe cordifolia*, *Rosa* 'Aimée Vibert' and valerian on the garden wall with a green-oak obelisk, ox-eye daisies and teazel.

Overleaf: Ox-eye daisies and Bacci the Patterdale terrier.

This page: Views of the dell showing
the green-oak urn, philadelphus,
the Neptune fountain cascade, and
(above) the handrail of a rustic oak
bridge made by Martin Gane.

Opposite: In early June, *Lilium regale*,
Argyranthemum Madeira Cherry Red
and *Nicotiana mutabilis* in a pot.

Top: Dahlias and sweet-pea teepees in the kitchen garden.

Above and right: The sweet-pea teepees earlier in the year, with pinks for picking (above) and zinnias (right).

Opposite: The chicken-house-turned-shed with *Rosa filipes* 'Kiftsgate' (top); the 1930s tin shed, made by Welsh miners who came to excavate the giant sewer through the hill to Keynsham (middle and bottom middle); the shepherd's hut (bottom left); the barbecue shack (bottom right).

Evening light, looking east, with
calendulas and sweet peas.

Pots of very dewy *Pelargonium*
tomentosum in front of the wicket gate.

Trematon Castle

The whole question of whether making a garden is actually a good idea in a given circumstance is one we find ourselves repeatedly debating. Trematon Castle may be the ultimate expression of my and Julian's compulsion to take on bedraggled houses and gardens, usually in the wrong place, but crammed with the right things; with charm, mystery, possibilities, dissipated grandeur, lost domains. The trouble with Trematon, is that it is such a magical world in itself, it was not obvious how it could be improved by gardening. We have lost jobs by making such arguments, by saying that what is needed is not more garden but less, less mowing, less planting, less art, less artifice. There is nothing more pleasing than an orchard, grass and trees; perhaps add to that lilac, philadelphus, some species roses, some 'non-planting' and near the house some pinks and some scented cottage garden plants. Partly this is sheer practicality; it is easy to plant masses of plants, it is the nurturing that takes the energy and devotion, and like museums and galleries what is difficult is keeping up the happenings long term. But is also to do with conspicuous consumption, the unnecessities of life, harking back to something simpler and trying to make the world a more pleasing place, productive and beneficial but not excessively showy. Gardening has become a commodity like everything else, and sometimes it is pretty sickening. Having said which, it cannot be denied that when a lovely opportunity offers itself, it is fatal for Julian and me.

Trematon was just such a *coup de foudre* and it struck us twice over. Firstly, in 2003 when we fell hopelessly in love with it but went away and properly assessed the foolishness of moving to Cornwall with three barely teenage sons and a business to establish. Secondly when we were in a false limbo, had sold the heavenly Hanham Court to move to a parsonage in north Norfolk with a metre of delicious sandy topsoil and this time she entrapped us. Trematon is a saucy mistress, almost unique in its setting, topography, romance, architecture, and has history in spadefuls. The bailey walls dip and skirt round a basin levelled off in the centre to create the flat space upon which the pared-down regency villa sits, like a creamy pat of butter, commanding a view across the Tamar and Lynher estuaries three hundred odd feet below. An embattled gatehouse straddles the sunken drive. The motte rears up inconceivably shear to the shell keep a hundred feet above, pinned to earth by two monumental holm oaks, *Quercus ilex,* which cast a deep Italianate shade over its southern lower slopes, and bisected by the colossal bailey wall, the very bottom of which is punctured by the tiny door of the 'Sally Port' or back entrance to the Castle. Thick with moss and lichen, toothy, jagged, glistening wet in places, the walls are populated with jackdaws and polypody ferns singular to Trematon, all things that are magical about Cornwall. The 'garden' mostly slumbered under winter heliotrope, a pernicious nineteenth-century introduction, which, having had free reign for many decades, rampaged through the flower beds, lawns, shrubberies, and up two sides of the mount, blotting out the ancient English wild flora which had embroidered these vertiginous heights since the days of the Edward, the Black Prince.

The garden was what we wanted to get our teeth into, including the shallow apology for a bed round the croquet lawn, the beds either side of a path leading to a deeply mysterious and enticing tunnel that went under the bailey wall and out into what was barely an orchard, some young poorly staked fruit trees, and a handful of very elderly apples, branches be-furred with rippling blue lichen. There was a neat vegetable patch hard against the high back wall of a long-gone glasshouse and next to it a little white wooden greenhouse. However, in the great curve of the curtain wall that embraced the gravelled entrance side of the house, there were the remains of a border, reputedly set out by Norah Lindsay in the 1940s. Possible remains of those glory days were several magnolias, one with a punchy pink outer and pure winter inner petal much like *Magnolia* 'Pickard's Ruby'. There was a handsome *Cornus capitata* or Himalayan strawberry tree, whose fruit looks like very large lychees. There is also a chunky wisteria.

Left: *Echium pininana* and *Matthiola incana*.

Overleaf: Our view over the Hamoaze, the estuary of the River Tamar.

Its flowering tendrils trailed, just as one would wish, a hundred foot along the ramparts, and we are working on it to make this the most thrilling and longest wisteria in the west with hard 'vine' pruning so that it can flower magnificently. The area faces broadly east but is sheltered from the bitter English Channel winds by the house. This was the place to garden with flowering plants, as they can be enjoyed from the house without any competition from the panoramic views on the estuary side.

Grey skies, grey granite, grey shaley soil, bitter and wet it was, and the boiler was bust, when we landed with a lot of furniture in a heap from Bristol. We kept the shutters shut which added to the gloom in a house which is generally a sea of windows and light. There were no snowdrops and no aconites to cheer the soul, but a great mound of *Sarcococca confusa* in the 'border' greeted us with its welcoming scent of sugar and spice. The thin soil turned out to be surprisingly limey, as the Castle has collapsed in on itself over the centuries and the 'garden' is really a well of lime mortar and rubble. It was goodbye to any fantasies of blue hydrangeas. Camellias blazed along the drive, marvellously brazen in the winter gloom, planted by our predecessors along with a host of rare rhododendrons, acers, paulownia, davidia and a grove of wonderful tree ferns. To keep our spirits up we planted snowdrops and aconites in the green, and magnolias in huge holes, big bold colourful Jury hybrids such as 'Apollo', 'Atlas' and 'Vulcan' and, for their delicacy and mysterious scent in June, many *Magnolia sieboldii* and *M. wilsonii;* these are struggling and given the cost of them this is frustrating. Matthew and Emma Rice were the first to alight from the train at Saltash on day three and bring their cheer and their blessing on the new project. In March I was fifty and we celebrated by the sea in a March heat wave and picked *Acacia pravissima*, the hardier mimosa, for the house. At Easter the 'Kanzan' cherry flowered, heartening and ravishing but for the purple

Above: The first year we grew Blue Wave Pictorial Meadow mix annuals in a new bed, intended for peonies, beneath the gatehouse.

leaves which, to us, always seem to be at war with everything else that is happening in spring. Julian dedicated himself to knocking out the winter heliotrope (*Petasites*), spot-spraying it again and again. He climbed like a mountain goat up and down the mount's near vertical slopes, the ramparts, and the woods down to the creek, and the abandoned double-walled garden knitted through with ash, sycamore and brambles.

The Cornish climate is really not that different from the rest of England, but the real winter, the time when one must expect to get frost, is shorter and every time of year is wetter. Autumn lingers, with nerines, dahlias, gladioli and rudbeckias, and the sweet peas keep on flowering. But spring came early and hotly sunny that first year and revealed the motte and the woodland awash with wild daffodils, bluebells, campion and ferns unfurling. But it also revealed the lack of so many things – not showy or rarefied plants, but there were no pheasant eye, and no fritillaries. The lack of old friends made us hanker. After the hot spell in March no summer came, just a deluge; everything melted to a mush in weeks of unremitting rain. Only the encouragement of our neighbour Alice Boyd kept us going. She would turn up with big smiles and armfuls of unbelievably special daffodils or buckets of *Scilla liliohyacinthus* bulbs. With the help of Mike Clark, a trainee gardener, we began to dig out the petasites on the mount and the banks and other things, such as shrubs that always survive decades of being ignored like *Viburnum rhytidophyllum*. The cyclamen, which had been under a huge and venerable beech tree on the bank beside the lawn before it had split open a decade earlier, had to be crated up and reserved while the bank was divested of a thick tapestry of heliotrope, ground elder and bramble. More positively we began to dig dustbin-sized holes, wrenching out boulders and putting back clods of manure and fresh soil, into which we tenderly planted a huge number of rambling roses: 'Wedding Day', 'The Garland',

Above: The newly planted bailey wall border. Two hundred tons of earth were brought in to make a steeper bank and a flat path between front and back borders. It is thought that the wisteria, magnolias and dogwood are remnants of plantings advised by Norah Lindsay in the 1940s.

'Rambling Rector', 'Sir Cedric Morris' and 'Cooperi' to clothe the ramparts. This clothing
of the ramparts is beginning to show now as we enter our fifth season and we have high
hopes, but we are still adding new roses. We are now beginning to discover which roses
work best in Cornwall: Ayrshire roses, Rugosas, but also a host of new discoveries and
old favourites like the seven sisters rose (*Rosa multiflora* 'Grevillei'). Along the drive
went all the philadelphus we could lay hands on including varieties new to us such as
'Starbright', 'Snowbelle' and *P. lewisii* 'Snow Velvet'. We needed the smell of *Viburnum
carlesii* and *V. × carlcephalum*, of *Ribes odoratum*, and of all those stormy coloured
lilacs. Again, these are getting going now after three seasons but we keep adding more
when we can. We missed the sacristy smell of the incense rose, *Rosa primula* and the
appley-eglantine-leaf-smelling *R*. 'La Belle Distinguée' so we planted them along the path
leading to the tunnel. A big *rockii* tree peony had come with us in a giant pot, and tree
peonies seem to like Cornwall.

   We made a small start, with cottagey beds down by the tunnel, using scented
annuals, *Nicotiana sylvestris* and *N. suaveolens*, *Matthiola incana*, *Lupinus arboreus*
and *Coronilla valentina* subsp. *glauca* 'Citrina'. We planted the shoulder-high walls
with *Daphne × transatlantica* Eternal Fragrance, with 'Mrs Sinkins' pinks and with
trailing rosemary. This 'cove' faces south and is encircled by banks, so it is hot and cosy,
capturing scents which are then enticingly drawn through the tunnel out the other side.
On a bench here we could sit sometimes and enjoy the fruity bubble-gum fragrance of
Philadelphus maculatus 'Mexican Jewel'. But it turned out that the bottom of 'smelly path'
was a sump for the endless rain, and everything began to rot off in the drenching winter
months. There was nothing to be done but deal with the drainage and bring the levels
up. The following spring we replanted, adding *Bupleurum fruticosum*, *Azara microphylla*,

Carpenteria californica 'Ladhams' Variety', *Crinum × powellii* in pink, and many *Echium pininana* grown from seed. It is thronged now with seedling echiums and we have enjoyed their magnificent rockets so much that it is a delight to see them take over.

On the bank opposite, having taken out a lot of ancient sludge-coloured hydrangeas, we rather perversely replanted with hydrangeas, only this time 'Annabelle' and 'Limelight' mixed with the big philadelphus varieties and with our favourite *Ribes odoratum*, the clove currant, which smells of hot cross buns at Easter time. We planted the ragingly scented *Rosa spinosissima* 'William III', Rugosas 'Roseraie de l'Haÿ' and 'Blanche Double de Coubert', and *R.* 'Geranium' for a burst of single 'war-of-the roses' red. The Moyesiis are slow to get going, tiresome but in the end they should just do their amazing thing forever. Mixed in here are *Euphorbia characias* subsp. *wulfenii* which flows down from a planting of the same with sarcococca in the gravel above. Euphorbias are not thrilled with the frostless winter we have just had; they flowered at Christmas and now there is nothing for it but to cut the heads back and force them to regenerate.

As that first season soaked on we made lists of what was missing: the freshness of flower and scent, old favourites, plants that need not compete with the ancient architecture and the aching estuary light, but which would complement them and somehow introduce a note of husbandry. By bringing in tons of topsoil and manure in small trailer loads – the only transport which would fit through the lanes and the entrance gate – we made a double border which at its height becomes a single mass, like football fans waving, on the curving bank opposite the front of the house. But in the continuing rain all we seemed to be making was a mess.

But in the autumn things were brighter and dryer, the pernicious weeds were on the wane, and the beds were puffed up like duvets with tons of council compost and the farm manure. We had reduced the amount of close-mown grass, opting for 'meadow' and the chance to plant bulbs by the many thousand. We planted *Camassia quamash* (syn. *esculenta*) and *C. leichtlinii* and *Narcissus* 'Actaea' and *N. poeticus* var. *recurvus* all through the orchard, the drive, and up the mount. On the terrace we filled big terracotta pots with stripy tulips and wallflowers for the following spring. We had discussed taking out the 'Kanzan' cherry by the house but instead we raised the crown of it so that you could see the gentle mounded lawn beneath and planted crocuses and autumn crocuses, scillas and sylvestris tulips, snowdrops, aconites, fritillaries, and added back the cyclamen we had gleaned from the bank on other side of the house. We planted anything that would bring pleasure to the view from the kitchen window, trying to make a jewelled corner of 'preciouses', experimenting with lily of the valley, erythroniums and martagon lilies. Now we have done a similar thing at the other end of the house on the way down through the Sally Port to the stables, and here to my extreme excitement the lily of the valley is romping away with dog's-tooth violets and *Cyclamen coum* all in the good light dry sand beneath the holm oak.

Early in our second spring we drew out a trapezoidal path around the croquet lawn with boards and flinty yellow gravel. This bright gravel path has given form to the whole area and had the remarkable effect of making the lawn look much bigger, even though we have made it smaller. Another trick of scale is created by the pair of 'cannons' that we had made in green oak. These point at the naval dockyard at Devonport, framing the tidal reaches below. Onto the path beneath the terrace spill out waves of 'Mrs Sinkins' pinks, reliable Bonica roses – still flowering in November – and *Matthiola incana* 'Pillow Talk' jostling with *Agapanthus* Back in Black and the saturated pink *Nerine bowdenii* 'Isabel' in groups of thirty or forty. Singing on throughout November with the roses, the nerines' intense puce colour answers the mounds of *Pelargonium* 'Pink Capricorn' flowering in big terracotta pots on the terrace. These pots have helped boost the floweriness on this side of the house without compromising the big picture. This year we have grown *Salvia involucrata* 'Bethellii' in all the pots but, though fabulous, it is really too windy on the lawn side of the house as they desiccate and snap very easily in the wind. All the planting here has to achieve a balance between joyfulness and submission to the view, which is framed by gatehouse and ramparts. One day these ramparts will foam with the

Opposite: The motte in spring is a riot of bluebells, primroses, campion, ferns and early purple orchids.

rambling roses we have now planted and keep endlessly tying back on to the wall. On the bank beneath them is a sort of 'maquis' of cistus (*Cistus × dansereaui*, C. × *hybridus*, C. × *dansereaui* 'Decumbens', C. × *argenteus* 'Silver Pink' and 'Peggy Sammons') *Lavandula stoechas* and *Rosmarinus officinalis* 'Severn Sea' which is clipped into low blue-green mounds and already scents the air all about the terrace. Cornwall is good for scent, being warm and wet and, when the sun does appear, aromatic plants exude their turpentine tang. Into this subtle mix we could not resist adding some shimmering blues: *Iris pallida* subsp. *pallida*, which have become rather drowned, and *Agapanthus* 'Northern Star' which are more robust. Blue seems to speak to the sky and the estuary in a way that is very calming, and it complements the vibrant pinks which we have used a lot as a much-needed counterpoint to the granite, slate, and the iridescent moss.

When it came to planning the 'Norah Lindsay border' it was hard not to go beserk, but also we were testing out new ideas and plants. Whatever we did had to be maintainable with little labour, and we have learnt over the years to manage the lack of labour by putting in a lot of weeding work in the spring, followed by deep mulching and by planting densely. Bulbs such as alliums and lilies can come through the dense planting, but some areas are left free for annuals or biennials which add spice. Experimenting with achilleas did not work, but thalictrums have proved a fabulous flicker through everything and current fads are *Ferula communis* and *Molopospermum peloponnesiacum* now that we know how much the Himalayan cow parsley *Selinum wallichianum* loves our wet world. The planting has been a huge source of pleasure and surprise. The Castle walls provide a terrific back curtain. Opposite the front door we made a shallow flight of steps from green oak, leading to a big green-oak vermiculated obelisk. The borders needed solid dark punctuation winter and summer, so there are

Above: *Gladiolus murielae, which we treat like tulips and buy each year, in the border in September; it has fresh green spears of leaves, is deliciously scented and is also good in pots. It is seen here with late-flowering giant lilies* 'Anastasia' *and* 'Miss Freya', *and the Cornus capitata tree in the background.*

six clipped yews in 'onion' shapes a metre high in the front sections, while ranged across the back bed are eight tall columns of yew – over which red *Tropaeolum speciosum* is intended to romp a bit, though it is famously tricky to get going. These and the mature magnolias, dogwood and eucryphia trees are a foil and scaffold for the energies of the new herbaceous planting. A secondary level of evergreen 'body' is provided by 'Miss Jessopp's Upright' rosemary (though all rosemary is faring badly in Cornwall, a great sadness as we love it and bought a whole collection from the Herb Nursery at Bodmin), *Daphne odora* 'Aureomarginata', and *Sarcococca hookeriana* var. *humilis* to be clipped like loose box. All this stops the whole from completely falling apart in winter.

All the herbaceous planting was done with 9-cm or bare-rooted plants. Phlox seem to love it here and the asters too grew like rockets and fell over, but at least the show in September was radioactively magenta, mauve and lilac. *Symphyotrichum turbinellum* (syn. *Aster turbinellus*) seems much too late to be enjoyable even in Cornwall. Much more successful were the lupins, especially 'Masterpiece', which was the colour – and price – of a Rembrandt but draws gasps from everybody for weeks on end. Although some people resist them, especially in Cornwall, we think irises can work in a border, given enough space and good drainage. Stands of *Iris* 'Braithwaite', 'Jane Phillips' and 'Sable' and their glaucous swords contribute to the outline and definition of the border even in January. We are confident enough to be making a new place for irises in the orchard near the kitchen gaden. *Gladiolus communis* subsp. *byzantinus*, which grows on the dual carriageways hereabouts, is massed at other key points, but has not been a huge success, sadly. The colour scheme developed itself somehow; nothing very clever, but pretty: white, pink, shocking pink, purple through shades of blue, with pale sulphurous yellows to intercede in plantings of *Thalictrum flavum* and *Scabiosa columbaria* subsp. *ochroleuca* and a single primrose-coloured hollyhock. There are more white rambling roses up the back wall, but also the cool grey-violet *Rosa* 'Veilchenblau' against the craggy stone. For shrub roses, afraid of the rain and balling brown buds, we chose bonny blowsy pink ones like 'Madame Boll' ('Comte de Chambord' misapplied), 'De Resht' and 'Charles de Mills'. Boudoir pinks are also to be found in pools of peonies – 'Monsieur Jules Elie', 'Madame Calot' and 'Karl Rosenfeld'. For height and upward thrust, onopordum and artichokes. Threaded throughout as a counterpoint to the thick bursts of colour is a veil or filigree layer of umbellifers. The best of these is *Selinum wallichianum*, along with earlier flowering *Cenolophium denudatum* and *Ammi majus*, with *Crambe cordifolia*, pepped up by the acid greens of culinary fennel, *Ferula communis* and *Angelica archangelica*. Reliable border stalwarts keep the thing going: *Campanula lactiflora* 'Loddon Anna' and *Lupinus* 'Rote Flamme'. Never be afraid of red, it somehow works in a large composition. *Dahlia coccinea*, given to us by Mary Keen, zings things up for months. Later in the summer a wave of papal purple rises up in the form of *Astilbe chinensis* var. *taquetii* 'Purpurlanze' with *Phlox paniculata* 'Blue Paradise', *P.p.* 'Eva Cullum' and *Salvia buchananii*. These brassy blasts of colour are tempered and the shadows lightened by the calmer woody green and white areas. The very middle, round the obelisk and steps, is cooler. *Cardiocrinum giganteum* amid *Hydrangea paniculata* 'Limelight', Iceberg roses fronted with white agapanthus, equally scented white crinums and hundreds of deliciously scented *Gladiolus* (or *Acidanthera*) *murielae,* also given to us by Mary Keen, add a wonderfully fresh note to the end of the year. We have taken to doing these in pots as well so excited by them are we. It is not complex or rarefied planting but, even in its infancy, it has perhaps conjured something of the illuminated manuscript, Bocaccio and the *Romance of the Rose*, heightened a pre-Raphaelite mood about the Castle and recalling the bold days of the Black Prince.

Below: Sweet peas on hazel teepees in the peony border, with a green-oak cannon behind.

Above: Springtime behind the battlements; the roofs of the stables lean against them.

Right: An aerial view of Trematon with the Forder viaduct and the rivers Lynher and Tamar in front of Devonport.

Top: Three medieval Cornish granite doorways.

Above: Lichen-covered fruit trees in the orchard and the picket fence around the kitchen garden.

Opposite: The keep, which towers over everything, partly obscured by two colossal holm oaks, probably planted in the late 19th century.

This page: Mixed annuals with emerging echiums (top); borders beneath the bailey wall (above); wisteria on the wall and, in the foreground, *Iris pallida* subsp. *pallida* (left).

Opposite: Keep, motte and gatehouse in fading December light.

Above, left: Giant pots of *Lilium regale* and scented *Pelargonium* 'Pink Capricorn'.

Above, right: *Dahlia coccinea* 'Mary Keen', a present from the eponymous gardener, and alliums in seed.

Right: *Thalictrum rochebruneanum* with *Salvia nemorosa* and alliums.

Far right: Erigeron daisies growing through an iron bench, with lemon verbena and *Matthiola incana* 'Pillow Talk' around it.

Opposite: *Euphorbia characias* subsp. *wulfenii* and the gatehouse at dawn.

Overleaf: The motte towering over the orchard.

Epilogue

'Design' is not something one wants to be too aware of, not in a garden and not in a book. But of necessity this book has focused on the pictures that one hopes will startle or draw you in. Photography is one thing, gardening another. What makes a garden good is not necessarily going to be there in photographs. This book is only part of the story. Unfortunately, it probably adds to the impression that we make 'designery' dramatic gardens. We do like to think bigger and bolder, but we are also always advising people to hold back, to stop the 'pollution' of gardening. We have both always been very at home with the Robert Kime dictum, 'Hooray for nettles!' uttered when we were all touring round an endless and super-sophisticated 'tour-de-force' garden. Equally we have done many smaller gardens, but these and many larger gardens we have made will all have to wait for volume two. It would be great to put together another book, rather different in timbre, although, sometimes, like everyone else, we feel like giving it all up, becoming hermits and living in a cell.

Gigantic thanks are due therefore to Dunstan for photography and design, for his complete understanding of what this project was all about and for his patience and boundless constructive help over a decade of working with us. For almost two decades Helen Phillips has been stalwart, a cornerstone, redoubtable in drawing, surveying, model-making, planning planting, and patiently putting up with us both. Valiant, come wind, come weather, there seems no discouragement can make her once relent. Thank you Helen. Thank you to Robert Hibberd and the men of oak. Thank you to Martin Gane and to Elle. Thank you to Danny Johnson who came to work in the Hanham tea room and made himself indispensable. And thank you to our three wonders, the boys Bannerman, who put up with an awful lot, but also had the luck to grow up in a house full of all these great people making things happen all around them. And finally thank you to Candida, to whom this work is dedicated, another such pilgrim, a beacon and a shining goddess.

Above: Helen through the looking glass, working at Trematon.

Opposite: The Ivy.

Index

Page numbers in italics refer to illustrations.
Numbers in bold refer to principal entries.

Picture Credits

The Publishers have made every effort to contact holders of copyright works. Any copyright holders we have been unable to reach are invited to contact the Publishers so that a full acknowledgment may be given in subsequent editions. For permission to reproduce the images below, the Publishers would like to thank the following:

Page 14 (bottom right): © Crafts Study Centre, University for the Creative Arts

Page 16: © British Architectural Library, RIBA

Page 228 (right); 231 (bottom left and right); 232-233: © Alex Michaelis

Page 281 (bottom): © James Walker